Found

Dennis Olsen

Copyright © 2024 by Dennis Olsen

All rights reserved.

No portion of this book may be reproduced in any form without written permission from the publisher or author, except as permitted by U.S. copyright law.

Contents

Prologue	1
Chapter One	5
Chapter Two	14
Chapter Three	23
Chapter Four	35
Chapter Five	44
Chapter Six	55
Chapter Seven	71
Chapter Eight	79
Chapter Nine	87
Chapter Ten	94
Chapter Eleven	106
Chapter Twelve	116
Chapter Thirteen	123
Chapter Fourteen	135

Chapter Fifteen	147
Chapter Sixteen	156
Chapter Seventeen	162
Chapter Eighteen	172
Chapter Nineteen	181
Chapter Twenty	192
Chapter Twenty-One	205
Chapter Twenty-Two	216
Chapter Twenty-Three	225
Chapter Twenty-Four	234
Chapter Twenty-Five	241
Chapter Twenty-Six	252
Chapter Twenty-Seven	259
Chapter Twenty-Eight	271
Chapter Twenty-Nine	278
Chapter Thirty	285
Chapter Thirty-One	296
Epilogue	302

Prologue

----

8 /4/11

HIS WORDS AREN'T making any sense.

He is talking and talking but not really saying anything. My pulse is increasing and my palms are slick with sweat. I am nervous...but why? We made love last night for the first time. I love him. It will all work out. But why do I have this nagging feeling in the back of my head that knows it is far from "working out".

Then his words really hit me. He. Is. Leaving. Me.

The new ink on my shoulder burns from this realization.

I can barely breathe. "Why?" I whisper to the ground, as a single chunk of my heart breaks off into a million little shards. I want to yell and scream and beg, but I can only whisper through the rain.

It's a light drizzle, nothing overly dramatic with crashing thunder and lightening or anything like that. Just a simple drizzle as if the gods above are echoing my whisper. I feel a single droplet land on my cheek just under my eye, and feel it slide down my neck and my shoulder and arm till it reaches my fingertips. And then it is gone. I'm not crying because the skies are doing it for me.

"Because we both knew it was never going to work Grayson." Another piece of my heart breaks. He never calls me by my full name. He's pulling away from me.

I meet his eyes. They are usually so bright and full of life. They always light up a room when he is laughing, or fill with joy and happiness when he's around me. But they are dead now, no happiness and no life. These are not the same eyes that held mine when he made love to me for the first time last night. Last night was everything, it was amazing...and now he is leaving me.

A slight shiver runs through my spine. "But what about last night? I thought—" I cut off unable to finish the sentence. I know that if I do I will just break even more.

His eyes pull away from mine. The rain drizzles on silently as if unaware of my heart being torn apart.

"Grayson, come on last night was fun. But it was just sex," he pauses. I know what he will say next will ruin me. "It was summer fun, it's not like I'm in love with you. I'm going back to college and you are still in high school. How was this is ever going to work?" He drives the knife in deeper as my skin prickles with goose bumps. My ears begin to ring, and I am short of breath. My whole heart burst into millions of scattered pieces, and he doesn't even care.

I didn't need the skies to cry for me anymore, because I can't stop the storm that floods my eyes.

His eyes soften slightly. "Come on Grayson, I will drive you home," he says softly. I wince at his words, hating the pity that fills every syllable for me.

"No," my voice edges with anger. I'm not an angry person. I never have been, and yet in this moment it consumes me. How could I've been so stupid to fall for someone like him? I knew he had the power to break me, but I never imagined he would. How could I be so naïve?

"Gray..." he trails as he steps closer and stretches out a hand towards me.

A sudden rage that shocks me at its force fills me. "Don't you dare Cale! Don't ever speak to me again!" I scream as I run at him, and shove him in the chest as hard as possible. My body is shaking. Vibrating with an anger I've never realized could exist. I can't feel any pain. The pain of my shattered heart is gone and replaced with this unfiltered rage.

He opens his mouth to say something and I immediately cut him off. "Fuck you Cale Hasting," I state with so much vengeance that he stumbles back a few steps. I've never spoken words like this before. I never curse, I never scream, I am never mad.

But I've never had a reason to be mad before today, and now I am reveling in this newfound anger. I hate the pain he's causing me. I hate everything about him, and I would rather be angry than feel my heart break anymore because of him. I hate him so much.

His eyes hold mine for one more second before he stalks back over to his stupid pick up truck where he first kissed me. The engine starts and he sits there for a few moments. But he finally accepts the message, and leaves me alone.

I'm alone in the rain and I don't care. I slowly lower myself to the ground and sit down in the mud, and curl up with my arms around my legs.

Fuck boys.

Fuck love.

And fuck Cale Hasting for making me love him and then taking it all away like I am nothing.

He's ruined me.

Chapter One

5/9/15

"ARE YOU SURE you can't come with me?" I ask for maybe the millionth time.

I don't usually whine, actually I always get on to Hayley for doing just that. But I haven't really seen my sister in four years, or that beach house, or that town. It all holds bad memories. I am already a bitter enough person without the reminder of that fatal summer.

I throw my last shirt in my suitcase, and sigh as I sit on my bed. I look over to Hayley hoping she will just tag along. She loves adventure, and will be able to keep my mind off that summer. The summer that changed me for the better I would say. I am no longer naïve about love or boys, but Hayley believes I need to be more naïve and have more fun.

"Gray, you know I would love to go to Florida with you—"

I cut her off. "Then come you wouldn't have to pay for a thing!" I plead. God, I sound pathetic. My shoulders slump at the realization. I am twenty years old, not sixteen anymore, and he is not even going to be there. So why am I still so apprehensive about stepping back into that stupid small beach town?

Hayley sighs and sits down next to me on the bed as her light green eyes meet mine. "You know I would love to come with you," she says. She wraps her arm around my shoulder and pulls me into her. "But I have to take this internship. If it wasn't important I would be right there with you. I always have your back G." She wraps her other arm around me and pulls me in tighter. Her naturally wavy hair tickles my shoulders, and she smells of peaches.

"You know I don't totally hate you right?" I ask as a small smile plays at my lips.

She lets me go and plants a big kiss on my cheek. "And I love you more Grayson Kennings."

I roll my eyes and pretend to wipe her kiss off. But she knows I love her more than anything, even if it is hard to say it at times. Hayley was the first friend I made in college. And even though she is the crazy party girl and I'm the furthest thing from, we mesh. We make each other better. We love each other despite our differences.

"Is it really going to be that bad?" she asks quietly. She knows what a touchy subject this is for me. It took me over a year to even begin to share with her what happened that summer. And even with that she doesn't know every detail. For me that summer will never be real if I don't have to confront anything to do with it.

I raise my left shoulder in a small shrug. "Hopefully not."

A petite redhead appears in the doorway of my room, or former room I guess I should say. I don't want to say I am bitter about Hayley filling my room for the summer. I know she needs to, an apartment in the heart of Chicago is not cheap. I just didn't think she would find someone so fast. A girl likes to think no one can live up to her. And that someone won't steal their best friend.

"Hey Maxine," I wave half-heartedly. I still don't see why Hayley chose her. She seems shy, and has barely said anything to either of us. Again I am no party child, but what Hayley and I do share is speaking our minds...and loudly.

She hugs herself as she speaks. "I finished bringing my stuff up just wanted to let you know Hay," she says quietly before turning back around and leaving.

"Hay?" I ask in a questioning tone. "I thought you hated being called that?" I say with a fake smile to cover up the sudden jealously that fills me. Can this summer really change everything? Will Maxine fill my best friend spot? I hate feeling insecure. I never let myself usually, but today was a day for unusual emotions.

Hayley's face twists, and I know she is annoyed. "Gray, don't be like that. She needed a place to stay. She is really sweet once you get to know her. Don't be that way," she pauses as she stands from my bed. "And I never said I hated being called that...it's just not my favorite," she shrugs. She then twists her hair quickly into a messy bun, and turns towards me with her hands on her hips.

It is a rare day when Hayley Mollgram is the one playing the mom role. And I guess today is one of those rare days, because I'm feeling more like a child as the day progresses. I take a deep breath, and stand up next to her and pull her into a hug.

"I am sorry. You are just my best friend and soul mate and I don't want to lose you," I pause. "Especially to some ginger who looks like a gerbil."

"Grayson!" Hayley exclaims as she pushes me away with a small laugh. Her face trying to cover her amusement and give me a stern look. She's used to my rude sayings, but I sometimes still shock her.

I yank her back to me, and give her one last squeeze. "I'm going to miss you Gray," she whispers as she takes a step away. A small tear hangs on her cheek, but she quickly wipes it away. She isn't one with emotions, even with me. She would rather go out, take a shot, and dance away the emotions. Where as I just bottle them in, and never let them show. But for some reason we are each other's weakness, we confide in each other. We really are sisters. "No one can ever replace you Gray. You are my one and only. But Maxine needs a place and a friend, so be nice. You might be surprised that you actually like her." She jabs me with her elbow.

I make a face at her. "Whatever, you know I'm not good at making friends."

She lets out a hard laugh. "You don't say, I thought you were a pretentious bitch when I met you."

I stick my tongue out. "And I thought you were a crazy slut, so it goes both ways babe," I say as I wink, and smack her ass.

She shakes her head as she chuckles. She grabs two of my duffels, and I grab the others. We both pause as our eyes meet, tears watering both of our eyes. Two years we have been together. Every break, weekend, and day of the week we spend together. I still can't believe we don't hate each other by now. But she is my sister, and it sucks to have to leave her for a whole summer. So much can change. I don't want to miss her crazy stories, the random nights when we just drive around, or when we sneak onto the rooftop and look at the stars. I just don't want to come back and feel left out. I know it's a juvenile thought, but I can't stop it from running through my head.

"Nothing is going to change G. I love you." She blinks away her tears as the words leave her mouth. I want to believe the words, but for some reason I doubt them. I can feel change, and I can't tell if it will be good or bad. But I push the feeling away, hating the thought of any change.

A small smile touches my lips. "Love you more," I pause and add, "Hay." A big fat smile coating my face just to annoy her.

She shakes her head at me before saying, "Lets get your bags out before I throw them out the window." She leads the way out of our-now just her-beautiful loft apartment. I'm just happy stupid Maxine didn't follow.

* * * * *

5/10/15

"EASTON 20 MILES" the green sign reads as I fly by on miles and miles of flat interstate. I have my windows down, with the wind flowing through my golden locks, and the radio blaring Taylor Swift's newest single. The drive is over sixteen hours, so I stopped once in Tennessee to rest for the night at a hotel. But considering I'm by myself the drive isn't as bad as I initially thought it would be. I like being alone with my thoughts. Being able to eat shitty road trip food and not feel bad about it. And even scream at the top of my lungs to awful pop music, and not have anyone to tell me to turn it down.

No, road trips are not a bad thing at all. They're liberating, and I feel free.

I hear my phone buzzing so I quickly roll up the windows half way. Turn down the radio, and grab my phone and swipe my finger against the screen. I hold the phone up to my ear with my right hand. "Hello?" I answer.

"GRAYSON!" I'm met with the squeals of my sister, as I pull the phone away from my ear with a cringe. Sometimes I can't believe she is two years older than me with all of the squealing she does.

"Yes Bailey?" I ask trying to keep the annoyance out of my voice. I know she misses me, and I honestly do miss her. We used to be so close, but after that summer I pulled away from everyone. Including my best friend and sister.

"How far away are you? I can't wait to see you! Agh! I am so excited! I have so much to tell you!" Her words come out fast and loud as I again cringe at her voice. When we were younger I used to make fun of her for her squeaky voice. She hated it. The parents pretended they didn't agree.

I put my right turn signal on as I merge over to Exit 23. I turn left, and I know what will be greeting me in less than thirty seconds. And there it is. A huge bright blue sign that reads, "WELCOME TO EASTON. THE TOWN OF MEMORIES."

The irony is so palpable in that moment I think it might reach out and slap me.

I let out a shaky breath. "Just passed the sign sis."

I hate that he had to ruin this place for me. I used to love coming here with my family in the summers. This place holds so many great moments in my heart, and it sucks that one big memory had to stomp the rest of them out.

But he won't ruin today, I decide in this moment. I can taste the salt in the air, and already feel the heat on my skin. This is also my home, and he won't ruin this for me. This is my chance to reunite with my family. It has been four years, and I refuse to let some stupid boy who won't even be here still dictate my life.

I ignore the babbling buffoon also known as my sister, and hang up on her. She will only be mad for a few seconds. I just have to take everything in. Every shack, person, and stranded flip-flop. I roll the windows back down and turn the radio as loud as I can. The feeling of freedom rips through my bones, and lights my veins on fire. It has been so long since I felt this feeling of total abandon and pure bliss. I don't want to let it go.

The fear of this trip is gone, and excitement fills my every cell.

I round a corner before pulling down our street. A street unlike any other. Rows and rows of beautiful beach houses lined right up against the sand almost touching the shore. It's breathtaking.

Quickly I pull into our long driveway noticing my sister's car, and another one I didn't recognize. I ignore it knowing she brought a friend, and slightly pissed again Hayley couldn't tag along. I hop out of my car. I look up at the two story beige house with a million windows looking. Everything looks the same from all those years ago, and that instills a sense of comfort. Change can be scary.

A smile lights up my face as I skip up the front steps, and whip the door open to the smell of lemons. I'm immediately giddy knowing mom made fresh squeezed lemonade, which is my favorite. I run to the fridge while also grabbing a glass from the cabinet by the fridge, and yell, "BAILEY!"

I grab the gigantic jug of lemonade and place it on the counter. I dig for ice for my glass out of the freezer. It is so weird how at home and natural I feel here after a four-year hiatus.

I hear footsteps descending from the stairs behind me. "Sissy!" she squeals and I roll my eyes at her childish language.

I glance over my shoulder. "Hey Bai, you excited for the summer? What's the big deal about coming here? Everyone is okay, right?" I ask her as I finish digging up ice. I'm going to have to get my dad to fix the dispenser, because it is way backed up.

"Yes, everything is fine," she pauses. "Can you look at me Gray?" she asks as her voice climbs an octave and I grab a lemon from the fridge. I begin to slice it to add to the drink. Our family takes lemonade very seriously. Bailey and I always used to have lemonade stands, and no joke we would rake in some serious cash. My mom's lemonade is famous in this small town. It honestly is the perfect drink for a day at the beach. Well now that I am older so is a pina colada, but I will settle with the non-alcoholic drink for now.

"What's so important? Hey do you want a glass also?" I ask. Though I already begin to grab a glass with a slight pause wondering if her friend wants one also.

I open my mouth to ask Bailey, when she cuts me off. "Come on Gray, just turn around I have to show you something!" she's now whining. Seriously you are twenty-two Bailey, act like it.

I smirk as I say, "Unless you have a huge rock on your finger and a hot guy on our arm I'm going to finish making some lemonade for us." I laugh to myself. The last person she was talking to was some pompous ass that went to Yale, and that was almost a year ago now. We have both been severely single lately.

A throat clears, and it sounds male. "Well..." Bailey trails. No, I think. She has to be lying! Could she really be?

"What?" I ask confused as I grab both glasses, which look beautiful if I do say so myself.

I turn around.

But what catches my attention isn't my sister's bright blue eyes. Or the gorgeous rock that lies perfectly on her left hand, like she was born to bear this type of jewelry.

No, what catches my attention is the hand she's holding. What catches my attention are bright hazel eyes. He catches my attention, because I haven't seen him in years. Four years to be exact. He catches my attention because he is still so handsome, and even more so now.

Don't say it. Don't say it. Don't say it. I think over and over hoping it won't and cannot be true, even though it's blindingly obvious.

She pulls him closer as she looks up at him. "Gray, this is my fiancé Cale. Cale, this is my sister, and soon to be maid of honor Grayson," she says with a little squeal of excitement. My blood freezes, and my heart stops at her words.

"Fuck," slips out of my mouth as the glasses of lemonade slide through the grasps of my fingers, and smash into a million pieces on the floor.

Life sucks sometimes.

Chapter Two

5/10/15

"LANGUAGE GRAYSON KENNINGS!" my mother's voice echoes from the front door.

She was never one for explicit language. It is "dirty and improper," she always says.

"Sorry," I mumble out feeling ten years old again. Not even in the house a few minutes and I've already had my mind tossed upside down, broken glasses, and been chastised. There goes my carefree summer of fun.

My mother's petite frame pops around the corner with my father. My mother is stunning with her chestnut colored hair and fair skin. My father and her both share the same blue eyes that Bailey and I are blessed with. Bailey shares the same hair color and facial structure as our mom, soft and round, always looking like an angel. But while my sister takes after my mother, I take after my father. He's a tall man, well over six feet tall with a strong build. We share the same bright blonde hair, and I have his strong facial features. Like a straight nose, and high cheekbones.

My mother and father sit the load of groceries they are carrying on the island in the kitchen. My mother's looking at the ground. "What happened in here?" she asks her face pinched. She quickly grabs the broom and dustpan from the pantry, and my father begins to pick up the larger chunks. I just awkwardly step out of the way.

I twist my hands not knowing how to answer.

"I told her," Bailey says happily.

I swallow the lump in my throat that is her news. "Yeah, and the glasses were slick..." I say nervously not wanting to look at the real reason as to why I dropped them. I then pause in confusion. "Wait you two knew?" I exclaim.

My father finishes collecting the glass, adding them in a separate bag with my mother's pieces she gathered. "No one walk in here without shoes on for the rest of the day," my father says ignoring my question.

"We just found out also Grayson, don't get you panties in a twist." That's my mother's favorite line to say.

"Was your drive good?" my mother asks after everything is cleaned up. I smile and nod, and both my mother and father immediately come over and engulf me in their arms. Because of my refusal to come down to Easton they rarely get to see me. They will occasionally visit, but they love the beach and can't understand my reasoning for wanting to go somewhere where it snows so much.

We grew up in Virginia and would always come on vacation in Florida. And one year we stumbled across Easton when I was young, and the family fell in love. We've had a house here ever since. It really did become a second home. I won't be surprised when my parents retire if they move down here full time. They are here more days out of the year then our actual home in Virginia. The air, the ocean, the feeling is just so different here. It makes everything seem better.

"We've missed you so much sweetheart," my father's deep voice rumbles.

I pull them closer. "I've missed you both more." And I really did. My family is a close one. I pulled away from everyone after that summer when I was sixteen. I didn't mean for it to happen, my heart hardened, and it became hard for me to be close to anyone. When we were all home and it was time to come back to Easton, I would make an excuse and stay in Virginia while everyone else left. He changed everything for me.

The reminder forces my eyes to snap to his. He's already watching me with those hazel eyes that still haunt me.

I pull away from my parents suddenly feeling extremely cramped with all the sudden emotions that fill me. I didn't like to feel many emotions. Emotions are messy, and I don't do messy. Messy creates problems.

But my parents, my sister, and Cale in one day, and in the span of ten minutes, it's too much. I look around the room and all eyes are on me. I panic. "I...um...I am going to go get my bags...."

I quickly start towards the front door when I hear my sister say, "Cale go help her."

My feet halt instantly and I whip around. "I don't need help." Especially yours, I want to add. My words come out a little hard.

Bailey waves her hand at me like I am being a child. "No, it's fine Cale will help you," she pushes. I roll my eyes and start towards the door like my life depends on it. I can't make a big deal out of this, or it will just look weird. But this whole situation is weird! I let out a frustrated growl. No one knows what happened that summer, no one knows of Cale and I, because I was just some dirty secret.

I make it to my car and open my trunk a little more forcefully than needed. I start throwing my luggage out of the car and onto the cement driveway. I can hear footsteps and I just hope it's my parents.

The sounds of footsteps stop right behind me, and I know it isn't my parents. I can feel him, feel the way my body heats at the proximity of his. I can feel the way my pulse jumps, and how my skin prickles with his nearness. I hate that my body still responds to him.

"Do you want help?" His deep voice rubs against me making me want to curl in a ball and cry with all of the memories that suddenly slam into me.

I throw another bag out of the car. "Would rather throw my body off a cliff," my voice says full of hatred.

I hear him take a breath. "Are we going to talk about this?" his voice hushed. That's right, can't let anyone know you fucked my heart and body one summer. Anger begins to pump through me, and the more I think about him and that summer the more it fills me.

He walks a few steps until he's to my left near the trunk, but still a respectful amount of distance sits between us. "Gray..." he whispers, trailing as if there are no words. And he would be right. There are no words because he said all of them four years ago. I don't need to hear one more word ever come from his mouth.

I throw my last bag out and slam the trunk closed, almost hitting his face before he jumps out of the way. I meet his shock filled eyes. "Don't call me that. You are not my friend, and you are not family. You are nothing to me. So don't talk to me, and I hope you rot in hell," my voice is calm, but holds a single waver of wrath in it.

He finally backs away from me. His jaw locked and his body stiff, I know he's pissed. But he has no right to be. I may be acting like a bitch, but I wasn't the one who ended things like he did.

"What happened to the sweet Grayson?" he mumbles as he turns his back and starts in on back to the house.

I snort. "She died four years ago," I speak aloud. He pauses for a mere second at my words before walking into the house and closing the door a little harder than needed.

If he thinks I will let the past be the past he's wrong. In public I will act like nothing is wrong. But if he ever tries to talk to me one on one I'll let him have it. Sometimes late at night I will imagine what I would say to him if I ever saw again. A small smile touches my lips, damn would it feel great to say those things to him.

It takes two trips and a lot of huffing and puffing to lug my many bags into my room, and I am just on the first level. I even hear my sister tell Cale that I'm, "like a feminist or something" and that is why I won't let him help me with my bags. Bailey sometimes makes me want to punch a wall. If she only knew the true reason.

My parents begin to put away groceries and yell that dinner will be ready at five. Which gives me thirty minutes to begin to unpack. Bailey and Cale go upstairs to do god knows what. The thought alone sent vivid flashes of images that have me so sick I almost hurl.

I close the door to my room and just stand there for a second taking in everything. This room used to be my haven. I loved this room with its pale yellow walls, with my white furniture, and pale pink comforter. The whole right wall is cork and filled with pictures and mementos from over the years. The whole left wall is floor to ceiling windows that double as doors and overlook the beach. I used to open them during the day and let in the natural light and sea breeze. It took a lot of negotiating for me to get this room.

My parents are on the other side of the house on the first floor. They technically have the master though their room doesn't have quite the view mine has. Bailey's room is on the second floor with the guest bedroom. She loved being up there as a teen because she could sneak boys up to her room easily and the parents didn't sleep up there to even begin to notice. She always would taunt me saying the parents would always know when I had a boy over because their room was on the same level as mine.

And yet no one knew of that summer and Cale.

I sit down on the bed in my room. It's odd being somewhere I was once so comfortable, and now I hate being in this room. Cale and I shared so many nights together in here. Nothing crazy happened...just talking, and kissing, and cuddling, and more talking until the sun came up. I fell so fast and hard for him. I was young and stupid to even begin to see that he would never feel the same about me.

I stand and slide the curtains open, and push the doors open. A sudden gush of wind hits me and I smile. I love the feeling of being on the beach in my own room. I can hear the fluttering of pictures on the opposite wall. I turn and walk over running my fingers over all the memories I have had in this small town.

My fingers suddenly come to a halt on an old picture of my dog and me. I was twelve years old and Gus almost as old as me. He was a small dog. Only about five pounds, but he was the best pet a family could ask for. But it isn't the picture of me and an old dog that stops me, it's what is underneath. I lift the picture and a small gasp leaves me.

It's still here.

I lay down in bed with the biggest smile on my face.

I'm in love with Cale. I think I knew I would love him from the moment I met him. But I wasn't going to tell him that just yet, it is too soon. But

I know he will love me to one day. I can feel it, we are meant to be. The age difference means nothing to me. He's only three years older. Heck my grandparents are fifteen years apart.

But I know it worries him. Being three years apart in ten years doesn't mean much. But being three years apart now.... I'm sixteen years old about to be a junior in high school, where as Cale is nineteen about to be a sophomore in college.

Three years doesn't seem so big. But high school to college...yeah that seems like a big difference. But when we hang out it doesn't seem to matter anymore, when he holds me, and kisses me...nothing matters.

I sigh and lift my hand to touch my lips. They feel swollen but in a good way. I can still feel him pressing his lips to mine. Every kiss feels like the first and I love that. I have never felt this way before and it scares me and excites me all at once.

The sound of a rock hitting my window startles me out of my trance and I shoot up in my bed. I look over to my windows wondering if Cale's coming over for the night again. No one is there though. My shoulders slump in disappointment. But another rock against the window catches my attention and I stand up from my bed and walk over to the windows. I look around and again see nothing. I grab my curtains to close them suddenly feeling uncomfortable when a small note tapped to the window catches my attention.

I open the door and rip off the small white note and close the door quickly whilst closing the curtains also.

Behind Gus lays us. The note reads. A small smile lifts my lips. I know it's from Cale. He loves his stupid little riddles.

Gus? My dog that died a few years back.... What does our relationship have to do with a dead dog?

I only have one picture with Gus and it's on my cork wall. So I walk over and run my eyes over the wall before finding the single picture of Gus and I when I was twelve. I lift the picture still confused what is beneath the picture.

When I lift it a small gasp escapes me. It's a picture of Cale and I. It is from the Fourth of July weekend. My friend Kylie had snapped a picture of us. Cale has always been weird about people taking pictures of us. I know he isn't ready to tell his parents about us. I think he's afraid someone will post it somewhere and it will get out. I hate that we are a secret, but I wouldn't trade him for anything. I love him.

I thought Kylie deleted the picture but I guess not.

I was looking at Kylie with a huge smile on my face, while Cale looked down at me. His eyes are bright and he looks at me like I am his everything. And I want to be. I want to be everything and anything he ever wants. God I have it bad.

But I now have a piece of us. Something I can look at and know for sure that this isn't all just a dream.

I pluck the picture from the wall and run my fingers over it again and again. I flip it over to make sure nothing is on the back and smile at his scratchy handwriting that resides on the back.

I can't wait to kiss you again.

My heart beats a little faster.

I never want this summer to end.

But it did.

It ended in a horrible crash.

I rip the picture from the wall and throw it in the trash. I want to scream and throw things and scream some more. But I know it won't do anything. I meant nothing to him. I was just a stepping-stone onto bigger and better things. Like my perfect size two, 5'4", angel faced sister.

I was nothing to him and I hate that he was once my everything. I hate that I let him rip my heart into so many pieces that I never got them all back. My heart will never be the same. And I blame him. It may have been four years ago, and I should probably move on. But I can't. I never got to say what I wanted to say.

But I would this summer. It's time for me to move on. To finally take those pieces of my heart back and live my life.

"Dinner!" my mother's voice echoes.

I look at the picture one more time before I walk out of the room.

Chapter Three

5/10/15

"IS THERE ANYTHING I can help with?" I ask as I step into the kitchen. Cale and Bailey have yet to come down stairs.

My mom's opening the oven and checking in on the twice-baked potatoes, and my dad has just come in with a pan of deliciously smelling grilled salmon. Everything looks and smells amazing and I realize how much I've missed a good home cooked meal. There will always be something about your own parents and how they cook that is the best. It's the best because it reminds me of home.

"Salad please Gray. Everything is already cut up just mix together," my mother requests as she worries over the asparagus on the stove.

I snatch a large glass bowl from the cabinet and place it on the island. I walk over to the fridge and gather all the ingredients for the salad. I unload them onto the countertops and spread them out to see what I am working with. Mom has a fresh bag of spinach and cut up lettuce. I empty them both into the bowl first. I then litter the salad with sliced baby tomatoes, chopped onions, mushrooms, and various other greens. I pour on the homemade dressing my dad always makes. I honestly don't know how he does it, but it tastes amazing.

My parents and I work silently but in comfort. The breeze of the ocean coming in from the kitchen windows mix with the country music softly playing in the background. I feel more at home than I have in a very long time.

I grab the wooden tongs and toss the salad thoroughly making sure to coat the leaves with the oil based dressing. I then top the whole salad with a light sprinkle of fresh shredded mozzarella.

"Dinner!" my father bellows. I know what he's guessing is happening upstairs and anyone can tell he isn't pleased by it. My parents are a tad old fashioned.

"I finished the salad," I say as I bring it over to the table. My mom follows with the potatoes on one plate and the asparagus on the other.

I can hear the two lovebirds come down the stairs before I can see them. I look up to see my sister patting down her hair and Cale fixing his shirt. Super classy. My stomach churns in disgust. "Wonder what you two were doing?" I mumble with a sneer.

"What?" my mother and Bailey ask at the same time.

I sigh. "Nothing just talking to myself," I say waving it off.

I help my parents finish setting the table up while my sister and Cale continue to be nauseatingly annoying.

Finally everything is finished and we all sit down as one big happy family ...minus Cale. Everyone starts to dish up their plates and I am waiting for who will bring up the elephant in the room first.

Throat clearing from my father means he is volunteering. "So," he pauses. "How did you two meet?"

"How did he propose? And when is the wedding?" My mother pipes in happily.

Bailey's face lights up like she's been waiting for this question all day. Cale smiles at her but it never reaches his eyes. His gaze flickering over to mine before turning back to his plate. Good, I'm glad he is uncomfortable. I don't want him here anyways.

"Well you all know I came down here right after school ended last year to be with friends and to get over some things—"

"Grant, was it? Catching your boyfriend with another girl can be a buzz kill," I say as I take a bite of the salmon that is the definition of perfection.

Silence. I am met with silence. I look up from my plate to see all eyes on me. "Sorry was that rude?" More silence. "Please continue," I say with the wave of my fork before stabbing another piece of fish.

"Well, we met that summer. He lives here." Bailey's face is a little flushed still because of my comment. I will admit it was a rude and low blow. But my mind is still a little distracted from the big piece of male shit that sits across from me. Still I do feel bad and that isn't what this summer's about.

"Where's your house?" my dad asks actually interested unlike me.

"I have an apartment downtown, but my family is from The Grove sir," Cale responds. A small snort slips from me, but at least no one hears, or they don't care. I had only gone to his house one time that summer, but I forgot he grew up on The Grove.

Of course he lived on The Grove with the wealthiest of the wealthiest. Most people think our beach house is large, and then I show them The

Grove. Our house looks like a shack in comparison. He would come from money. I mean I know he has money he is a Hasting. But we never really talked about money or those types of things, so it never really hit me that he was a Grove boy back then. We talked about life and family and school...not money.

We kept things simple. Too deep brought serious conversations that brought questioning of the future, which brought fighting, which brought a hot make out session. We did more kissing and fondling than serious talking that summer.

I miss part of what Bailey says. But the gist is they meet and fall "madly in love", her words not mine. I really don't need the details of how she used him as a rebound and then they decided they actually liked each other. Shocker. Two attractive people falling for each other.

"Proposal?" my mom asks with wide eyes. She's a sucker for the stories. I for one want to throw up...all over Cale.

"You wanna tell this one babe?" Bailey asks Cale.

His eyes once again flicker over to mine, and something in his eyes tells me I'm not going to like this story very much. But he answers, "Of course."

He clears his throat. "Well it was just a few days ago. I took her to the beach for a walk around sunset. It was a beautiful night, perfect for a proposal. I had the ring for a while now but just didn't know when I was going to ask the big question. But something about this night just felt right," he says as he looks down at my sister. The way he looks at her almost makes me cry. He used to look at me that way.

He continues. "I brought her to this little cave on the beach where you can sit and just watch the tide come in and out. And next thing you know we fell asleep and when I woke and saw her just beautifully laying there I knew I had to do it. So I pulled out the ring and slid it on her finger. She woke a few seconds later confused but then saw the ring and said..." he pauses looking at her with a smile on his face.

Bailey's whole face lights up with the story. "I said yes of course!"

My mother and father continue asking questions while a piece of my heart breaks off and floats over to Cale. He already has so many pieces of my broken heart that I will never get back, and yet he still finds ways to take more years later.

Cale's refusing to look at me, and only I know why. I can't believe he would take her to the cave. But then again since the day after he acted like I was nothing and walked away from me I can believe it...I just don't want to. I thought he made love to me for the first time in that cave, but no I was fucked in more ways than one in that cave for the fist time. And him taking my sister to that cave to propose to her, and probably have sex with her makes my heart hurt so badly.

I begin to pick at my food not listening to them talking anymore. I don't need to hear any more stories, because I am far beyond gone. I'm breaking all over again and I hate that he still has this power over me. And a small part of me knows he always will. First cuts are the deepest.

"So the reason it was so important for everyone to come is we want be married by the end of this summer!" Bailey squeals.

Well that catches my attention.

"Are you fucking kidding me?" I ask seriously.

"Grayson language again!" my mother scolds. "What has college taught you?" she mumbles.

"I am sorry but they have barely known each other for a year and then they want to get married so soon...are you pregnant?" I ask. And it may have sounded rude, all right it is rude, but it's also a valid question. Why is this all happening so fast?

"Grayson!" my mother and father yell.

"Oh my goodness!" my sister squeaks her face engulfed in flames of embarrassment.

"Good god..." Cale moans.

I raise my hands in defense. "I am sorry! But you all know it is a valid question!" I wasn't usually this much of a loose canon. I like order and thinking before speaking, but this whole conversation is putting me off my game.

Bailey shakes her head still appalled. "Of course not. We are in love and want to start our lives together as soon as possible. Is that a crime?" she asks annoyance clear in her voice, and her eyes shooting daggers at me.

My mother leans over and rubs her arm. "Of course not honey, we all support you."

I want to object but feel after all I've said today it will really cross a line. My mom claps her hands together excitedly. "Well, planning has to begin right away! Have you thought of anything? Venue? Dress? Flowers? Date? Wow I can't believe this is happening it is so exciting my eldest getting married right here in Easton!"

I don't think I've seen my mom this happy since they opened a Target down the road, and she really loves Target.

Bailey nods along with my mother. "Venue is going to be the beach either here or The Grove we haven't decided. Date is August eighth, the first Saturday of the month. Options for bridesmaid dresses have been selected and pulled at the store downtown, but no shopping for me yet. I have been waiting for my maid of honor," she says looking at me. "And my mother to come with me obviously."

I smile at her though I can't tell if I am genuinely happy about being her maid of honor, or apart of this wedding in anyway. Let's be real I'm not. And that makes me an awful sister, and made of honor, and human being in general.

"Oh baby, you have done so much in the last couple days!" my mom claps proudly. Like it's the most amazing thing ever that Bailey planned something. It always was this way with her, praise for the eldest no matter what.

Bailey shrugs. "We have to, we don't have much time till the wedding." And then she stops and looks at me. "That is okay Gray right, that you are my maid of honor?" Bailey asks with wide eyes and a pleading smile.

I nod, "Of course, I am honored sis." And I am. I just wish she wasn't marrying the one person in this world I hate more than anything.

After the wedding chatter dies down a bit everyone helps clean the table up and put the leftovers away. It goes quickly with five of us. Cale and Bailey start making their way upstairs again when Bailey shouts, "Oh Grayson, you have to go try on dresses tomorrow so we can get it fitted in time for the wedding! And we have a meeting with the florist!" And then she's gone.

Oh, fun now I'm going to be drowning in wedding magazines and color palates for the summer. What ever happened to my carefree summer? Oh yeah Cale Hasting had to come crashing down and ruin everything...again.

I need some fresh air after dinner so I make my way down to the beach. I roll the cuffs of my boyfriend jeans higher and shrug off my cardigan and wrapped it around my waist. The slight breeze rolls over my shoulders and the setting sun flickers off the waves of the water making the ocean glitter. Damn I missed it here.

I find a spot and sit down in the sand. It has been so long since I touched sand. I forgot how soft it feels and the way is squishes between my fingers and toes. It feels like home. With my eyes closed and the warm summer air washing through me I feel at peace. Even with everything that has happened, in this small moment I feel calm.

His fingers lace through mine. It is the first time he has ever held my hand and I can't get the smile off my face. I feel giddy and alive. He's older than me but I don't care. I have never met anyone like him before.

Cale is the type of guy who's dangerous. He will either love fiercely and forever, or break my heart and leave me in a big pile of broken shards. But something about his smile and the way he looks at me...I know we can love each other. There is just that something. I always thought it was a myth, but it exists. The pull, the way my skin prickles when he is around, and the way my heart races when his skin accidentally brushes mine.

God if this feeling was a drug I would be an addict. I crave him, and I have only known him for a week or so.

"Do you want to grab something to eat?" his deep voice rolls over my skin making me shiver.

It's around two in the afternoon and the sun is blasting down on us. I can feel the sweat dampening my skin. I try to not look too much at Cale because I can see the beads of sweat on his skin, and it makes me want to lick them off of him.

I clear my throat and try to clear my mind of these thoughts of his sweaty body on mine. I have never had these types of thoughts before, and it is new and exciting. "Um...yeah sure," my words stumble out. I am always such an ineloquent mess around him, mother would not be happy.

"What would you like?" his hand squeezes mine lightly.

"Anything cold," I say looking up at his hazel eyes that make my heart melt. His eyes hold mine before flickering to my lips once and then back. Dear lord I want him to kiss me so bad. I have only kissed a few guys and it was all right. But Cale is experienced and just the feeling of his eyes on my lips makes me tingle, I know the real thing might kill me.

"Alright lets go get something to cool you down," he smiles. His hand pulls me in the direction of his truck. It's black and shinny and I love the way he looks driving it. I know that's weird, but some guys are born to drive certain cars. Cale was born to drive this truck. He isn't a hick or a cowboy. He just looks sexy as hell in it.

He opens the door for me and I smile at him. I have never had a boy treat me this way. It makes me feel all tingly inside. He slides into the drivers seat and the truck roars to life and then we are off. Off to god knows where but we are off. The windows are down and the radio is blaring some cheesy pop song that we both sing obnoxiously loud to. Sometimes our eyes meet and I will look away with a blush creeping up my face. I still don't know why he picked me that night, but I know that I am just happy he did.

Cale goes through a small drive through of a run down shake joint. Though it looks sad and small they hands down have the best custard and shakes in town. Cale orders me a vanilla chocolate twist in a cone and he gets a cherry shake. He pays and I protest but he says, "My mother would shoot me if I didn't pay on a date." And I immediately shut up. He said we were on a date. I can't wipe the silly smile off my face. The few times before this it was just hanging out, but this is a date. I'm not really sure what constitutes as a date and what doesn't, but I don't care as long as it is one.

He hands me my cone and grabs his shake before driving down a ways till we end up at a surf shop. He pulls into their parking lot that perfectly overlooks the beach in Easton. A know a lot of couples come here to do...you know. I get a little nervous at that, but try not to show it. I mean if he tries something I will like it right?

He turns the engine off but keeps the radio playing in the background. He reaches for his shake that has been residing in the cup holder when I snatch the cherry that's lying on the whipped cream of his shake.

"Hey," he chuckles. I lick the whipped cream off of the cherry and his laughing dies down immediately. His eyes are locked on my mouth. I feel alive and in charge...and a little dirty. But I like the way my blood boils and the hairs on my arms rise when he looks at me like this.

"I can tie the cherry stem in a knot you know?" I comment as I pluck the maraschino cherry off and eat it.

His eyebrows raise. "Really?"

"You don't believe me?" I ask as I plop the stem into my mouth and start to twist and turn the stem. Not even thirty seconds later I take the stem off my tongue and show him the small knot I have made.

His eyes have darkened slightly. "You know what they say about that?"

A small giggle leaves me. "I know my mom hates when I do it, it's not lady like apparently."

Cale shrugs. "Being a lady is for your thirties," he says as he sips on his shake.

I nod as I lick the side of my cone that has started to melt. I turn to Cale to make a comment about the surf shop and ask if he surfs because it is a dream of mine to learn when my comment dies in my throat.

Cale's eyes are black as he looks at me. He sets his drink down and reaches his hand out towards my face. "You have some ice cream right here..." he mumbles as his finger reaches out to wipe a small part of my lower lip and chin. Then he brings his finger to his mouth and licks it. My whole body's on fire from his touch, his gaze, the sight of his tongue, and the ideas I am beginning to get in my head.

"Taste good?" I ask a little breathless.

He groans, "Lets see." Before his hands pull me closer to him and he kisses me.

I drop my cone on the floor...completely worth it.

Not really worth it I would say now.

I dust myself off as I stand from the sand. Why am I being punished with these memories? I don't want to remember anything from that summer! I wish it didn't even happen. Maybe I would be a normal twenty year old who would know how to have relationships then. But I don't, because I'm scared of ever even letting a guy that close to me. So scared he will break me into a million little pieces that I may never get some back.

I walk into the house through the patio door and make my way to the kitchen to grab some water. I hear heavy footsteps behind me and I can feel it's him. Don't ask me how, I just know. And I hate that I know. I hate that I know his scent, his touch, the way his chest raises and falls when he sleeps. I hate that I know him at all.

"Do you still have the truck?" I would have noticed that truck and knew he was here when I pulled in if it had been outside the house.

Silence. I don't know if he is shocked because I know it's him or that I am talking to him...probably both.

"In the shop. That one is my fathers," he says.

I nod as I head back to my room. His voice quietly calls after me. "Are we talking?" he asks.

I shake my head and say," No." Then I slam the door behind me.

This is going to be one long summer.

Chapter Four

5/11/15

I ROLL OVER to the sound of my phone buzzing from a text message.

Rubbing the sleep out of my eyes I try to get my contacts to focus. I really shouldn't be sleeping in them, but I do anyways. I hate myself in glasses.

I grab my phone and swipe my finger across the screen to be greeted with a text message from Hayley.

Hope you made it there safely! I won't be really able to talk this week because the new internship is bat shit crazy but hopefully by next week things will settle down for me to talk your ear off for hours! Lots of love

I text my love back with a little encouragement to help her get through the week. It's weird being away from Hayley and not knowing what is happening every second of her life. I feel disconnected from my best friend and I don't like it. I wanted to call her right away when I saw Cale and tell her, but a part of me still can't believe it's real. I am hoping it was all one big bad dream.

But I wake up to my room in Easton and I know it all is real. My sister is marrying a man who broke my heart into so many pieces one summer without even blinking an eye. I loved him more than anything, and he just wanted to use me for sex and then break it off.

A part of me knows I will always love him, and a part of me knows I will always hate him. I will always have feelings for Cale Hasting because he was my first love. I might not have been his love at all, but he was mine. First loves are wild, young, and reckless, and they run the deepest. First loves are love in its purest forms. And for a lot of people they should never love the way they loved for their first love, it is dangerous and unsteady.

I loathe Cale for what he did to me. But I'm not stupid enough to ignore the fact that he will always own a piece of me. A single piece I am going to try and regain back this summer. It is time from me to move on from the pain he caused me all those years ago. It is time for me to try and become a whole person who can fully love without fears. And maybe be a little less bitter.

I roll out of bed pulling my hair from its messy bun that resides on the top of my head. My long hair comes tumbling down over my shoulders in waves. I'm in a small tank and undies when I cross my room to use the bathroom. The one thing I hate about my room is that my bathroom has two doors. One from my room and one on the other side that guests can use if they are downstairs. My bathroom always has to be kept clean and nice for guests. Unlike Bailey's whose bathroom is always scattered with makeup and hair products.

I don't pay attention to the fact that the light is already on when I swing the door open to reveal Cale in all his sweaty glory standing there in just a pair of running shorts and nothing else.

Nothing happens for a few seconds. A small gasp falls from my lips, but other than that for a few moments we just stare at each other.

I can't look away. His dirty blonde hair is almost lighter than before from the sun. His hair always has that just rolled out of bed look to it, the look that makes any girl want to run their fingers through it and even pull on it a bit. I remember I used to, and he loved it. His body is even more in shape than it was four years ago. His arms bigger, his muscles more defined, but still lean and tall. The wave tattoo on his ribcage is still the only ink his body holds. His body's glistening with a thin layer of sweat, and the few beads that slide down his body makes my skin flush at the sudden flashes of images that run through my head. Very dirty images.

I'm flustered and my pulse is running wild with the way he's looking at me. I haven't been looked at like that in years. Like someone wants to devour me, but in the best way possible.

I lick my dry lips and force words to leave my mouth. "What...um...what are you doing in here Cale?" My voice comes out breathless and scratchy. I can't think straight. I didn't think he could still do this to me, I didn't think he would still hold this power over me. But he does.

My whole body lights on fire, and my core has this ache that runs so deep I know I will need a nice cold shower to get rid of it.

But the way he's looking at me isn't helping. His hazel eyes are black as they run over my bare legs to my small tank that barely contains my breasts. The want in his eyes is beyond evident, and I hate that my body's responding to him like this. My nipples harden, my skin's hot and flushed, and I know he can see my chest heave with shallow breaths.

I try again. "Cale. Why are you in my bathroom?"

His eyes run over my legs one more time before he snaps out of his trance and turns towards the mirror. His body is shaking slightly as if he's trying to control himself. He runs a single hand over his face a few times. That is his tell, he's anxious.

He inhales a sharp breath. "I went for a run and was just splashing some water on my face. The sun was a little overkill today. I forgot that this was your bathroom," he pauses as his eyes hold mine through the mirror. "I'm sorry."

I know that "sorry" is his way of apologizing for years ago, and I don't want it.

I narrow my eyes in on him. "I don't want your apologizes. Just get the fuck out of my bathroom," I rumble.

He flips from the mirror to face me. The bathroom isn't that big and in the small space he's suddenly too close, too real, and all in all just too much.

Cale opens his mouth to say something but I cut him off. "Never mind I will just leave," I say as I turn around to leave my bathroom.

His hand shoots out suddenly and grips my waist pulling my body in that moment to his. My back against his front. Too little of clothing and too much heat makes my body all too aware of his.

I close my eyes trying to clear my head of the things I want to do to him…his body. I hate him. I just have to remember that, and it works. For a few seconds I forget about the heat, and my body tries to slide from his strong grip. "Let me go Cale," I growl.

But his grip only tightens on my waist, pulling me closer till I am so pressed up against his body I can feel every plane, dip, and curve of his torso. The feeling of his hard body against my back makes my thighs quiver, and an ache twist in my stomach. I also feel a little something else that's beginning to poke at my back. And I hate that it turns me on even more than I already am. He broke me. Hell, he is engaged to my sister! Ugh, this is so wrong!

"Cale, you are engaged to my sister!" I say repeating my inner thoughts. "Let me the fuck go!" I whisper yell at him.

He releases one hand, his right, to swipe my long locks off my shoulder to reveal the small tattoo I have. His fingertips leaving a trail of sparks in their path. No one knows about it, only Hayley. My parents would freak and Bailey would want to know the meaning behind it. It was a stupid mistake to get it when I did. But now it serves as a constant reminder that no matter what happens, I can only depend on myself.

"When did you get this Grayson?" His voice is quiet but fierce. A small wave of anger clear through his words. His fingers like a soft feather tracing the small wave that resides on my right shoulder. The smaller version of the exact wave that lay upon his ribcage.

I struggle against him again and this time he lets me go. I turn to face him my eyes hard and my jaw locked. He doesn't deserve to know anything. He's nothing to me, and he has already proven I was nothing to him.

I cross my arms defensively. "It doesn't matter," I barely whisper. I don't understand why he gets to be the one who is mad here.

Two steps. That is all it takes for him to have me pressed against my bathroom door and his body hovering over mine. "Like hell. Tell me," he demands. The vein in his neck is standing out, and his nostrils are flaring with irritation. The tension in the bathroom so thick I can almost feel it pressing our bodies closer.

I shrug like it's nothing when we both know better. "After the cave. You dropped me off at home and I left a while later to go get some food when I passed a tattoo place that I knew wouldn't card me and I got it." And then I came to meet you at the beach and surprise you with it, but you dumped me like the trash on the road. I didn't say it because we both know what happened, but I was damn sure close.

I can feel the tears prick from under my eyes. I hate feeling vulnerable. I'm the strong, independent girl who's in charge and knows what she wants.

But he makes me feel weak and sixteen all over again. I lick my lips and pressed my fisted hands into my thighs to keep the tears at bay.

His eyes soften, as he took a step back and looks around trying to process what has happened. "Gray..." is all that escapes so I cut him off before he can say any more.

I shake my head and swallow the lump that clogs my throat. "It was stupid and a mistake. Just forget about it, and leave me the hell alone," I speak quietly before slipping back into my room.

I know he won't come in. It would be crossing too many lines too soon.

I head over to my bed and crawl back under the covers wishing I had Hayley to lean on as tears slip silently over my cheeks.

I hate what Cale Hasting has done to me.

* * * * *

"Are you serious?" my sister yells into the phone. I have just walked into the kitchen to grab an apple when she comes storming down the stairs in a cloud of aggravation.

"Ugh, yes I guess that is fine, but I better be receiving a discount for the inconvenience!" She pauses listening to the person on the other end of the phone call. "I don't care that the wedding is less than three months away, you will do it!" Her voice demands as it reaches a new level of squeakiness in that moment. I feel bad for the other person on the line. Bailey isn't easy to deal with when she wants something and they obviously aren't seasoned in the art of keeping crazy brides calm.

She hangs up and slams the phone on the counter. "Fudge," she mumbles. I shake my head, god she can't even curse like an adult. She runs her hands through her hair and begins to whine like a dog.

I roll my eyes. "Everything okay Bai?" I ask not really caring to be honest. I don't think planning a wedding should be this stressful, and if they pushed the wedding date back it honestly wouldn't be. But the two lovebirds just have to get married as soon as possible.

Her bright blue eyes look a little crazed as they meet mine. "The florist was supposed to meet with us at two because you are choosing a dress at twelve. Everything was worked out. But now they have to move us up to twelve also. I can't be in two places at once!" Her words coming out fast, and a tad jumbled as she speaks frantically.

"It's going to be okay, maybe mom and I can go to the bridal store while you and Cale go to the florist. It is all going to work out. Breathe, and be calm," I tell her as I walk over and wrap my arms around her petite frame. It's awkward at first not going to lie. Bailey and I haven't been super touchy feely in a long time so it's weird to embrace her. But I know she needs it, and as soon as she hugs me back I realize I need it just as much. She may not know what hurts me, or what I used to cry about at night, but when she holds me it feels like she almost does. Like she for just those few moments gets me.

It makes me wish I could tell her everything.

"Everything okay?" Cale's deep voice echoes from the staircase down at us.

But then I make eye contact with Cale, and remember why I can never tell her anything.

I pull away from Bailey suddenly feeling uncomfortable that he is in the room. The bathroom fiasco was only a couple hours ago, and too fresh on the skin and heart for my liking. Again hatred pools under my skin making my skin flush. Hatred for not only what he did to me, but for putting this wedge between my sister and I without her even knowing

"No, I mean yes now. My maid of honor just came up with a brilliant solution to the problem I was having," Bailey says. She smiles as she wraps her arms around me one more time for a quick squeeze.

I can't help but smile back. I hate Cale and I hate this wedding, and my sister annoys me a large part of the time. But I do love her more than anything. We use to be so close that we would tell each other anything and everything. But I pulled away and our relationship has suffered. We talk on the phone and text every couple weeks, but the conversations are short and sometimes forced. She makes more of the effort to be honest. I should try more, and sometimes I do. But then I pull away if she mentions something that reminds me of that summer. I hate that I recoil from that reminder, but I do. I'm still weak. I hate being weak.

"And what is that?" he asks as he grabs some juice from the fridge.

Bailey has a huge grin on her face. "You and Gray are going to go to the bridal store, while mom and I go to the florist!" She says enthusiastically with a clap of her hands.

Cale stops pouring his drink. My heart stops. I have to spend time with him...alone? Hell no.

I shake my head. "I said that you and Cale should go to the florist and mom and I should go to the bridal store," I clarify.

Bailey just smiles and waves her hand. "Yes I know you did silly," she laughs me off, and she says no more.

I stare at her waiting for an explanation. I glance over at Cale who's gripping his glass of milk so hard I am surprised it hasn't burst already. He's avoiding my gaze. "I don't get it Bai, why can't I just go with mom?" I ask my tone a bit more clipped than I would've liked.

She sighs. "Because you and Cale need to get to know each other, and this is a perfect opportunity," she starts as she begins to tap on her phone. "Plus mom used to work at a flower shop so she knows her stuff and I have already picked certain dresses for you to try on." She stops and locks her blue eyes on me. "I don't really need to be there, the flowers need me today Gray." I try to hold in my scoff. I don't want to be stuck "getting to know" Cale. Little did she know just how well he does know me.

I look up to meet Cale's hazel eyes, his jaw locked, and his lips thinned.

Yeah, we know each other just a little too well for my liking.

Chapter Five

5 /11/15

CALE AND I WALK out the front door, his truck immediately catching my attention.

I hate the way my body tingles and warms at the sight of it, memories crashing down on me. "I can drive," he offers as he starts towards his car.

"No," I shoot out right away. Like hell I will ever step foot back in that stupid truck. I can't face those memories right now. Or maybe ever.

He pauses and flips to meet me. "It's no problem come on Gray, I can drive," he pushes.

I shake my head with my eyes narrowed in on his stupid truck. I lick my lips, "Fine then we can drive separately. But I am driving my car Cale." I open my car door about to get in when I add, "And how many times do I need to tell you to not call me Gray?" I slam the door behind me as I start the car.

I roll the windows down and turn the radio to a country station. There aren't many radio stations here. Pop, country, christen, and some oldies.

The occasional alternative song will slip on that's three years old, but the hosts will claim is new. I sigh annoyed at this whole situation. I don't know how to be around him let alone go shopping with him for the day. It actually pains me to be around him, and it pains me even more to see him with my sister. They both look so happy. When was the last time I was happy?

I look at the rearview mirror to see him still standing there before he grumbles something and regretfully walks to my car. He slides into the passengers seat without a word. I pull out of the driveway and onto the street. The wind blowing through the windows and brushing my skin ever so lightly, I love this feeling.

I stop at a stoplight when I look over at Cale. He's staring straight ahead, but I know he can feel my stare. It hurts. Looking at him hurts. He's still so beautiful, and I know I shouldn't refer to men as beautiful, but he just is. He's rugged and sexy and beautiful. I can't deny it, and he's so aged well over the years. Cale isn't just a stupid teen anymore. He's twenty-three now. His hair is still its crazy mess that I have always loved. But his eyes are wiser, his body bigger, his jawline littered with scruff that makes my stomach dip. He's older, so much older, and yet at the same time he is still the same Cale from all those summers ago.

"I will never get in your truck ever again," I say. The light turns green and I pull forward and turn left through the intersection.

He doesn't answer for a while. Which I don't mind, I honestly don't need an answer. He just has to know, he has to know that I will never get in that truck and not think about the kisses, the touches, and the nights where he held me. The thoughts would consume me, and it hurt that those memories will always haunt me.

I hear him take a breath before saying, "Are you ever going to get over that summer?" His voice is a little hard.

I flinch at the edge in his voice, tears rising to the back of my eyes. Shit, I hate getting emotional, and especially over someone like him. "It's hard to get over something that completely broke you," I state simply. And it's the truth. It may have been four years, but he the hurt he inflicted will always be with me. The first cut is the deepest they say.

The sounds of a Carrie Underwood song fill the air between us. I itch to flip the station, but that will just make me look weak. Her voice speaks about how she will move on like he has when the deserts flood and the grass turns blue. How she will always love him.

I hate him. I hate him. I hate him.

I repeat this in my head until the song ends. I will finally have closure this summer and I will move on. I'll find love, and leave Cale in the past. Because that is exactly what he is...the past. He was never my future.

"I'm sorry," he murmurs quietly. I almost don't hear him between the wind and the radio.

Anger floods my skin. "I don't want your apologies Cale. Haven't you realized yet that they mean nothing?" My words are harsh, but they're the truth. No "I'm sorry" can ever fix what happened that summer.

I flip my blinker on and turn right.

"Can we please try and move past this and be friends?" He sounds unsure of his words. Like he's even hesitant of his proposition. Can we even be friends?

I say nothing.

"Please?" he pleads.

I continue to ignore him. Us, friends? Maybe when pigs fly.

Then he says the magic words, "For Bailey?"

He knows he has me. Because after everything is said and done I love my sister more than anything and would do anything for her.

Including befriending the one person who broke me and still has the power to do just the same.

I turn into the parking lot of the outdoor mall where the bridal shop resides. I turn my car off and look to my right. "I can try," I say before I slip out of the car.

He quickly scrambles out of the car and his hazel eyes hold mine as his lips turn up in a small smile. I refuse to acknowledge the fact that my pulse races at the sight of his smile. "That is all I am asking for."

"Come on. One date? One dance? One kiss?" he pushes with a huge grin on his face, his eyes brows wiggling suggestively at the last offer. I hate how pretty his face is.

I roll my eyes as I turn away from the keg and start walking down the beach. I'm never rude to people, but I have a few drinks in me and I know his reputation. My parents will kill me if I get involved with a Hasting boy. But he quickly follows suit. He obviously isn't going to let this go.

I halt my steps and turn to look at him. "Why me?" I ask seriously. "Why not Ashley or Maddy?" They are his age or close and way more his type.

I know of the Hasting boys. All attractive, and have humped well over half the population of girls and women in this town. I'm not looking for a summer fling. They always end in hurt. I have never been hurt and I definitely don't want my first heartbreak to happen with a Hasting boy.

He reaches out and twirls a piece of my blonde hair before letting it drop. His hazel eyes holding mine and the look in them is so intense I can barely breathe.

"Please?" he pleads. "I never beg," he pauses as the fat grin grows on his perfect face, "you must be really special."

I chew on the inside of my cheek before conceding. "One date," I agree. I honestly don't know what makes me say yes. His smile, the way my heart races at his nearness, or the fact that he is a Hasting boy.

He bites his lip like he's trying to hold back his excitement, which makes me giggle. I have never had a boy this eager to take me on a date. I feel giddy all over.

His hand brushes mine. "That is all I am asking for."

And I know from that moment. I know there will be more dates. I know I will fall for him.

I know he will have the power to break me if he wants to.

But I also don't think he will.

How wrong was I.

We both walk into a store named I Do. It's a small boutique, but widely known for their gorgeous wedding, prom, and bridesmaids dresses. I walk straight up to the main desk as Cale follows.

A middle-aged woman with black hair smiles at me. She has a few wrinkles but other than that is extremely beautiful. She's one of those women who age in a way everyone is envious of. "How can I help you dear?" She has a slight twang to her voice. I wonder where in the south she's from.

"Just here to try on some dresses—"

She claps as she cut me off. "Oh is this your fiancé? What a beautiful couple. I am a little old school, but I do enjoy how you young women bring in your future hubbies. They should get a little say in the wedding you know!" she babbles as she chuckles to herself.

I shake my head as my cheeks flush. I turn to face Cale who's awkwardly avoiding my gaze. "No I am here to try on bridesmaid dresses. He is my future brother-in-law," I say as I point to Cale.

Her eyes widen. "I am so sorry! I sometimes just rattle on. My apologizes!" she speaks as her hand flies to her chest in regret.

I smile. "It's okay!" I assure her. It was a mistake...an awkwardly painful one, but a mistake nonetheless.

"Name?" she asks as she flips through an appointment book.

"It should be under Kennings, Grayson Kennings," I tell the lady.

Her eyes light up immediately. "Oh, we have you all set up Ms. Kennings!" She waves at us to follow her towards the dressing rooms. "The bride has picked out about ten dresses or so for you to try on. All ranging in colors, but if you want a dress in another ones color, no problem. We can do anything you would like here today!" The lady says this all as she has us follow her to a large dressing room filled with dresses, shoes, and even some under garments.

"By the way my name is Helen and if you all need anything please let me know!" Helen gushes as she goes back up to the front desk.

My hands play with the hem of my top nervously. "So um...just wait out here I guess and which ever one you like or you think my sister would like we can get," I say turning to walk into the dressing room.

"Or which ever one you like," he offers. His words stopping my steps.

I swallow the lump in my throat and turn to face Cale. "This isn't my wedding. Doesn't matter what I like," I state before sliding the curtain close.

I take a deep breath trying to calm my nerves. I am alone with Cale and it is weird. I know nothing will happen, neither of us will ever let that happen. Plus he doesn't even want me anymore. It's just odd after all these years to be alone with him again.

I look at all the dresses. They're all flowy and short, perfect for an end of summer wedding. The colors are all pale pinks and nudes and tans. The dresses are all delicate and very feminine. My sister may be slightly annoying, but she always has had great fashion sense. Even in high school I would steal her clothes because she always had the best of the best.

I slip on the first one, which reaches the tops of my knees. It's strapless with a lot of ruching on the top. It has a deep V in the back, which makes it easy to zip up by myself. The nude almost pink color of the dress brings out the natural blush in my cheeks that I like. It's a tad too tight in the bust area, but other than that it isn't a bad start. The dress pulls my waist in making me look tinier than I actually am.

The thought of my tattoo crosses my mind. But I brought heavy-duty concealer to cover it up just in case. Glad it's coming in handy.

I swipe the curtain open and walk out a few feet for Cale to see the dress. He's looking at his phone when he finally looks up. The look on his face makes my heart pound so hard I think it may actually leave my chest.

His eyes are glued to every part of my body with this wide-eyed dark glare. He looks at me as if he wants to worship me and eat me up all at the same time. The look in his eyes bringing me straight back to four years ago, and I hate how one look from him and I am coming undone. I hate how in this moment I want him all over again. His Adam's apple bobs slightly up and down as his eyes finally lift to meet mine.

Memories of us together begin to assault me.

His tongue licking the inside of my thigh.

"Wow Grayson," his raspy voice rolls over my skin in the most delicious way. He opens his mouth again as he tries to find words.

My nails digging into his back as he enters me for the first time.

I shift uncomfortably under his strong gaze. "Please don't Cale."

The way the vein in his throat sticks out when he groans my name.

He clears his throat, his deep gaze still trapped over my skin making me flush. "Don't what?"

His teeth nipping at my breasts.

I look down still feeling his hot eyes all over me. "Look at me like that."

My teeth pulling at his bottom lip.

He stands up and takes a step closer. "How am I looking at you?" His voice is deep and thick as it hits me. I hate how he's getting to me.

His mouth moaning naughty words into my ear.

I lick my lips to look up and see him only a few feet away from me. "Like you want to do things to me." Dirty things to me, I want to add.

The moment between seems to last forever until it's broken by the clapping of dear old Helen. We both take a single step back from each other, back from the moment and back into real life.

"You look amazing Ms. Kennings! Wow you are just one beautiful young lady," she smiles at me as tears litter her eyes. She sets two water bottles down on the table next to where Cale had been sitting. "I brought you two waters." Cale thanks her as he grabs the water and takes a big gulp.

"Thanks Helen," I smile.

She shakes her head as a small smile lifts her thin lips. "How come you aren't marrying this one mister?" she says playfully as she jabs Cale in the arm. "She is as pretty as an angel." I blush at her words.

I have never been one for compliments.

Cale catches my eyes as he says, "She is beautiful."

I hate that my heart beats faster for the man who stole so many pieces of it. The man who is now giving his heart and last name to my sister.

I am supposed to be the strong one. I've been home for two days and I've never felt so weak. He makes me weak.

I refuse to be weak anymore.

* * * * *

I pull into the driveway of the beach house and neither Cale nor I make any movement to leave the car. Silence falls over both of us.

We ended up picking out a dress for the wedding and Helen took my measurements for the dress to be adjusted. Cale was adamant on the first dress after I tried on ten more after. I wanted to disagree and pick a different one. But the way he looked at me in that dress had me sold.

I sigh. "These moments that keep happening...they can't Cale. You can't look at me like that anymore." And it's the truth. If I ever want to move on from Cale Hasting every time we are alone he can't look at me like he wants to eat me.

"I know," he agrees. His eyes are locked straight ahead.

He's biting at his lip and twirling his thumbs. "I know we have a past, but it is just that. The past," I tell him. Saying those words aloud hurt more then they should. Cale is the past...even though I once thought he was my future.

He turns his head to the left, his eyes holding mine. "The past is the past. And I am marrying your sister so..." he trails, and I close my eyes for the briefest second at his words. I would've never guessed him saying he was marrying Bailey would hurt so badly.

I nod. "So we both understand."

He nods in return. But the burning question that has been with me since I saw my sister and him is burning to bright to bear anymore. I have to ask. But do I want to know the answer? I know the answer could dig me deeper in my pit of Cale-loathing. I have to know though.

Cale reaches for the passenger's side door when my words stop him. "Did you know?" Is all I ask hoping he can guess what I'm getting at.

He shifts in his seat uncomfortably and then looks down. "No," he says the one word so quietly I almost miss it.

A small pain lifts from my chest at his answer. "So you didn't..." I can't even finish the sentence.

His eyes suddenly shift to mine and hold them intensely. "I didn't know she was your sister until a few weeks in. I would have never intentionally—"

I cut him off. "Doesn't matter anyways," I mumble as I start to get out of the car.

But Cale's hand jumps out and stops me by grabbing my upper arm. Not hard, but a solid enough grip to catch my attention and make me face him. Make me face his words.

"It does matter Grayson," his words coming out slow and deliberate as if he's trying to get me to read into them.

Tears sting the back of my eyes and I clench my jaw. I will read nothing into his words. Cale and I are no more. So what does any of this matter? I shouldn't have even asked, it was stupid to.

I break away from his grip and gaze stepping out of the car and slamming the car door shut, but not before saying, "No it doesn't."

I walk into the house.

Cale doesn't follow me.

Chapter Six

5/15/15

"I THINK HE still secretly loves you," Hayley's voice says from the other end of my cell phone.

I roll my eyes. "Yes, and he wants me to bear his children and he's going to propose...no, no, wait," I pause dramatically, "that's my sister you dimwit."

"Alright bitch, glad to know your great personality is only growing with distance from me." I can practically feel the daggers she's glaring at me with.

I sigh as I sit on my bed and straighten out the skirt of my dress. "Sorry Hayley. But Cale never loved me and never will." I bite the inside of my cheek. "It's just the physical attraction, nothing else." The truth is I know I still have some unresolved feelings for him. But Cale...I don't know what he feels and doesn't feel for me.

Hayley clucks her tongue, which I hate. "I'm sorry babe. But if a man is so in love like you say him and Bailey are he shouldn't be acting like a man starved around you. If he really loves Bailey that attraction shouldn't matter anymore." Does that mean he feels something for me? Ugh, Hayley just gave me hope, and I don't need that!

Hope brings heartache and break, and I am supposed to be finding myself and breaking free from Cale. Not falling more into the pit that is Cale Hasting.

So I change the subject. "How is Maxine doing?" Not that I really want to hear about the redhead who's stealing my life, but it's a whole hell of a lot better than talking about Cale.

"She's great. Still a little shy but I'm doing my best to get her out of her shell. But it's a little difficult because she works at night so we can't go out a lot. But other than that she's been super sweet, and if your bitter ass would give her a chance you would love her," she says. Awesome now I am being scolded by Hayley about some tiny irrelevant ginger.

I hear my parents and know we have to leave soon. Not that I want to. I honestly would rather hang out with Maxine then go to this dinner tonight. But sadly I don't have that option. "Hayley, I love you...sometimes. But it may take hell freezing over before I enjoy the company of the leprechaun."

Hayley barks out a laugh I know she tried to cover. "Grayson, I sometimes can't with you! And with the way you're going hell may be freezing over a lot sooner than you think." I smile at her words, because I miss her, even when we are bickering. She really is my other, and slightly better half.

We say our goodbyes no matter how hard they may be. My heart squeezes a little as I slide my finger against the screen and hang up on my best friend. The last few days have been filled with wedding this and wedding that, and trying to avoid Cale. Which overall has been mostly successful. Since the talk in the car neither of us has made an effort to talk let alone look at one another. I can tell my sister is starting to notice the awkwardness between us, which only makes her push more for us to hang out together.

I run a hand through my hair and stand to give myself another once over in the mirror. Its not like it really matters what Cale's family thinks of me, but I always imagined meeting them. Not that anyone knows that. I hate that I even care, but I do. I will never say this aloud, but I want them to like me.

I'm wearing a simple black dress. Nothing super fancy, but I look nice. It's a shift dress that flows to the tops of my knees with a high neckline. I have light makeup on, and my hair is just naturally falling around my shoulders. I bend to slip on a pair of my favorite black wedges, and quickly stand. I turn to check my shoulder one last time making sure not only makeup but also my hair is covering the tattoo.

I run my index finger of the small tattoo, though it looks like a small skin toned scar now.

I trace the lines on Cale's ribs. The waves so simple yet beautiful. I bite my bottom lip before I do what I've been dying to do since I saw his tattoo. I lean down and brush my lips lightly against the strong but delicate lines that inhabit his skin. His skin is hot against my lips. I can hear his breath shallow with my lips on his body. His hands slip around my waist and pull me closer if that's even possible.

My tongue flicks out and tastes his skin, which is salty from the ocean. His hands squeezing my hips at the action. "Gray," he groans. "If you don't stop that I'm not going to be able to stop myself from fucking you senseless." His words light my body on fire. I can't help the small gasp that leaves my lips at his words. I also can't help but think about having sex with this perfect man. I want to...I really, really want to. But I'm also scared. It will be my first time and what if when I tell Cale that he is turned-off and never wants me again.

His hands grip my waists a little harder only making my body push into his more. Cale slides my body over so that I'm no longer lying next to him, but lying on top of him. My hips line up perfectly with his and he presses my body even further into his to show me how much he wants me. I stare straight into his eyes, and run my tongue up his neck and press myself against his length. It's a bold move for me considering how inexperienced I am. But Cale makes me bold, makes me want more, and makes me take what I want. He narrows his eyes, and pulls me into a passionate and deep kiss that I can feel all throughout my body,

I pull my face away from his with a gasp, and bite my bottom lip. I love how I can still taste him. I cross my arms over his chest and rest my chin on my arms. My eyes meet his dark ones, and I wonder how long I can really hold out till I let him have his way with me.

"What does it mean?" I ask with a tilt of my head.

Cale places his hands behind his head and relaxes against the blankets. We are in the bed of his truck, one of my favorite places to spend with him. He's parked on this hidden part of the beach away from everyone and anything. It's our own little world over here, and I love it. I can be my bold self with Cale here. Not the quiet respectful Grayson everyone knows.

He reaches out with his right hand and tucks a strand of hair behind my ear, while rubbing his thumb against my cheek. I lean into the palm of his hand. Every touch, look, and kiss from Cale only makes me greedier. I always want more and more with him. Something about Cale is different from every other boy I've ever known. Besides the fact that he's older, he makes my heart race, and looks at me as if I'm everything he's ever wanted. He makes me feel beautiful and sexy and wanted all at the same time.

He makes me want to forget that this is just some summer fling and fall head over heels in love with Cale Hasting.

He runs the pad of his thumb against my cheek once again. "My tattoo?" he asks.

I nod once.

He rests his hand on my back tracing circles with his fingers making me squirm a little. Cale lowers his head so he's looking at the night sky with his left hand still tucked under his head.

He doesn't say anything at first, and I just silently wait. I don't want to push him. I know when he is ready he will tell me.

"Waves are an interesting thing Gray. For some they wash away the past and represent a new beginning. But for others they represent the past, and the past never really leaves but just washes up on a different shore. I don't know I've always loved the ocean and what it can represent." His words are soft almost hard to hear. But the way he speaks of the ocean makes my heart skip a beat.

"Water purifies," I mumble. It's something my dad always says whenever we go to the beach.

Cale lifts his head so his eyes meet mine. "I wouldn't say I'm pure Grayson." His eyes fill with humor, but serious at the same time. The way he says my whole name causes a shiver to fly through my spine.

My eyes hold his until he lays his head back down.

"Would you ever get a tattoo Gray?"

I pause before blurting the first thing that comes to mind, because yes I would. And I know exactly what I want to get now, but I don't want to freak him out. So I just say, "Maybe one day," and leave it at that.

I should hate the tattoo. But honestly I don't. It does remind me of that summer and Cale. But it also reminds me of new beginnings and being strong on my own. For those reasons alone I don't hate or blame Cale for my tattoo. Honestly I would thank him...not that I ever would.

I grab my phone and slip it into a small clutch and head out of my room. I walk into the kitchen to meet my parents. They both look up as smiles spread over their faces. "Grayson you look lovely," my mother says and then pauses to look up at my father. "Doesn't she honey?" she asks my father as she pulls him closer.

He looks down at her, and the look in his eyes could bring tears to the coldest of hearts. I would know. He looks at her like she is his whole world. "Both of my girls look beautiful tonight," he says. He then leans down to place a small kiss on my mother lips.

It use to gross me out when my parents would do things like that in front of me. But now it just reaffirms my faith that maybe, someday I can find what they have. That someone like me can be just as happy. My mom and I may not look alike but we are more similar than people think. She is the one who thinks before acting, everything in the world has its perfect place, and she doesn't like disorder or anything messy. Which will forever make me wonder how she was drawn to my father. The man is the definition of messy, he is the soft one, the one who is impulsive and loves new things.

I use to be a nice mix of my mother and father. Not anymore.

I shift in my heels before asking, "So where are the two love birds, shouldn't we be leaving?" I glance at the microwave clock one more time before letting my eyes flicker to the staircase.

My mother pulls away from my father, and gives her hair a quick fluff before grabbing her purse from the counter. "They left already, wanted to get there a little early to see if Cale's family needed anything."

And with that we head out to my parents car and are off to The Grove.

The car ride is quiet at first, just the low lull of the radio and sounds of other passing cars. The dark streets only lit by old street lamps that flicker when it rains. The dark waves looming on the beach as they crash against the soft sand. I close my eyes for a few minutes and try to prepare myself for tonight. No one knows how long I've actually waited for this moment, how many times I imagined it. How I would play the different scenarios of meeting his parents, and how they would love me, and give Cale the blessing to marry me right then and there.

Damn I was a naïve sixteen year old.

I smile at the memories and try to remind myself that tonight isn't about me, not one bit.

All of the sudden my mouth is open and I'm asking, "So what do you really think of Bai marrying a Hasting boy?" I didn't realize till the question was out that it had been burning inside me just waiting to be asked and answered.

My parents never really spoke badly of anyone, but when the Hasting boys ever came up they would always tell us to never fall for boys like that. That they were entitled and just left a pile of broken hearts in their path.

They were right about that.

But what do they really think now?

"Well..." my father trails off not really knowing what to say, his hands shifting awkwardly over the steering wheel.

But my mother knows just what to say. "This is a small town Grayson, everyone knows everyone and if you don't know them, you know about them. The Hastings are from The Grove. We knew they were rich and had four spoiled boys. We also knew those boys liked to party and climb anything in a skirt." Dad chuckles at her words. "But it's been years, and obviously the boys have grown, I mean look at Cale!" She exclaims.

I roll my eyes. I have, I think.

But she continues. "He has a great job and can support Bailey and he obviously loves her...though it was all a little fast," she concedes at the end.

"And you wonder why I asked if she was pregnant?" I say with an expression of annoyance.

She shakes her head. "Now that was just rude Grayson, and you know better. I didn't put you through etiquette classes for nothing young lady," she chastises.

My shoulders slump. "Whatever, you know you were thinking it," I murmur.

Again my father chuckles, and see him nod at me, but not before my mother jabs him with her elbow.

The rest of the car ride is fairly quiet until we turn down a street and then the car goes deadly silent.

We have entered The Grove.

I've been here once because of Cale, and I've driven by it many times. But to actually be in it after all these years is amazing. These are the houses celebrities, CEO's, and trust fund babies own. Every house the car passes could fit four or five of our house inside it. I honestly don't know what people do with all the space...and the people who have to clean it! Wow, that just sounds awful.

The car finally stops in front of a three-story brick house. It looks as if it is made for the deep south with the large wrap around porch, and white columns. Everything about this house screams old money, but nothing about this house screams beach. Which I guess makes sense for The Grove. The Grove is about showing how much money you are worth, never about the gorgeous beach that surrounds these amazing houses.

We pull into their large driveway that wraps around and leads to multiple garages. This place is massive, like nothing I've ever seen before. I have only been here once, though slightly drunk, but I still remember everything. Like the way Cale touched me in the kitchen up against the fridge, and then on top of the island. I bite my lip at the memory and blush.

My parents and I make our way up to the double French doors and knock. Mrs. Hasting opens the door immediately beaming with a smile from ear to ear. "Hello!" she chirps. "Welcome, please come inside!" She moves aside as we walk into the foyer of the house.

My parents begin to introduce themselves to Mrs. Hasting, who insisted they call her Jayne. She is a beautiful woman, with her long dark blonde hair, and bright hazel eyes. Her face is soft and sweet, and the way her eyes light up when she speaks makes her easier to approach, as if she radiates this warm light.

She turns to me. "And you must be Grayson," she says as she leans and hugs me, and I respond with a hesitant hug back. "Bailey talks about you all the time," she gushes, "and good things I promise!" I smile back though a small piece of my heart cracks. That summer years ago, I dreamed of meeting Cale's family and his mom and his dad. I never dreamt I would be here for my sister's engagement to him.

"Ahh and here they all are!" Mrs. Hasting exclaims as Cale, Bailey, and whom I am assuming are Cale's father and brother.

Cale definitely gets his good looks from his father. For his age he is still attractive, undeniably a silver fox of the George Clooney kind. He shakes all our hands and asks us to call him Daniel. I smile at his words, but know

I will still address him and his wife formally as Mr. and Mrs. Hasting. It's how I was raised, and I still feel like a child around adults, even at the age of twenty.

Then whom I'm assuming is Cale's brother introduces himself. I knew Cale had three other brothers and I had seen a few pictures, but I never actually met them. Though back then they were the talk of the town. The Hasting boys were another kind of boy. All hot, and all players, and all forbidden...well at least by my parents. They ruled this town, and every girl would willingly cut off a limb for a chance to be with one of them. I don't know if things had really changed, but I know I have.

His name is Chase, and I can't deny he is hot. Like extremely. He is tall like Cale, but less muscular, still toned though. His hair is longer than Cale's, but the same dirty blonde color. Anyone could plainly see they were related. If I didn't know any better I would assume they were twins.

His hand is soft in mine as he shakes my hand. He smiles at me, not in a creepy "I want to get you naked" way, but in an "I think we can be friends" sort of way. His eyes are warm just like the rest of him, which makes me smile right back at him. He finally pulls always but I can't keep the smile off of my face. I need some friends if I'm going to survive this summer still sane. And a small part of me is so happy he didn't try and check me out, I don't think I would be able to ever date another Hasting boy without comparing them to Cale. Which isn't fair for anyone, but especially his own blood.

"Alright, well dinner is almost ready so why don't we all head to the kitchen for some wine and appetizers," Mrs. Hasting says as she motions everyone to follow her through a large archway.

I pause. "Sorry I was wondering if I could use the bathroom first?" I ask quietly with a raised hand to gain the Hasting's attention.

Mrs. Hasting turns and nods in understanding. "Of course. The one down here is under construction," she pauses turning to my parents. "We're expanding a little," she explains. My parents politely nod and smile, but I can tell they're thinking similar thoughts to mine. Expanding? Like this house really needs to be any bigger. But to each their own I guess.

She motions to her right. "Cale can show you to the guest bathroom upstairs," she says. Mrs. Hasting smile is bright and warm, but god did I want to scowl at her for her choice of son to show me upstairs.

I smile softly back. "I don't want to intrude, I'm sure I can find it myself." And I can find it, it's not my first time at the Hasting residency. Not that anyone needs to know.

"Are you sure? It's no problem for him to show you." Her eyebrows scrunch together in worry.

I give a reassuring smile, and head up the long staircase.

As soon as I hit the top step I know I should head to the left for the guest bathroom. But I feel a tug in my body and go where I know I shouldn't. I turn on my heel and head right towards Cale's room. I slowly push open the cracked door and step into the dimly lit room. I close my eyes as my body lightly shakes. I'm suddenly flooded with the memories of Cale and I in his room. He only brought me here once, but it is a day I can never forget. My eyes land on his king size bed in the left corner, the same navy blue down comforter coating his bed. I walk over and run my hand down the comforter, still as soft as I remembered.

He's taking my shirt off. The first time I've ever had my top off in front of a boy. His eyes lock on my chest as he reaches around and unhooks my bra. I feel nervous but needy. It's like no other feeling I've ever experienced, and I never want this heat to stop. Next thing I know Cale's lips are on my neck, with his hand trailing up my thigh forcing my body to catch aflame. My heart beats wildly.

I close my eyes and live in the fire that is Cale Hasting. I never wanted his touch to end. I could stay in his bed all day.

And we did.

The memory of the only time I ever spent in Cale's room warms my cheeks in embarrassment. I shake away the thoughts of his lips and hands, and inspect the room some more. It has been so long since I was near my family, near Cale, near this town of Easton. I've missed so much.

I chew on the inside of my cheek as I made my way around the room. I stop at a picture of him and Bailey on his nightstand. She is looking at Cale, big smile, and wild blonde hair crazy in the wind. While Cale looks at the camera, his bright hazel eyes serious, contemplative. I swallow the lump in my throat that forms at the sight of their picture together. I obviously know they are together, but seeing a picture, seeing it documented makes it real.

I tongue the inside of my cheek and turn to face the wall covered in pictures, posters, medals, and plaques. It reminded me of mine, though his has a larger collection of items.

I run my fingers over the medals he received in middle and high school for every sport imaginable. His dad really pushed him into football, but his real passion was soccer. He was amazing with the ball, the agility of his feet, how fast he could run. Cale loved playing pick up games on the beach. He was always trying to teach me weird tricks that I could never do. I stop at a few pictures of him when he was younger, maybe sixteen? His hair was longer, his tan deeper, his smile brighter, he was young, wild, and free. I wish I knew him, not his reputation, but really knew him back then. Though he wouldn't have given me a second glance since I would've been thirteen at the time. Those three years don't mean anything now, but back then they meant the world. They held our relationship in its hand, and crushed us. Cale let it crush us.

I brush my hand over a few pictures and one falls from beneath a picture of him and his brothers. I mumble, "Shit." As I bend down to pick up the picture. I didn't want anyone to know I'm snooping around in Cale's room and knocking pictures off the wall is not the way to be so discreet.

A gasp leaps from my lips as I flip over the picture and see that it's a photo of me. It's of me sitting in the sand, my hair flying in the wind as I look over my shoulder and smile at Cale. My face has a shadow casting over it, but if you know me it's obvious. It was one of the few times Cale took pictures of anything, let alone me. He would get in these wild moods where he would kiss me in public, and take pictures of me. Those were the nights we would get so heated we would get so close to sex. But then something would pull him back, would rein in his wild streak, and usually delete the pictures.

I hear the sound of footsteps entering and my head snaps up to meet Cale's gaze. His eyes staring at the picture in my hands, his jaw locked, and his fists tightened. His eyes lift and blaze into mine. "Why are you in my room, and going through my stuff Grayson?" His voice is strained as he speaks through his teeth. He's obviously upset, but he doesn't have much of a right to be.

"I was just looking at your pictures and it fell," I state. "I think the real question here is why you still have this?" I raise an eyebrow at my question.

He takes a step forward to yank the picture from my hands, but I move it out of his grasp clutching it against my chest. "You have no right to go through my things," he speaks. He's close to me and his anger radiates of him.

I shake my head, annoyance climbing through my veins. "And you have no right to have this picture after what you did to me." I pause before whispering, "You broke me." My eyes shift from his unable to look him in the eye while admitting that small truth.

Silence wraps around us at my admission. I can hear him swallow, and the sound of me shifting in my heels is louder than normal. I hate myself for continuing to show him how weak I am. But he continuously tears down the many walls I built. I see his feet take a single step towards me, and I slowly lift my eyes to meet his. His face flickers with emotion and his mouth opens like he wants to say something, but just can't seem to find the right words.

He shakes his head with a sigh. "Gray—"

He starts to speak but is cut off by my sister's squeaky voice. "Baby, where did you go?" Her voice trails in from the hallway.

I glance one last look before taking a singular step backwards. Away from Cale, and away from whatever lies might leave his lips.

Bailey appears in the doorway as I tuck the picture behind my back. I'd forgotten I was still holding onto it, and obviously didn't want my sister seeing the photo. The tension is thick in the room and her eyes flicker between us before a smile lights up her angelic face. "What are you two up to?"

Cale is about to say something when I step in, "I stopped in here after using the bathroom because I noticed the adorable picture of you two on his nightstand." I motion over to the table with my free hand.

Bailey's grin grows and she walks over to link arms with Cale. "It's one of my favorites." Her gaze lingers on the picture before tugging Cale towards the door and waving at me to follow. "Dinner is ready and we don't want to keep anyone waiting."

I follow her and Cale down the stairs, but not before tucking the picture into a random drawer on my way out. I'm trying to contain the anger that fills my body. I hate that Cale still has that picture of me, but it also makes me question everything. Why does he still have it after all these years? Does he look at it? Or did he forget it was even there? I shake my head and try to forget about the dumb picture, because it doesn't even matter. It doesn't matter if he still looks at it, or if I mean anything to him, because he's marrying Bailey.

We all make our way to the Hasting's extravagant dinning room and sit down to begin dinner. The Hastings sit at each end of the large table, with my parents and I on one side, and Bailey, Cale, and Cale's brother Chase on the other side. Their wait staff serves us a delicious dinner comprised of steak, potatoes, greens, and seriously the best rolls I've ever had. And I take my breads very seriously.

I'm buttering my fifth roll, when Mrs. Hasting calls my name. "Grayson, I hear you attend Northwestern," she remarks.

I turn to my right to face her, and nod. "Yes, I'll be a junior this year," I smile. "I love it there," I say honestly.

Her smile widens. "That is just wonderful!" she exclaims as she claps her hands together. "Because Chase here is transferring there this year and will also be a junior! And it would be just lovely for him to already know someone there." She motions between the two of us, but pauses, "Well not just someone, family!" she laughs.

I look across the table to face a red-cheeked Chase. I smile at him in reassurance, and he offers a timid smile back.

Mrs. Hasting turns back to me and with a quick wink, and whispers, "Well not family by blood." And I actually feel Cale's eyes burn into the side of my face.

I ignore Cale and face Chase once again. "We definitely need to get lunch together then! And you will love my best friend and roommate Hayley. Between the two of us, you'll be set." I say with a wave of my butter knife, before stuffing a sixth roll in my mouth.

Judge me.

Chapter Seven

5/17/15

I GRAB MY tray with a soup and salad on it from the counter.

The local café is crazy busy at this lunch hour, but luckily Chase has already snagged us some seats on the patio. It's a beautiful afternoon with clear skies and a bright sun, and a perfect day to spend outdoors. I weave my way through the crowded lines and finally make my way to Chase and sit down with an exaggerated huff.

Chase smiles. "Mayhem breaking lose in there?" he asks with the tilt of a head.

I nod with wide eyes. "Just a little, and by little I mean straight hell." We both laugh at my words, and begin to dig into our food.

I wasn't lying or trying to get a rise out of Cale when I mentioned Chase and I having lunch together. Well I can't lie, a small part of me wanted to gain something out of it. But I still am only looking for a friendship with Chase, and from our interactions it seems the same goes for him. We texted all day yesterday and made the plans to meet up today for lunch. He was a little hesitant at first, but once I peeled back those layers he is the male version of Hayley in every way. And having someone to talk to, especially someone that reminds me of Hayley, might actually make this summer bearable.

I swallow a bite of my salad before asking, "So what is your major? I never asked."

He spins his fork in his pasta a few times. "Environmental engineering."

My face pulls in confusion. "So what does that mean? Like what do you want to do with that?" Besides Hayley's fashion classes, and my communication classes I have no idea what the rest of the school does.

He smiles. "I want to travel around the world, especially third world countries, and help with crops and make sure they have clean drinking water," he pauses to take a drink of his tea. "I've been given so much in life, and I just really want to help others."

I shake my head in amazement. "That's awesome Chase," I say honestly. "You could really make a difference, and having that opportunity to travel is invaluable."

He shrugs. "Tell that to my father. He thought me saying I wanted to go into environmental engineering, meant I was also going to attend law school after graduation. And then join him and my brothers at the family company. But that's not the path I want to follow." He sighs into his food.

"That's okay that you want to take your own path Chase. You have to be your own person," I admit.

He rolls his eyes. "Well my father would rather me be like my older brothers," he barks out a dark laugh. "Cale, Colt, and Clayton all went to college for engineering, and then either specified with law or public health or management. And all because that's what my father wanted."

Mr. Hasting is the founder and CEO of one of the largest construction and engineering companies in the country. His children are all set to be his successors, and all three brothers sit currently on the board of directors. That has to be a ton of pressure on Chase to follow his older brothers, but he doesn't need to.

"But you want a different path Chase. Your father has three sons to take care of his company after he no longer can. He can live with you traveling and doing better for this world." I smile at him, and then add, "And think of all the amazing publicity it would bring his company. Would make them look at philanthropic and shit." I add with a thumbs up.

Chase breathes out a laugh. "Philanthropic and shit," he quotes me. "My father would love that reasoning."

"Well he's gonna have to, because you're meant for other things in this world Chase," I say. I smile as start to finish of my salad. I love how natural things are with Chase. Even with the mention of Cale, my body and heart barely responds. And I know this is because I have a friend. I was able to push all feelings and memories of Cale aside in college because I had Hayley to distract me. And Chase is that new friendship that is the perfect distraction for this summer.

Chase's face flushes slightly at my words. "Thanks Gray."

I wash down my food with a swig of my soda. "Anytime."

Chase and I continue to finish our lunch while he asks me more questions about Northwestern and the classes and the people in Illinois. The conversation flows easily and the café becomes less crowded the longer we talk.

"Gray...? Is that you?" a woman's voice questions from behind me.

I turn to my head to make eye contact with Kylie, my best friend from all those summers ago. She lived here year round, and we grew up exploring this small town together. She was even there when I fell head over heals for Cale. She was the only person who really knew about us, and she was the best friend a girl could have. And when I left Easton to never come back, I also left Kylie.

"Kylie," I whisper. "Ohmygod it's you!" I cry out gaining attention from other patio tables.

Her eyes water slightly. "I never thought I would see you again, especially after Cale—"

My eyes widen at her admission in front of Chase. "I...no...umm..." I stutter, and turn my head to motion at Chase whose face is scrunched in confusion.

"Oh," Kylie gasps and slaps a hand over her mouth. "I'm sorry I didn't even see you there," she says to Chase.

Chase then stands. "What about Cale?" He asks me with narrowed eyes his gaze flickering between Kylie and myself.

I open my mouth to say something to turn the conversation away from all of this, but Kylie cuts me off.

"I'm sorry I mentioned him," she pauses and turns to me. "Is this your boyfriend?" she asks, worry painted deep onto her face.

I shake my head as my stomach drops at her words. "No, he is—"

I get cut off once again. "I'm Chase Hasting," he introduces himself while reaching out his hand to shake Kylie's.

Kylie's bright eyes meet mine. "Hasting?" she questions.

I lick my suddenly dry lips. "Yeah," I barely whisper aloud.

She raises her hand to motion between Chase and myself. " So how do you two..." she trails not even able to finish her sentence.

Chase stuffs his hands into his front pockets. "Her sister is engaged to my brother," he answers as if it's the simplest thing in the world. The awkwardness just seeps deeper into my bones. Worlds are colliding and I hate it. Oh wow, I hate everything about this.

Kylie's head tilts in question. "Which brother?" her question directed at Chase, but her eyes never leaving mine.

My skin prickles with the heat of embarrassment from the words that I know will leave Chase's mouth next. How did things go from so good to so bad so fast? I was having such a great day with Chase, but my past and present are now meeting, and life isn't so simple as it once was.

"Cale," he answers as if his brother's name meant nothing. But little did he know that Cale is the only name that will always haunt me.

Kylie's eyebrows raise. "Wow," she breathes in complete and utter shock.

I close my eyes and shake my head, refusing the feelings that want to crawl into my heart and build a little nest. "Yeah," I sigh. "Maybe we should all sit down and talk."

Kylie nods, Chase is obviously still confused, and I just sit in defeat of this whole situation.

* * * * *

Lunch lasts a little longer than I thought, but also went better than I could have ever imagined. I explained to Chase that Cale and I had a past, but didn't divulge too many details. I described us as more of a fling that broke up along the way. Not the real version where I fell for him heart first for him only to tear out my heart, and jump up and down on it.

I can see Kylie eyeing me along the way, but she never once jumps in and says anything to reveal my white lies.

After a long conversation about what Cale and I never were, we are finally able to move past what was and focus on us.

Kylie still lives in Easton, and student teaches at the local elementary school. She even still does freelance photography on the side. Kylie with a camera was just as dangerous as any weapon. She could capture the true emotion behind any individual. And when anyone looked at her pictures they couldn't deny the truth. Just like I couldn't deny the summer I fell in love with Cale. It was partially because of her and her photography that I truly had to admit to my feelings for Cale. I may hate him, but I could never hate Kylie for showing me something only she could see.

The three of us got along crazy well, and I have a feeling that the three of us will be seeing a lot of each other this summer.

After the chatter dies down Chase stands up from his chair at the table. "Well I've got to get going, but it was great to meet you Kylie," he says with a smile. I quickly stand also and Chase wraps his arms around me. "Don't worry I won't say a thing about Cale to anyone Gray," he mumbles into my hair. I smile at his words and give a small nod in appreciation.

He pushes in his chair, and with a final wave he leaves.

I sit back down and look over at Kylie. She places a hand on top of mine with a small squeeze. "I really missed you after you left," she says.

I squeeze my hand against hers in return before pulling away. "I know I missed you so much."

A sigh escapes Kylie's lips. "I was mad at you for so long when you didn't come back—"

"I didn't mean to hurt you Kylie, I was just hurting so much, and so angry for so long it clouded a lot of my judgment back then," I say cutting her off.

She wets her lips. "I know. I know," she mumbles. "It took a while for me to understand, but once I had my heart broken I started to understand where you were coming from." Hurt coats her face, and it pains me to watch.

"I'm so sorry Kylie, what happened?" I question hoping I'm not crossing any boundaries. We were once best friends, but so many years have passed it's hard to know where we stand.

She shrugs. "It was my first year in college, he was a senior. Thought I loved him, and he cheated on me with my slutty roommate." She rolls her eyes at her words. "It was awful, and I hated everything and everyone, and I suddenly knew why you never came back."

I nod. "I just couldn't risk seeing him again Kylie...even the thought of seeing him again hurt too much."

"I get it now Gray," she tilts her head as she really looks at me. "Are you okay?" she asks.

I pretend to not know what she's talking about. "Why wouldn't I be?" I say as I take a sip of my drink.

"Gray," she chides. "Come on, Cale is marrying your sister. That has to suck."

I let out a husky chuckle. "Yeah it sucks," I breathe. "But I have to move on, Cale has this hold on me even after all these years...and it's time I get closure," I say.

Kylie's lips press into a smile. "You deserve a great man Gray."

I push my blonde hair behind my ear. "I know I'm awesome," I laugh.

Kylie shakes her head. "You are awesome, and so am I, and we deserve better than these dumb Easton boys," she responds with a raised eyebrow.

"If I had alcohol I'd drink to that right now," I smirk.

"We need to get wine drunk together, and soon at that. I need a fun night," Kylie says with a lopsided grin.

A sit up straight as an idea forms in my head. "My birthday is this Friday we should go out!"

"Wait?" she pauses, her face pulling in confusion. "I thought your birthday was in the fall."

"It is," I agree. "But my family wasn't with me so they wanted to celebrate my half birthday with me. So we are doing a dinner together, but after I'm free to go out with you!"

"Really?" Kylie asks sounding hopeful.

I nod excitingly. "Yes! I was just gonna hang with my parents, keep it chill, but no! You, me, and maybe Chase should all go out and just have a night out," I say with a big fat grin on my face.

Kylie leans over and hugs me tight. "I'm so happy you're back," she whispers.

And for the first time since I've stepped foot into Easton, so am I.

Chapter Eight

5/18/15

"WHEN ARE BAILEY and Cale coming?" I ask as I walk around the dinner table placing the plates and silverware.

"Oh, they're not honey!" my mother's voice shouts from the kitchen. I quickly grab the extra plates and utensils and clutch them to my chest. I turn on my heels and walk into the kitchen trying to bury the anxiety that laces through me.

I set them down on the island and turn to lean against the edge of the counter. I cross my arms over my chest. "So where are they?" I ask, not caring who answers.

"Who?" my father questions as he begins to slice up the chicken.

I roll my eyes. "Bai and Cale..." I trail. No answer. "Hello? I'm sorry am I invisible to you guys?" I wave my hands in the air annoyed at this whole situation.

My mother looks up to me. "I'm sorry honey, but I honestly don't know where they are." She shrugs and continues to tend to the potatoes on the stove.

"They're adults and engaged now, we don't track their every movement," my dad answers. "We asked if they were going to join us, and Bai said no."

I bite at the inside of my cheek, and stare down at my bare feet that press against the cold hardwood floors. "So you don't care that Bai and Cale are having a lot of alone time?" I ask with a raised brow.

My father sighs, and my mother's eyes narrow in on me. "Like your father said honey, they are adults and engaged. We can say all we want, but they have to make their own decisions now. Not that it is any of your business Grayson." I blush in embarrassment of the use of my full name in chastisement.

I nod even though I would like to push the subject further. My parents have always been old schooled, and I know not knowing what their daughter is up to is killing them a little inside. Especially since she is with a Hasting.

I walk to the table with a bowl of steamed vegetables in hands and my parents in tow. We quickly begin to pass around the food to fill up our plates. I start to shovel chicken and potatoes into my mouth, when I receive another disapproving glare from my mother.

"It's not a race Gray, you can breathe between bites." I set my fork down and begin to chew slowly at her request. I love my mother to death, but I've never met another woman so stuck on manners.

I chew and swallow slowly, making sure to eat at a slower pace.

"So how was lunch with Chase yesterday?" my father asks.

I smile immediately at the mention of his name. "Great! I can't wait for him to transfer to Northwestern," I say truthfully.

My mother smirks at me. "You know your father and I met the summer before our junior year." I roll my eyes at what she is pushing. It's as if Chase and I are the only ones who see each other as friends. Everyone else has hearts in their eyes, and is trying to play matchmaker.

I shake my head, and stuff some chicken in my mouth. "No mom," I groan. "We are just friends, that is all. Promise," I push. I could never date Chase, even if he wanted to, I just couldn't. It would be a constant comparison to Cale, and that's fair to no one.

My father kisses my mother on the cheek. I smile at the small gesture, hating how my heart pulls in sadness and jealousy. All I want is to have a relationship like my parents, and be unconditionally in love with a man who wants me back. My father's eyes meet mine. "We aren't trying to push anything Gray. But Chase is a nice boy...maybe those Hasting boys aren't as bad as we once thought," he says with a single shouldered shrug.

I scrape my fork against my plate, hating and loving the awful sound at the same time. "He is nice, but he is just a friend..." I trail. "So moving on, I also ran into Kylie yesterday," I mention happily.

My parents faces light up at Kylie's name. They always loved Kylie, and are still close friends with her parents. Kylie always referred to my parents as her second family. And I know it hurt when I stopped coming to Easton, because Kylie also stopped coming around as much.

"Oh that is just wonderful!" My mother exclaims with a loud clap. "I've missed her coming around here so much, is she coming over? Oh tell her she must! I will make her favorite, lasagna! Wait is that still her favorite?" my mother rambles on and on, more to herself than anyone else. My father laughs at my mother's constant stream of words, and I just shake my head in amusement.

I breathe out a laugh. "Slow down mom. She will be coming over, and I'm sure she would still love your lasagna."

Dinner continues on with my mother going on and on about Kylie. My father goes on about some baseball game I could care less about. And I sit and watch my parents' small interactions with a warm smile. But the small voice in my head wonders if I will ever have the chance to find what my parents have.

What I thought I once had, but now what Bailey and Cale have.

* * * * *

I lay in my bed on top of the covers with a sigh. I quickly shoot Hayley a text waiting for the bubble to show she is texting back, but it doesn't appear. She doesn't answer back right away, so I know she is most likely still working. I chew on the inside of my cheek, and turn my head to look out my open doors. I have my side doors open, and the breeze from the ocean rolls in steadily. I bite my lip at the feeling of the salty breeze brushing over me.

"Stop making those sounds Gray," Cale grumbles at me. "You're killing me."

I smirk as I sit up on my elbows on the soft cushion of my comforter. The doors in my room are open, and the sun floods my room, filling it with bright light and smell of the ocean. Cale continues to massage my feet, though his fingers start to trail up my calves in slow seductive strokes. "You lost the bet," I point out. "So you rub the feet," I laugh.

Cale's fingers continue to press into the arch of my feet, and I can't help but groan in response. He seriously does have magical fingers. I blush at the idea of them on other parts of my body. After the kiss in his truck, Cale hasn't touched me much. We hang out almost every day, and we have so much fun...but dammit I want him to touch me and kiss me. That first kiss in his truck was the hottest thing I've ever experienced, and wow I want more. I've never had a guy kiss me as thoroughly as Cale Hasting, and I'm sure a no one ever could.

"How was I supposed to know you knew Spanish that well?" he exclaims.

I laugh. "I used to spend my free time watching Spanish soap operas," I shrug. "Learned a thing or two."

"Learned a thing or two?" he mocks. "More like became fluent."

I stick my tongue out at him.

Suddenly Cale's hands are wrapped around my thighs and pulling me towards him until I'm straddling his lap. His fingers continue to trace around the bottoms of my feet and the backs of my calves. I wrap my arms around his neck and pull my body closer to his.

Cale's eyes go dark, and his eyes trace over my body until they land right back where they started, my lips. I want him to kiss me, god it's all I want. I crave the feeling of his lips on me. The same lips that created a fire deep within my core in his truck. I lift one of my hands from the back of his neck, and begin to trace the lines of his face. I hate how beautiful he is. Sometimes it hurts how much I want him. But it doesn't stop me from wanting him more, and that should scare me more. But it doesn't.

"I think I deserve another reward for winning that bet," I whisper hoarsely. My finger finally begins to touch the skin around his lips. I don't touch his lips just yet, but I am so close, and I love the way his body leans in closer. The way his tongue darts out to wet his lips, wetting my finger at the same time. I feel the heat of his breath surround me, and all I want to do is melt into him and get lost.

Suddenly his fingers are wrapped around my wrist and stopping my fingers from touching him. I raise an eyebrow in question as to why he stopped me.

He leans in even closer, his lips just barely brushing mine. "I don't know if you deserve another reward." He cocks his head to the right and watches me with so much attentiveness I feel naked even though I'm fully clothed.

A small smile lifts the corner of my lips. "Ok," I shrug. "That's fine, Julio said I have beautiful lips," I lie. Julio only asked me how to get to the nearest grocery store. But Cale doesn't need to know that. Cale's eyes narrow at my words. I peel my hand away from his grip and crawl off his lap. "I'm sure he would give me my reward I'm looking for," I say as I start to get off the bed.

But before I can even place one foot on the ground Cale's arms wrap around my waist. He pulls back onto the bed as I let out an excited squeal. He places me on my back against the comforter and presses his hard body deliciously against mine.

He presses his fingers into my sides making me howl with laughter, and squirm and writhe underneath his evil fingertips. "Stop, stop, stop!" I scream out with laughter following.

His hazel eyes burn into mine. "No Julio," he growls. His jaw is clenched, and his face is hard, but a playful gleam shines behind his dark eyes.

I press my lips together, refusing to answer him. He presses his fingers further into my sides as I try to escape the wrath of his tickling. But his body is pressed into mine pinning me down with his hips, and his other hand has snaked around to latch onto both of my wrists holding them above my head.

"No Julio," he says once more.

He presses one last time into my side before I give in. "Fine, fine, fine, no Julio!" I shriek. "Please stop, stop, Cale—"

His name barely leaves my lips before he presses his mouth against mine, and if possible this kiss is even better than our first. His lips are soft, but they press into mine with such passion that I feel my skin tingle and my mind go numb. But his lips pull away way too soon for my liking. I let out an annoyed groan in protest of his lips leaving mine. "Did Julio really say that?" Cale questions.

I raise an eyebrow. "What if he did?" I reply back in a playful tone.

Cale's lips graze mine. "Gray..." he trails, my name coming out deep and raspy.

A laughter bubbles up and escapes my parted lips. "No, he asked where the closest store was," I say with the shake of my head.

A devilish smirk coats his face. "You will be the death of me Grayson Kennings." I loved the way my full name rolled off his tongue so naturally.

I push my body up into his, and lift my head off the mattress so our lips are barely separated. "Then you better kiss me while you can."

So he does, again, again, and again.

Cale kisses me until I'm so completely and utterly lost in him that I never wanted to leave that moment.

But we did. The moment ended and the memory faded.

I gave Cale everything, and he took it all greedily. And when he broke me, he didn't even have the decency to give back the pieces of my heart he took.

But I'm done giving him parts of me, because I'm done being lost in Cale Hasting.

I have to find who I am without him being a part of me.

And in this moment, with the my eyes watching the dark waves wash up on the shore, I decide Cale Hasting won't define me anymore.

No matter how much I wanted him to define me. No matter how much I wanted to get lost in him. No matter how much I never wanted to leave that bed.

I have to find myself, and I have to move on. I have to try.

Chapter Nine

5/22/15

"OKAY, RIGHT THIS way ladies!" Helen chirps.

My mother, Bailey, and I are back at the bridal store I Do. But this time we are here for Bailey to pick her dress. Bailey's been in a panic all day about having to pick her dress. She says she narrowed it down at the beginning of the summer before we all came down, but she just can't choose between the three left.

I've never understood woman and their need to have the "perfect dress" on their wedding day. It's a dress we wear for one day, and yet we are supposed to spend thousands on the stupid garment. Ugh, and all the crying that's involved with finding "the one" I hate it. How can a dress make a woman cry? Call me a cynic, but I find everything about weddings annoying and trivial. I used to be one of those girls who planned her wedding to the last little element, but that all changed years ago.

Helen walks us towards a large couch, and leads Bailey into the dressing room that sits in front of us. Before Helen pulls the curtain closed, Bailey shouts, "Now I want you all to be honest okay? I want Cale to cry the moment he sees me." She smiles at her words.

"Romantic," I rumble with a sigh. Helen pulls the curtain closed and the sounds of zippers and rustling fabric is all that is left to hear.

"Are you okay Gray?" My mother's voice questions to my left.

I turn to face her. "Why would you ask that?"

She purses her lips and shrugs. "I don't know, you've been a little weird the last couple days."

I nod in agreement, because I have been weird the last few days. Chase and I have texted a few times. I've barely talked to Kylie besides a little today. And Hayley has been too busy to talk for the last week. I feel alone and I hate it. Bailey only comes over sometimes, and if she does it's with Cale. So I can't even have one on one time with my sister. My parents have immersed themselves into the wedding planning, and I've never felt so left out.

I'm leaving Cale in the past, but that doesn't mean I want to help my sister plan her wedding to a man I once loved. To a man who crushed me beyond repair.

I chew on my lip. "I just don't want Bai to make a mistake with all of this," I say. And it's the truth. I don't want her to rush into something that can end badly. Cale hurt me in a way that I would never wish on anyone else, especially my sister.

"It is fast Gray, but she seems so in love," my mother smiles. "I've never seen her so happy, and Cale the way he looks at her—"

I cut her off, "Like she's the first shooting star he's ever seen." The words leave my mouth before I can stop them. I blush as I say those words. It's been years since I've muttered them.

My mother makes a face at my words, but nods slowly in agreement. "Yeah, he looks at her just like that," she mumbles suddenly deep in thought.

We sit in silence for a few minutes before the curtain finally slides open to reveal Bailey. All I can see is sparkle, sparkle, and more sparkle. She shuffles out of the room, resembling a waddling duck. Helen helps her onto the small round platform so she can face herself in the large three-way mirror.

The mermaid silhouette hugs her tightly, a little too tightly honestly. Her breasts are about to pop out of the low cut sweetheart top, and every single inch of the dress is filled with sparkling stones.

The dress looks tacky.

"Bai I think the guest might go blind looking at that," I say motioning to the awful dress that sticks to her body.

"Grayson," my mother says harshly as she gives me a pointed look.

I open my mouth in protest. "I'm sorry, but do you see what she is wearing?" I ask seriously.

Bailey rotates on the platform. Her body teetering side-to-side reminds me slightly of a toddler learning how to walk. Bailey faces me, "Gray I understand how you wouldn't get this dress." I raise a brow at her words. "It's expensive and glamorous and everything the Hasting family would love. I can't just walk down the isle in some plain white dress, what would they think of me," Bailey says with a small dismissive chuckle.

I roll my eyes at her words, but say nothing more even though I want to. Cale always hated anything and anyone over the top, or ostentatious. He always made remarks about how beautiful I looked without makeup, or how cute I was in a simple sundress. Cale loved simplicity. But maybe he's changed, and Bailey is right. Maybe she has too look expensive-more like gaudy-to look the part of a Hasting.

"I think what Gray means Bai, is that you don't have to look a certain way for anyone. You pick what you feel comfortable in," my mother says.

Bailey shakes her head. "It doesn't matter what I want. I'm high society now, which means it matters what other people think." Bailey looks at herself one last time in the mirror before Helen helps her off the platform. "I like it, but I'll try on the other two for you guys before we make any real decisions." Bailey waddles off into the changing room once again with Helen following behind her.

I cross my arms across my chest, and scoff lightly at what just happened with Bailey.

"Gray, don't even go there," my mother chides. "Bai's very nervous about marrying Cale and taking on the Hasting name, and she thinks she has to act a certain way. She will learn in time where her place is and who she wants to be." My mother while strict has always been supportive of us and very wise. She knows what to say, and when to say it. I know no matter what Bailey will always be herself, even if it takes some time adjusting to the Hasting lifestyle.

I nod at my mother's words. I know she's right, but at the same time I can't help but be slightly pissed at Bailey for her words. I know the Hasting's are high society here in Easton, but that doesn't mean she needs to act above our family name. Our family is well known and liked in Easton. And for her to act as if my mother and I know nothing, or wouldn't understand high society events really hurts.

"It's just fast mom, I think Bai is throwing herself into this relationship too soon," I say truthfully. "And I feel like everything is going to crumble and fall before she even realizes it." I would never want my sister to get hurt, but having her hurt by the same man who hurt me would be devastating.

My mother pushes her dark hair behind her ears, and settles back into the couch. "I don't know Gray. It is fast, but I can't say much about it. Your father and I only knew each other six months before we got engaged." I beam at my mother's words. When I was younger I used to make my parents tell me how they met all the time. Their story was like a fairytale, and made me want to find that fairytale love also. Which I thought I found one summer with Cale, but love isn't a fairytale I realized. It's hard, and something a couple has to work at every single day.

I naw on my lip in thought before answering. "Yes, but you also waited until you graduated college to get married," I point out. Bailey technically has a semester left of school, because she put off her gen-eds until the last minute. It's not much, but I guess Bailey was one to never want to really work after school. She never talked about having a career after college, only about starting a family. So I guess she got what she always wanted, her MRS degree.

My mother nods at my words. "True, but your father and I were at the same place in life back then. Cale is older and already gradated college, and has a great career with his father's company. So he is in a different place in life."

"Yeah, I guess," I half-heartedly admit.

Suddenly the curtain whips open, and Bailey comes out in the same sparkly over the top dress that she was in before. She has a veil in her hair, and tears in her eyes.

"What happened to the other dresses?" I ask confused.

She shakes her head. "No, I can't. This is it. This is the dress I want to get married in." She smiles as tears continue to fall down her cheeks.

My mother stands and quickly hugs her. "Oh you look amazing honey, Cale will fall in love with you all over again when he sees you in this dress."

Bailey nods in agreement as she begins to fan her face. I resist the urge to roll my eyes.

Bailey makes her way over so she is standing right in front of me. Her dark hair frames her beautiful face, and the too tight dress hugs her like a glove. Even with it's tackiness the dress looks beautiful on her. The truth is everything looks beautiful on Bailey. Her blue eyes lock on mine, the smile on her face so bright it's almost as blinding as her dress. I've never seen her smile so bright and true.

"You really love him?" I ask as I swallow the lump in my throat.

She nods with a small hiccup. "Yes, so much."

I wet my lips. "And you really want this life with him?"

She nods once again, and I step forward and wrap my arms around her petite body. A small tear escapes my eyes, and trails down my cheek. "Then as long as you're happy, I'm happy Bai," I mutter honestly.

I release her and take a step back to really look at her dress once more. "You look beautiful. You'll blow Cale away in that dress," I smile.

I wipe away at the lingering tear hating how real this wedding seems all of the sudden. But if Bailey is truly happy than that is all I can ask for. If Cale is what makes her happy, than I'm happy for her, no matter what I may feel for Cale. He once looked at me as if I was his shooting star, but he killed the star that once lingered in the sky. Bailey is his new shooting star, and I hope she stays in the sky long enough to really make a life for herself with Cale Hasting. I never want Bailey to hurt like I did all those years ago. If it takes my pain to create her happiness then I will accept that role.

I take a step away from everyone, and turn to grab my phone as it makes a small chirp sound alerting me to a text. I see a text from Kylie.

Sorry I've been busy these last few days, but r we still on for tonight's bday festivities?

A breathy sigh of relief escapes my lips as I type, Yes please!

I turn to see Bailey and my mother hugging again with tears in both of their eyes. I can hear Bailey say, "Like this dress looks so high society." I shake my head.

I then add, I need a drink asap!

I need to forget about everything for one night and let loose. And tonight seems like the night to do that.

Chapter Ten

5/22/15

"THREE...TWO...ONE!" Chase shouts as we all down our fourth shot of fireball. The cinnamon whiskey sends heat through my veins and warms my heart.

I smile. "Okay we need a dancing break or I'm going to get too drunk too fast," I tell Chase and Kylie. I grab both of their hands and lead them to the dance floor.

We are at this club downtown that's pretty new, and Easton doesn't get anything new...ever. So it's no shock that the place is filled to the max. The dance floor is crazy packed, but I don't even care in this moment. I have my two friends by my side, and I'm just slightly drunk that I can't wipe this stupid smile off of my face. I'm feeling good and could care less about Cale or Bailey or anyone else right now.

Going wedding dress shopping hadn't been on the plans for today. No, having my birthday dinner with my family was on the docks. Albeit it only being my half birthday, it was still something my family wanted to do with me. But instead Bailey moved her wedding dress appointment up to my day. The one day I wanted to be about me for the summer. I only wanted one day. Every other day is about Bailey and Cale, and I still couldn't have a day to myself.

So tonight is about me. Right here and right now is about me.

The music switches from the bass hitting electronic music suddenly to a song filled with light, upbeat fun. Chase immediately grabs my hand and twirls me around to the quirky and bubbly sound. We dance and spin and scream the lyrics at the top of my lungs until I'm almost out of breath. Kylie grabs my hand now and twists me until I land in someone's arms. Arms I know don't belong to Chase or Kylie.

I gasp at the warm contact, and look up to meet bright green eyes. I can't help the thrill that runs through my body as I look at the man before me. His pink lips turn up into a smirk, and I can't help but smile back. My hands that are still on his chest squeeze around the fabric of his button up on instinct before I pull away flushed. I run my now sweaty hands over the body of my dress trying to calm the sudden nerves that fill my veins.

"Sorry I ran into you," I mumble hating the sudden bat of nerves that flutter through me.

I don't know why he's making me nervous, but on some weird level I like it.

"It's really no prob—"

His words are cut short when some drunken moron slams into the mystery man, and pushes him back into mine. His hands wrap around my body to shield me from the impact. His hands on my lower back, and his body pressed into mine causes butterflies to erupt all over my body.

I quickly pull away again, but not before making sure the man was steadied.

"I guess the world just really wants us together," he jokes lamely.

I roll my eyes. "Do those lines ever work for you?" I ask eyeing him suspiciously after that cheesy one liner.

He laughs with the shake of his head. "Never, but it doesn't stops me from trying."

I can't help but laugh back. "I do like a man who doesn't give up," I admit with a small smile.

"Can I buy you a drink?" he asks with his eyes narrowed in on me like my answer to his question means so much.

I look back at Chase and Kylie who are watching with full attention on me. I raise an eyebrow as if to ask them if it's okay to step away for a bit with this guy. Chase smiles and nods, and Kylie obnoxiously throws two thumbs up at me.

I chuckle.

I turn back to face this man who has me standing in a fit of nerves and say, "Yes."

His big hand wraps around mine and leads me towards the bar. There's only one bar stool available and he lets me have it like a real gentlemen. "Thank you," I murmur.

He places his hands on the bar in front of me so that his arms have me caged in. His hot breath brushes against my neck making me shiver. "My pleasure," he whispers.

I hate and love how the hairs on my neck stand up at the deep rumble of his voice. A part of me hates it because I know it's not Cale behind me. But the other side of me loves it because it's not Cale. It's someone new, and I need new.

New and exciting.

"What can I get you two?" The bartender asks as he continues to whip up a mixed drink for some girls down the bar.

Mystery man leans forward to say, "I'll have a beer, whatever's on tap." He turns his head to lock his eyes on mine as he waits for me to speak up.

I wet my lips. "Vodka cranberry is fine."

His eyes have me breathless. His dark hair and lightly tanned skin and pink lips have my attention. But those eyes hold me more than anything, I could get lost in them forever.

He nods at my words, and repeats them to the bartender before he settles back behind me.

I turn my body on the stool so I can look face him and take him in more. "So what is your name Mr. Lame Lines?" I ask with a teasing smile.

He tilts his head and leans in closer. "Max, and you Miss Ego Squasher?" he plays back.

I bite the inside of my lip for a second deciding if I should give a real name or not. But I just decide to go for it, "Grayson."

Why not? I think to myself. He's cute, he seems nice, and it's definitely time to move on.

"Grayson..." he trails, as he tastes my name on his lips for the first time. I like it a little too much I must admit.

"What?" I question.

"The name fits you," he claims.

"How?"

"It's different," he answers with a single shoulder shrug.

"And I'm different?" I chuckle.

"Yes Grayson, you are different," he smiles as his eyes hold me still.

Our heads both turn to the bar when we hear the sounds of glass sliding against the sticky bar. "Here you guys go," the guy states as his eyes are already looking down the bar to see whom he has to serve next.

Max shakes the bartender's hand, and discreetly slides some cash into his waiting palm. Then the busy bartender leaves.

Max turns his attention back to me. "Thank you," I murmur with the straw against my lips. I take a long sip from the drink basking in the chill that slides down my throat, but warms my heart at the same time.

"Are you from Easton?" he asks after a quick swig of his beer.

"I'm from Virginia. But my family has a beach house down here, but I haven't been down here for a long time. School has taken up a lot of my time lately," I explain as my eyes continue to soak in the man in front of me.

"I just moved down here a few years ago. That explains why I've never seen you around before. I would've remembered a girl like you," he drawls.

I shake my head. "Again with the cheesy lines," I scold jokingly.

He laughs. "So where do you go to school?"

"Northwestern," I answer.

He raises in an eyebrow in surprise. "You went a far ways away."

I shrug. "It was time for a change," I say truthfully.

I watch Max's throat as he finishes off his beer. I hate how strong the urge is to kiss my way up his thick neck. I just met this man, and yet the urge to reach out and touch him is overwhelming. He sets the bottle down on the bar before turning his attention back on me. His hands resume their place on the bar caging me in once more. I can see his tongue run over his lips and his bright white teeth, and I can't help but watch every swipe of his tongue.

He clears his throat as my eyes jerk away from his pink lips. He knows I was staring and is enjoying his power over me a little too much. "So what brings you back to town Grayson?" he asks with a small tilt of the head.

It's my turn to drain my drink. "Sister is engaged. Wedding at the end of the summer," I say with a tinge of annoyance coloring my tone.

"Fun," he smiles.

My lips pull to the side in thought. "I guess for some people."

A wide grins spreads across his obnoxiously attractive face. "Wanna get married to piss everyone off and upstage your sister?" he jokes with a wiggle of his eyebrows.

A breathy laugh escapes my mouth at his words. "Wow you really don't stop, do you?"

His eyes graze over my face. "Never," he breathes.

And for that moment our eyes lock and all I can see is Max. All I can see is his dark wild hair, his strong jaw that I for some reason ache to pepper with kisses, and then his green eyes that pull me into a deep jungle of heat. This heat is new and exciting, and at the same time I fear it.

He leans his body into mine until his lips graze my ear. "All jokes aside Grayson. I've wanted to kiss you since the moment I laid eyes on you. And your fiery personality only makes me want you more." His words are deep and hoarse and make me flush.

He pulls away so that his face and lips are just inches from mine. I have to lick my now dry lips to even speak. "Fiery personality, eh?" I joke with a raised eyebrow.

"Yes, Miss Ego Smasher. I somehow find your personality addicting," he admits.

"Addicting?" I breathe.

He nods. "Yeah, I want more."

"More of what?" I ask quietly in the too loud bar, and yet he hears me anyways.

"You," he whispers before he leans in to press his lips lightly to mine.

But before the kiss can progress to anything more I hear my name being shouted.

"GRAYSON! GRAYSON!" I close my eyes for a second in disappointment. I know it's Kylie shouting my name, and I want to punch her for her timing. But I pull away from Max nonetheless.

"I'm sorry," I exhale.

He nods but pulls away also. "Me too."

I look over to see Chase holding up a drunk Kylie, and waving at me to come over. I sigh, but quickly nod in acknowledgment at his wave.

I turn towards the bar grasping ahold of a random pen and turn back to Max. His eyes squint in confusion, but soften as I grab his hand. I scribble my number down on the soft pad of his hand. My eyes flicker up to Max's blazing ones. The way he watches me makes me squirm and I love every minute of it.

"I wanna finish what we just started," Max grumbles at me as I drop the pen back on the bar and hop off of the stool.

I walk a few steps away before turning back to face him. "Call me and you just might get that chance."

Then I walk away.

But I'm weak and can't help but glance back at Max. He's still standing watching me, and his eyes hold mine as the sexiest smile spreads over his face.

I shake my head and walk towards Chase and Kylie.

What a night, I think to myself.

* * * * *

"Grayson! I love you so much! And I'm so happy we went out tonight! And wow Chase you're just too cute...and I might throw up..." Kylie trails her face suddenly uneasy.

Chase and I are on either side of Kylie holding her up, leading her into my house. "How'd she get so drunk?" I ask Chase. "I wasn't gone that long was I?"

"She just kept wanting to do shots and shots and more shots," he explains. "And yeah you were gone flirtin' it up for a while," he laughs.

I shake my head with a giggle. "He was cute," I say casually.

"Yeah," I hear Chase mumble in agreement.

I ignore his change in demeanor, not reading much into it. "You find any cute ladies tonight?" I ask instead.

We finally reach my room and place Kylie on my bed. We thought it would be better to just take her home with me, so that I can keep an eye on her for the night. She passes out immediately, her body curling into a ball on the edge of the bed. I quickly grab a trashcan and a glass of water and some Advil, and place it on the nightstand next to her. Hopefully she doesn't get sick tonight, but if she's does we are prepared.

"So did you?" I repeat.

"What?" Chase questions.

"Find any cute girls? Anyone who caught your eye?" I clarify.

He shakes his head. "Oh no..." he trails.

"What about Kylie?" I half joke, half truthfully ask.

"No. Great girl but not my type," he says with an uneasy smile.

"What is your type Chase Hasting?" I tease as I playfully punch his arm.

He smirks. "You'll never know."

I laugh. We walk out of my room and to the open from door. "Thanks again for tonight Chase, I had a great time." I pull him into a hug and hold him tightly for a few seconds.

He pulls away and places an innocent kiss on my cheek. "Night Grayson."

"Night Chase," I sigh before closing the front door and locking it.

I walk over to the kitchen wanting a snack before bed when I spot Cale leaning up against the fridge. His hazel eyes hold mine and for some stupid reason I feel guilty. Guilty about giving my number to Max, and guilty about Chase kissing me on the cheek. All of which I shouldn't feel guilty about. But the way he watches me forces the emotion to course through my body.

"Have a fun night?" His words are cold against the warm air.

I look down hating the look on his face. He looks at me as if I've betrayed him and I've done nothing of the sort. Far from it actually. He's the one who betrayed me and I shouldn't be feeling bad about having a fun night.

I lift my chin and push my shoulders back with a new wave of confidence washing over me. "Yes I did. What about your night?" I ask as I push my way around him and grab a cold water bottle from the fridge.

The chill of the refrigerated air causes goose bumps to cover my skin. I close the door to find Cale right next to me. He's so close, yet so far emotionally.

I suddenly smell liquor and turn to face Cale. "Have you been drinking?" I ask suspiciously.

His hard eyes hold mine. "What does it mean to you?"

I roll my eyes with a sigh. "Nothing Cale. I couldn't care less." And it's the truth. If he wants to drink he can, he isn't mine to watch over anymore.

I crack open the water bottle in my hand, and take a swig the cold water washing through me. A single drop of water misses my mouth and run down my neck and into the valley of the top of my dress. It should be something small, something so innocent and insignificant.

But it's everything.

Cale's eyes burn into my skin as he watches the drop of water slide down my chest and into places that once belonged to him. His eyes burn a path until they are on my lips. I hate the thoughts that course through my mind. When I was with Max, Cale was the last thing on my mind. But now Max and all his infectious happiness is gone, and nothing is blocking the raw emotions that Cale brings out of me. And I hate it.

The words that leave his mouth next shock me.

"What would you do if I kissed you right now Gray?" His words are deep and gravely and roll over my skin like silk.

"You're drunk Cale." I try and reason.

"Answer the question," he growls as he takes a step closer to me.

"I would push you away," I say truthfully. Or at least what I want to be the truth. In all honestly I want to have the power to push him away but I don't know if I could. And it makes me hate myself all over again.

"Would you?" he asks huskily.

His body is so close to mine, staking me, urging me to do bad things with him. But I can't. I won't. I love Bailey and I refuse to cross this line with Cale again. But Cale's dark eyes, messy hair, and swollen lips draw me in.

I nod suddenly unable to speak.

"Answer me Gray. Would you push me away?" he pauses to lean his towering body over mine. "Or would you fall into me like you've always done. You always used to moan when I kissed you, do you still do that? Do you still like it when your neck is being kissed?" His lips move to my ear as his dark words continue to consume me. "Do you still like it when I whisper dirty words in your ear?"

I hate how my body trembles at his words, and his demanding presence.

I shake my head but we both know it isn't true. I would give in. I can't help but to give into this man. I want to be a better person. I want to move on and fall for men like Max who give cheesy one-liners.

"Tell me you would push me away," he whispers into the dark.

I'm supposed to be moving on, only focusing on the future. But here I am living for these few seconds of the past So I don't tell him anything like I should. Instead I live in the past for a few seconds longer and say nothing.

Chapter Eleven

5/22/15

I'M DROWNING.

Drowning in lips, tongue, and teeth. Drowning in Cale.

I know I should pull away. I know this is wrong. I know he is engaged to my sister. I am aware of so much, but in this moment I only care about the taste of this man. It's been so long since I've tasted him I almost forgot the soft caress of his lips, the minty taste of him, and the overwhelming feeling of always wanting more from this man.

The realization that I want more is enough to send a shock through my system, and I jerk away from Cale. My hands pull out of his now deliciously tangled hair, and I take a couple steps back from him.

Ten agonizingly long seconds pass. We say nothing to each other, not one word passes as we just look. Our eyes are caught on each other, and the undeniable tension roars between us like the crackle of thunder just begging to release the rain from the clouds. And just like those clouds my body is begging for a release from Cale.

His hand runs a single finger over his lips before dropping his hand forcefully. His hand slaps against his jean-clad thigh and the moment is over. Our eyes break from each other, and air finally seems to make its way into the room again.

"I...umm..." I mumble unable to find the right words for this horrendous moment.

Cale runs a hand over his face in shock at what just transpired between the two of us. The high from the kiss we both shared is quickly coming down, and the feeling of dread is sinking in instead. If Bailey ever found out about this it would destroy her, destroy us. And all my fears about Cale breaking her are gone, and replaced with the fears that I will be the one to break her. That I will be the one that creates her heartbreak and fear to fall in love with any other man or to trust another woman.

The reason for her heartbreak can't be me. If I'm the reason for breaking her I will never recover.

"Gray, I'm sorry that should've never happened. I don't..." Cale trails trying to find the words to fix what just happened. But we can't fix it.

What we did is unfixable, and that's the scariest part.

I shake my head. "No, yeah," I agree awkwardly.

Cale takes a step back stumbling uncomfortably away from me. "I'm going to go upstairs and this can never—"

"Be mentioned," I finished for him. "I get it. Believe me, I get it Cale," I state as I turn to walk away from the kitchen I can now never look at again without picturing his hands on my body.

Cale's hand shoots out to grab onto my arm to stop me. "I'm sorry Gray. I'm drunk, and it was stupid, and it won't happen again," he swears.

I know it can't happen again, I am conscious of this. And yet at those words a pang of sadness shoots through me.

"Same. I'm drunk too," I lie. I'm not drunk. We both know it's a lie, but we let my words try and cover up the damage we just caused. Cale pulls away from me, and we both walk away from each other.

Walk away from the one thing that feels so right, but is so wrong.

I walk back into my room my head still reeling from the way I just betrayed my sister. I hate Cale for initiating the kiss, and I hate myself even more for letting him kiss me and liking it.

I crawl into bed next to a passed out Kylie. I check over her to make sure she's okay and hasn't puked all over herself or even worse. Her snores are clear as day, and she's curled herself up into a ball. She looks peaceful, and I envy her peace in this moment.

I grab my phone and text Hayley.

If u have time to talk plz call me. I did something really bad.

I press send and lay back onto my bed. The kiss was everything, but it also made me realize one thing: I can't have him. Cale is the definition of untouchable. Even if he called off his wedding with Bailey tomorrow I still couldn't have him. Cale will never be mine. Doesn't matter that I still hate him for the way he broke me years ago, doesn't matter if I forgive him, I can't have him.

And finally coming to that realization hurts and calms my heart at the same time.

Suddenly my phone rings, and I run with my phone into the bathroom as to not wake up Kylie. Not that it would with how dead to the world she is.

"What happened Gray?" she asks immediately.

I swallow my nerves. I know Hayley won't judge me, but saying out loud what happened tonight makes it all too real.

"You want the good or the bad new first?" I ask lamely.

She chuckles. "Always the bad! Do you even know me G?"

I smile weakly. God I miss her so much it actually hurts. I squeeze my eyes shut as I say the words that make even my own heart stop. "I kissed Cale." I continue. "Or Cale kissed me, but I kissed him back so what difference does it make who kissed who?" I ramble.

I hear her gasp. "I told you he wants you!" she shouts so loudly I have to pull my phone away from my ear.

I grimace. "No Hayley. He doesn't. It was a mistake...a huge one and it won't happen again obviously. It just—"

"Felt amazing?" she asks finishing off my sentence.

I sigh. "It did." I groan at my admission. "Agh, but that doesn't matter Hayley! He is engaged to my sister and it doesn't even matter. Ask about the good news please, I need to stop focusing on something that can and will never happen again," I say gloomily.

"But do you want it to happen again?" she pushes.

"Hayley," I growl.

"Fine, fine, fine!" she gives up. "Give me the good news."

"I met a guy tonight," I confess. "It was better news before Cale kissed me, but yeah I met a guy. A great guy, a really cute guy, and we even almost kissed." I explain to Hayley.

No gasp this time. No answer. No nothing.

"Hayley. You still there?" I ask uneasily.

I hear her exhale. "How is he good news when you are caught up on some other guy."

I shake my head at her words. "No. I need to move on Hayley, and I can't have Cale. I know that. So moving on with cute guys seems like good news to me."

I can almost hear the smile stretch over her lips. "How cute we talkin' over here?" she teases.

"Very cute," I admit.

"Details. I need details Gray."

I smile and lean back against toilet I've been sitting on and get comfortable. Because talking about cute boys with my best friend is exactly what I need in this moment.

I need to let go of the past. So I sit back and give all the dumb details of cute guy from the bar to Hayley, and don't speak one more word about Cale or that damn kiss.

* * * * *

5/23/15

My heart hurts.

I park my car back in the driveway, and just sit as my heart burns from the memories of last night. I just dropped Kylie back off at home, and even her cheerful yet slightly hung-over spirit couldn't lighten my mood.

I am the worst sister in the world.

The absolute worst. I don't know how I'm going to face Bailey or even face Cale or even walk into that kitchen again. As soon as I woke up this morning the waves of guilt and disappointment washed over me. And suddenly I wasn't drowning in Cale; I was drowning in fear and guilt.

I sit in my car for a few seconds longer trying to gain the courage to walk inside and face these people. I've even disappointed my parents. They might not ever know what happened between Cale and I, but I know I've disappointed them. They didn't raise me to be this kind of woman. They didn't raise me to screw over people like I did last night. They didn't raise me to hurt the people I love.

I climb out of my car and slowly walk into the house. I can hear only one voice. The one voice it physically hurts to hear. The one voice I've hurt in a way I never wanted to.

"I'm just gonna grab a vase," I hear Bailey say to someone.

I step into the kitchen, hating how the immediate onslaught of images of Cale and I hit me. I clear my throat, and push the haunting thoughts to the back of my mind. Bailey turns to face me, and for a quick second I think she may know. But she just smiles her brilliantly white smile at me as if there are no worries in the world.

And to her there aren't. If only she really knew.

"What do you need a vase for?" I question, trying to sound causal even though I am anything but.

Bailey grabs the vase off of the counter and brings it over to the island where I stand. The vase is filled with beautiful lilies, my favorites. "Wow, they're gorgeous," I breathe. "Where did you get them?"

Before Bailey can even open her mouth to answer me Cale walks through the back door. My eyes immediately cast to the floor avoiding him, and I find my body itching to leave the situation.

Bailey beams when he walks into the room. She wraps her arms around him, and plants a small kiss on the same lips I kissed just last night in this very kitchen. The blood rushes to my face in embarrassment and guilt, and I feel my face grow red and hot. I can't watch the intimate moment, no matter how small. Bailey wouldn't be kissing those perfect lips right now if she knew what happened last night. But Cale and I both agreed we wouldn't tell anyone. I can't be the reason Bailey hurts, but watching them is hurting me.

I decided yesterday at Bailey's bridal appointment that her happiness was worth every ounce of my pain. And it still is, though the pain just suddenly got a lot harder to handle.

"Cale got them for me this morning, isn't he just the sweetest?" Bailey says hanging all over him.

I finally look up to meet Cale's bright eyes. But they aren't bright anymore. They are dark and filled with anger towards me and only me. Those flowers are apology flowers, and he knows it. It's his way of saying sorry, without having to say sorry or admit what he is sorry for.

"Well they are your favorite babe, just thought I do something nice for my future wife." He leans over and kisses the top of her head after he murmurs his words.

They're not her favorite, I think to myself. Bailey loves tulips, always has and always will. My favorite flowers are lilies. But I don't say anything, because it's not my place to correct him.

Bailey's smile falters just slightly to where most people wouldn't catch it. But I do. She pulls Cale in closer. "They are, thanks babe." She lies, because she would rather lie than point out the truth. It makes me sad for her that she would rather lie then have her fiancé know the truth.

I wet my dry lips. "That's very sweet Cale." My words come out cold and distant. I want to sound happy, but I can't.

Bailey finally pulls away from Cale and starts fiddling with the flowers. "You have fun last night Gray?" she asks.

I don't look at Cale. "Yeah. The club was fun," I say vaguely.

"You got back pretty late Cale said." She continues with her attention fixated on arranging the flowers.

I can feel the heated gaze of Cale on me, but I refuse to acknowledge him. "He did, did he?" I comment, saying nothing more or less.

"Yeah, he said you and Chase seemed really close," Bailey emphasizes insinuating something more.

My face pulls in shock and annoyance, and this time I do look at Cale but he is looking at the ground. "No," I clarify. "Chase and I are just friends, I promise."

Bailey finally tears her gaze off of the dumb flowers. "But wouldn't it be so cool if we dated and married brothers Gray! We would be double sisters!" she exclaims.

I scrunch my eyebrows together. "I don't think that's how that works Bai..." I trail.

"Just think about it. Chase is cute and you two obviously have a connection, and Cale saw him kiss you on the cheek—"

"We are just friends Bailey god!" I snap. I didn't mean to, but I hate how everyone keeps trying to push Chase and I together. Why can't guys and girls be friends? Why does everyone have to assume that there is something going on when nothing is? Why did Cale have to bring Chase and I up to Bailey at all? Why did he kiss me last night? God, why?

Silence promptly follows my words.

Bailey's face falls in hurt, and I immediately feel like a bitch. "Bai, I'm sorry—"

She shakes her head. "No, I'm sorry Grayson." Her use of my full name shows that she is really upset with me. My shoulders sag in disappointment in myself. I didn't want to hurt her, and yet here I am being a stage one ass to my sister who has done nothing wrong.

She grabs the vase off of the counter. "I am just going to take these upstairs." With that she disappears up the stairs before I know it.

I feel Cale's body close to mine, but I don't erupt in tingles or excitement because I know this isn't about us. This is about me and Bailey, and how I just acted.

I look up to narrowed eyes. "Why do you always have to be such a bitch Grayson?"

I feel like a child getting reprimanded and I hate it. "Cale I didn't mean—"

He holds up a hand to stop me. "No. I am sorry about last night, and that will never happen again. But you treating my fiancée and your sister like that is unacceptable." His words ambush me with embarrassment. "Have you ever thought that maybe I wasn't the big asshole in this situation. That I wasn't the one with issues, that maybe I left all those years ago because I couldn't stand you anymore." His last words are filled with anger and all but growled out.

I fight to hold back the tears that fill my eyes. I fight to hold back the urge to slap him. I fight to stay standing, because all I want to do is crawl into a corner and cry my eyes out. I close my eyes to keep the tears at bay. "It's over," I say as my voice cracks.

He nods. "It is."

"Finally, after all these years," I say.

"Finally." And with that Cale turns on his heal and goes upstairs to his future wife. To my sister, the one he chose, the one he loves.

I was a moment of weakness and nothing more. Cale and I were never anything, and will never be anything ever again.

I'm free, and I should feel happy about it. But instead I feel lost.

Chapter Twelve

5/25/15

"YOU READY?" I ask Bailey as she comes down the stairs.

It's been a little awkward between us for the last few days since I yelled at her. But Bailey has always been one to bounce back quickly. She's a forgive and forget type of person. I wish I had inherited that same gene.

A small smile spreads over her lips. "Yup, just lemme grab my purse."

She walks over to the hooks by the back door and grabs a light coat and her purse. She pushes her dark hair behind her ears, and motions me with a thumbs-up signal that she's ready.

I nod and we head out to my car.

Today is just going to be about Bailey and I. We haven't had anytime for just us and I feel as if I've lost touch with my sister. Having Cale around is definitely not helping our relationship grow. But I'm also not helping. I haven't stepped up as much I could have, but I am now.

I'm about to be the best goddamn sister and maid of honor ever.

"Turn on whatever you like," I say motioning to the radio. I pull out of the driveway and head towards downtown Easton.

She messes with the buttons for a minute before settling on some indie station.

"Thought you would've picked country," I joke.

"Well you don't know me very much anymore do you?" Her tone edges with annoyance.

My eyebrows rise in shock at her words. Not at her words exactly, but at the fact she even said them. Maybe Bailey is right. I don't know her much anymore. But I can mend that, and I can try harder. So that's what I'm going to do.

"You're right. I don't. But I would like to fix that Bai," I tell her earnestly.

It's now her turn to look shocked. She probably expected me to fight her but I'm done fighting. I'm done being immature, and I'm done living in the past.

"Let's just focus on today and have fun, okay?" I tell her.

I flick on the turn signal and turn right and head towards a strip of restaurants. I park outside this little Italian place. It's our favorite, or it used to be.

"Do you still like Abbiocco?" I double check knowing I shouldn't assume much anymore with Bailey.

She nods with the touch of a smile on her lips. "Of course."

We climb out of the car and head in to the old restaurant. When we first started coming down to Easton our family fell across this tiny hole in the wall. As soon as we walked in the owner Adela, a small sixty-year-old woman, wrapped Bailey and I in her arms and fed us until we were stuffed. She's like a grandmother to us, and no matter how long we are gone for she treats us as if no time has passed.

As soon as we step in, Adela's daughter Clara rushes over. "Bailey! Grayson! Oh it's been too long!" Her long dark hair, and beautiful chocolate eyes beam as she takes us in. She's beyond gorgeous, and is the spitting image of her mother when Adela was young.

Clara turns to me and pulls me in for hug. She smells of flour and a light citrus perfume. "And where have you been all my life Gray?" she asks with the tilt of her head.

"School has taken up a lot of time," I half lie. It's the excuse I've used for years, but it's never been the truth.

Clara shakes her head. "I'm sure that's the reason." Her eyes narrow in on my as if they know the real reason I stopped coming around years ago. But she couldn't know, no one does.

"Is Adela around?" I ask trying to change the subject, but also excited about seeing my favorite lady.

Clara grabs us some silverware and a couple menus as she leads us to our favorite table. "No mamma's been out recently because of a cold. But she'll be back soon no worries!" She sets down our menus and silverware and turns to face us. "But she will be sad she missed you both."

"We'll stop by again, but tell her we miss her also," Bailey smiles.

"And tell her to feel better," I add. "She has a wedding to attend at the end of the summer." I motion over to Bailey at my words.

Clara smiles. "Believe me, we wouldn't miss it for the world!" She then motions at us to sit. "Come on get comfortable! I'll get you both some waters to start and then Fin will be your server. You both better not forget to say goodbye when you head out!" she points a finger in joking chastisement.

Bailey and I nod with a chuckle in agreement. Clara is only older than us by a decade or so, but she feels like such a wise soul. She was the older sister to Bailey and I that we craved at times when we were fighting and had no one else to go to.

I glance out over the deck that we sit upon, and out into the abyss of sea that surrounds us. The coolest part of this restaurant is their outdoor seating. It is so close to the ocean we might as well be floating around in it right now. The smell of Italian spices and the salt of the ocean mix around to create a calming sense of home.

I look over to Bailey and see her staring out at the ocean also. "I've missed this," I mumble out.

She turns to face me. "It wasn't the same coming here without you Gray. I'm glad we decided to have this day to ourselves."

Bailey's hand rests on the table and I squeeze it gently. "Me too."

* * * * *

"Ugh, I'm way too full!" Bailey exclaims as she tosses her napkin onto the table. She places her hands on her stomach and holds her food "baby".

"Is it a boy or a girl?" I ask teasingly.

"Might be twins with how much we just ate," she chuckles.

I just shake my head with a smile. This lunch had been much needed between Bailey and I. We really got to catch up with our lives in a relaxed environment without our parents and without Cale. Today was perfect, and I felt like I finally had my sister back. I know things haven't been easy, but no matter what we are here for each other.

Bailey suddenly stands. "I'm going to run to the bathroom real quick. You need to go?" she questions.

"Nope I'm good!" I tell her.

She heads inside the restaurant leaving me alone with the ocean and the last roll of bread. I slowly chew on the roll as I feel a wave of contentment roll over me. I grab my phone from my purse checking to see if I have any missed notifications. I'm scrolling through some random texts when my phone starts ringing.

It's a random number but I immediately answer. I know people are weird about answering unknown numbers, but I love it. I think it's funny to mess with the telemarketers, or sometimes it ends up being someone I actually need to talk to.

"Hello?" I answer as I swallow my last bit of food.

"Grayson?" A deep voice fills my ear.

"Yes, this is she," I answer still unsure of who is on the other line.

"Hey, it's Max," he pauses awkwardly. "From the club," he clarifies.

A smile immediately spreads across my face at the mention of his name. "I remember." A tinge of excitement runs through me at the fact that he finally called. A part of me was disappointed when he didn't call right away. I really had been looking forward to finishing that kiss.

There's another pause. "Did you want something?" I ask unsure of what to say. It has been a while since I've actually liked anyone. I keep most men at arms length, and never really talk to them unless I need them for one night of fun. After Cale I stopped trying with all males, but Max is different. Max makes me want to start trying again.

"Umm...yeah sorry I guess I'm not as smooth over the phone," he says lightheartedly.

I giggle. "I think you're doing just fine."

I hear a breathy laugh come through the line. "I just wanted to call to see if you wanted to go out sometime?"

I bite my lip and my heart squeezes as my whole body fills with bliss. "I would love that Max," I say truthfully.

"How about sometime next week?"

"Sounds good to me. I just have to check to see what days I'm free." I acknowledge, knowing my schedule is usually filled with back-to-back maid of honor duties.

"Wedding stuff?"

"You guessed it," I sigh.

"If this date goes well my offer still stands to upstage your sister and get married first," he quips.

I laugh. "How about we see how this date goes first?"

"Sounds perfect." I can hear the smirk through the phone and love the way my heart skips a beat.

"Okay, I'll call you later then."

"I look forward to it. Bye Grayson," he breathes.

"Bye Max," I whisper as I pull the phone away from ear and hang up.

I feel giddy and anxious all at the same time. I haven't felt this way in years about a guy or even about a date. But Max is unlike any guy I've met lately. He's funny and sweet and damn sexy, and he makes me forget about my past with Cale. In fact he blots out all of Cale when I'm around him. So I'm moving on, and moving on with a man like him is about all I could ask for and more.

Bailey comes back from the bathroom and slides into her chair. "What's with the smile? You look really happy..." she trails.

I roll my eyes. "Am I not allowed to be happy Bai?"

She waves her hand as if to dismiss me. "No you just look extra happy, like you're glowing," she observes honestly.

"A guy just asked me out," I confess. For a second I feel awkward sharing this information with Bailey. I never really talk to her about boys. It's always Hayley I run to with these kinds of conversations. But the ecstatic smile that breaks out on Bailey's face lessens my worries instantly, and makes me happy I'm sharing this part of myself with her.

"OMG! Who?" Bailey freaks, and I can't help but laugh. Her squealing not as annoying as it once was.

"Just a guy," I say vaguely not wanting to talk about the night of the club.

"A cute one?" She asks.

"The cutest," I admit.

And for the first time in a long time I'm excited about the idea of dating a guy who doesn't have the last name of Hasting.

Chapter Thirteen

5/30/15

"UGH, ARE YOU sure this looks good?" I ask as I turn around looking at myself in the mirror.

I turn over to my computer screen to see Hayley rolling her eyes at me. "If you change one more time I swear I'm going to crawl through this screen and punch you."

I purse my lips. "That doesn't tell me if I look good or not Hayley," I mumble.

I hear a sigh as I turn back to the mirror. "Yes, you look amazing Gray! I promise, you know I wouldn't lie to you!" She exclaims.

"I know," I hum in agreement.

I'm wearing a simple white sundress that stands out against my tan skin, and strappy wedges. My blonde hair is pulled back into a ponytail, and I spent a little more time on my makeup than I usually do trying to make myself at least seem put together.

"Don't be nervous G," Hayley tells me.

I twist towards my computer screen. "I'm not nervous," I lie.

Hayley smirks. "It's just a date."

I nod. "I know. But I haven't been on a date in a while and—"

"You actually like Max?" Hayley asks cutting me off.

I bite at the inside of my lip as my face flushes. "I do." I don't know why this date is making me so nervous, but it is. I mean it's just a date, nothing more. And yet, the idea of spending time with Max makes me feel all anxious inside.

"It's okay to like him you know?" Hayley points out.

I turn away from the screen now not wanting to face her. Or more not wanting to face her words. "I know," I say.

"Because I know Cale hurt you and—"

I flip around stopping her with a raised hand. "Please Hayley, let's not go there right now," I beg. "I just want to focus on Max and this date and nothing else, okay?"

Hayley tilts her head with a small smile. "Okay."

I run a hand down my dress, and sit down at my desk so I'm in front of my computer. "How's the internship so far?" I ask.

Hayley's face immediately lights up. "It's so much work—"

"And you love it," I finish for her.

She nods eagerly. "I do, I do! I'm learning so much and it's tough at times but wow..." she breathes. "I don't think I've ever loved this city more honestly."

I cast my gaze down hating the tears that threaten to overflow. I know I should be happy that Hayley is having the summer of her life, and I am. But I can't help but be a tad envious that I'm not there with her. Experiencing the real world, and falling in love with the city again. It's something I wish I could be doing with her instead of being stuck hundreds of miles away.

"How's the ginger?" I ask teasingly.

Hayley narrows her eyes at me. "Maxine," she emphasizes for me, "is doing wonderfully actually."

"Good for her," I say unenthusiastically.

"Don't G," Hayley sighs. "Come on you should be getting excited for your date right now."

I play with the raw hem of my dress. "I am," I murmur.

"You know you're my favorite always," Hayley says with smile.

"I better be," I say with a small playful pout.

She laughs. "Go finish your makeup and have a wonderful date!"

I frown. "My makeup is finished!" I shout.

Hayley tilts her head. "More lip-gloss, and a little more blush," she critiques.

I roll my eyes. "Yeah, yeah," I say sarcastically.

I reach to close my laptop as she yells, "Remember it's not slutty to put out on the first date, and you better text me every detail Gray!"

I chuckle. "Bye Hayley!" And with that I shut my laptop.

I dab on some more gloss and brush on a little more blush, knowing Hayley is usually right about this kind of stuff. I then stand up from desk, and tighten the hair in my ponytail. I do a once over and take a deep breath to ease my nerves. I'm nervous to go on a date with Max, but I'm also so excited it makes me even more anxious. I slide on a few bracelets, and grab my purse and head out of my room.

I walk out into the kitchen to see my parents and Bailey and Cale all sitting around the island. I immediately avoid Cale's gaze. Neither of us has said one word to each other in five days, and it's been awkward as hell between us. But I can't care about our awkwardness anymore. I have to focus on Bailey and mines relationship. After our lunch together I've been making more of an effort to hang out with my sister and be more supportive of her. I know I've lacked in many ways as a sister, but I'm stepping up now and I hope that's what counts.

I inwardly roll my eyes at my family. "Seriously, you guys aren't obvious at all," I say as I walk over to join them.

My mother smiles at me. "Gray, come on we are just excited for you!"

"Why?" I mumble as I mess with my phone.

"Well, it's not like you went on any dates when you were younger," my father points out.

My eyebrows knit together. "That's not true," I say defensively. Hating how my face heats up at that admission in front of Cale. I don't care what he thinks of me, I don't!

"It's okay honey!" my mother comforts. "We never minded when you were a teenager, but now that you're older we love seeing you put yourself out there."

I shrug at her words having nothing to say because she is right. I never went on dates or even let guys entertain the idea of having a chance with me.

After that summer with Cale I was so broken I couldn't even think about opening myself up to anyone else.

"Do we get to meet him?" Bailey asks excitingly.

I chuckle at her words. "Yeah right."

"Why can't we meet him?" My father questions with an eyebrow raised.

"Because it's a first date! It might not go anywhere and I'm not gonna have you meet him if it doesn't," I say.

"Well if there is a second or even a third date we are meeting him," my father says strongly.

I nod. "Okay, okay," I relent.

There's a knock at that door and everyone shifts to move. I raise my hands. "Uh uh, no!" I state. "Everyone sit, and no one come to the door with me," I say sternly.

Everyone begins to protest, and no one makes a move to sit back down. I shake my head. "Sit!" I shout at them like they're dogs.

This time they listen, though they look annoyed. I grab my purse from the counter and walk to the front door. I turn around to see everyone's heads crane around to catch a glimpse of my date. Well everyone besides Cale, not that I cared.

I open the door to reveal Max. His smile sends my heart racing and I can't help but smile back in excitement.

"You ready?" he asks as his eyes take in my dress. His eyes linger for a second on my legs and I love the way my skin tingles at his gaze.

"You have no idea," I breathe.

I step out of the house and quickly close the door behind myself. I follow Max down the steps towards his car and rake my eyes over him. I take in his grey jeans, and his navy sweater with a plaid shirt sticking out from beneath. He looks good I can't lie. I like how put together he looks, how clean cut he comes across. But when I look into his eyes all I can see is the wild passion that lies within him.

His eyes catch mine. "You look beautiful by the way Grayson." I can't help but blush at his words.

"Thank you," I respond with a blush.

Max opens the passenger door for me, and I thank him before sliding into the leather seats. His car is clean and sleek and smells like pine. He slides in to the drivers seat and starts the engine.

He pulls out of the drive way and heads towards downtown. "Where are we going?" I ask curiously.

His eyes flick to me before they end up back on the road. "It's a surprise," he smiles.

I sit back in my seat as excitement courses through me at what the surprise could be. "I'm really glad you called me Max," I admit. I was nervous telling him this, but I want him to know how I excited I am about this date and him.

His tongue wet his lips. "I would've called sooner if I had known you were going to wear that dress," he smirks.

I shake my head. "Wow, you really do never give up," I comment.

He laughs, and the sound is beautiful. It's deep and melodious, and makes my skin crawl with a deeper need. "I never give up on the things I want."

I bite my lip at his words.

Max stops in front of Abbiocco the Italian restaurant Bailey and I just went to for lunch a few days back. I smile at the restaurant, though I decide not to say anything because I don't want to ruin whatever Max's surprise might be.

He comes around and opens the door for me, which I love. A man with good manners is something that is always sexy. Max then takes my hand and leads me inside the small festive restaurant. His hand is big and feels warm against the skin of my palm. I realize I like the feeling of his hand in mine, and it kind of scares me.

As soon as we walk in Adela the owner's eyes meet mine, and she storms over to me immediately. "Grayson!" Her thick Italian accent shouts at me in excitement.

Max looks over at me confused, and I just shrug with a knowing smile lifting my lips. "So I'm guessing you've been here before?" he asks in realization as he runs a hand through his dark hair.

Adela rushes over and wraps her arms around me in a hug. She is a tiny little woman, but she is stronger than she looks. Her hair tickles my neck, and she smells like oregano. She places her hands on my cheeks and smiles brightly. "Oh Grayson, how excited I am to see you!" she says. "Clara told me she saw you and Bailey a few days back and I was so sad I missed you!"

I placed a hand on top of hers that still rested on my face. "Yeah, she said you were under the weather. Are you feeling better?" I ask concern lacing my words.

Adela nods. "Just getting old that's it," she says dismissively. And then her eyes slide over to Max who still stands beside me. "And who is this?" She questions with a knowing gleam in her eyes.

I wrap my hand back around Max's body and pull him closer. "This is Max," I tell Adela.

Max sticks out his hand to shake Adela's. "It's nice to meet—"

But Adela cuts him off as she pulls him into a hug instead. "A friend of Grayson is a friend of mine always!"

Max chuckles at Adela's words. "Well it's great to meet you," he says honestly.

"So what brings you lovely children here?" she inquiries.

"We're on a date," I whisper playfully to Adela though loud enough that Max can hear me.

Adela raises her eyebrows at Max. "He is a pretty thing," she comments.

I let out a breathy laugh. "He is," I agree feeling Max's gaze on me making me flush.

Adela grabs some menus and silverware for myself and Max. "I can take you to your table—"

"I...uhh...actually," Max stutters awkwardly stopping Adela in her tracks.

Both Adela and I face Max, as his face turns red in embarrassment. He runs a nervous hand through his dark hair, tugging at the ends. "I actually had my friend Fin set up something for us..." he trails.

Adela claps her hands and let's a small squeak. "That's for you?"

Max nods as I look at him quizzically.

"Well follow me this way," Adela says eagerly.

Max laces his fingers through mine as we follow Adela through the upbeat restaurant. This place is always packed, but on the weekends it's a whole other ball game. A live band plays, the bar is packed, and food and wine are consumed at crazy levels. It's as if in this small town we have a small gateway into Italy, and it's beautiful.

Adela leads us out to the patio, which is filled with couples. But she takes us to a separate part of the patio that I've never been to before. It's usually reserved for parties or even weddings, but never general seating.

We reach the reserved area and a small gasp falls from my lips at the sight in front of me. Sparkling lights are strung up everywhere making it look as if the stars are surrounding us. A single table sits in the middle of the fallen stars with lilies placed in a vase at the center.

I turn to Max in surprise. "What? How? I don't...." I mumble unable to find the words to describe how I feel.

It's like a dream. I've never had a guy do this for me, or anything even close and I'm shaken from the way my heart squeezes.

Max's green eyes light up. "I had to do something big to impress the one girl who doesn't impress so easily," he smirks.

I wet my lips and blink away the few misty tears that linger in my eyes. I am so thrown off and filled with an excitement I didn't even know lived in me anymore.

"This is perfect," I say quietly.

He steps closer to me. "So you're actually impressed?"

"Beyond."

* * * * *

"So how did you know I like lilies?" I ask as Max leads me to the front door of my house.

It was late. We stayed at the restaurant until they were closed and then some. Max and I could talk for hours and it felt so natural. Besides Hayley, I've never been so comfortable talking to someone so quickly. We could talk about nothing or we could go as deep as we needed. It was honestly amazing, and surprising.

Max shrugs. "I didn't know they were your favorites honestly," he admits. "They're my mom's favorite."

I stop before we reach my front steps and look up at Max a little taken back by his words.

"What?" he asks confused by my sudden pause.

I smile. "I thought you would give me some line," I say honestly. "But you got me your mom's favorite flowers." I knew how important Max's mother was to him. He graduated college early and came back to town to live with his mother. She was getting older, and had had a few surgeries recently. So Max was living with her for a while to help her out. So the fact that he got me his mother's favorite flower makes my heart do weird things.

His eyes squint. "Is that wrong?" he asks nervously.

I shake my head. "No, I love it."

His hands pull me up the steps to the front door. "Would you rather me give you a cheesy line?" he chuckles.

"Nope," I smirk.

"You sure?" he pushes with a raised eyebrow.

I laugh. "I'm sure."

Max's thumbs rub against the skin on the outside of hands warming me. "I had fun tonight Grayson," he says. His green eyes hold mine and I can't help but step closer. He's pulling me in, and I can't help but want to fall. It's scary the idea of falling all over again, but at the same time I just want to take the dive.

"Yeah me too," I agree as my eyes flicker to the ground. His eyes are too vibrant, his smile too bright, and I don't want to fall too soon so I take a small step back.

He takes my step back as me not wanting to take anything further tonight. But that is far from the truth. I want Max to kiss me so bad, but I am nervous. We have a great connection and our conversation is great, but taking it to that next level makes it so real.

Max's hands drop from mine and he itches at his ear awkwardly. "Well it was fun yeah," he pauses before heading down the front steps. "I'm gonna get going," he says as he points to his car.

His back is facing me and he is almost to his car when I say the words that have been on my lips since the night I met him. "Aren't you going to finish what you started?" I rush out loudly.

Max's body flips around to face me. His head cocks to the side in confusion. "What?"

I clear my throats and swallow my nerves. "Aren't you going to finish what you started at the bar?" I ask referencing the night I met him when our kiss was stopped short. I force a small confident smirk to play on my lips, and place my hands on my hips. I push away my nerves and let what I want wash over, and what I want is Max.

His eyes light at my words, and in two steps he's up the front steps and his lips are on mine. His hands land on my cheeks and he pulls my face in closer if possible. My body sways into his as my hands wrap around his firm waist. His lips are soft against mine, yet they press into me with a rough eagerness. I love the way he feels pressed up against me, so I press into him more.

Max deepens the kiss as his tongue plays with mine. My nails dig into the skin on his hips making him growl with a need that wraps through me. His teeth nip at my lips before diving back in for more. The kiss makes my head spin and I love the way he draws me in.

In the back of my head I'm aware I'm above water still. I'm not drowning like I do with Cale, but at the same time I don't know if I should be.

Chapter Fourteen

6/5/15

"IS EVERYONE READY?" I ask as I grab the keys for Bailey's car off of the counter.

Bailey nods along with Kylie and Chase, and Cale mumbles an answer I don't care to hear. I haven't talked to Cale at all since before my date with Max and I'm okay with it. My date with Max was perfect, and when I'm with him I forget about the part of my heart that is missing because of Cale.

"Awesome," I say. Kylie tosses me a thumbs-up, and I toss her beach towel at her.

"Perfect! Let's head out." Bailey waves at us as she heads towards the door.

We all follow Bailey out the front door. I hand her keys to her before we all slide our ways into Bailey's jeep. I end up in the middle seat, which I hate but I make no comment. Today is about having fun and not complaining about the little things. Kylie and Chase squeeze in next to me. "Glad none of you have hideous body odor," I mumble.

Kylie is the only one who hears me as she laughs, though others might of heard me but just decided to ignore my snide remark.

Bailey pulls out of the driveway and starts off towards the highway. We decided to head towards a more popular beach about an hour away from Easton for the day. Easton's beaches are beautiful of course, but we wanted a younger crowd to hang out with.

"So Bailey, give me the details," Kylie starts. I look at her puzzled as to what she is getting at. "Because Grayson won't tell me about her date with Max," she finishes. I roll my eyes at her and sit back in my seat continuing to be squished between Chase and Kylie.

Bailey laughs. "Like she would tell me. She hasn't given me any details either besides the fact that they kissed and it was good." I stiffen slightly at my sister's words, but don't react any further or look at Cale.

I don't care about his reaction to her words, I don't.

"Ohhh you kissed…" Chase teases me as he elbows me in the side.

I shove back at him in response. "Shut up loser," I mumble.

"So?" Kylie questions.

I raise my eyebrows. "What?" I ask.

She waves her hands eagerly. "Come on I want the details!" She exclaims. "Are you going to go on another date with Max?"

I shrug. "Maybe." And it was the truth. I might go on another date with him, but he hasn't asked yet. We've texted a little bit back and forth since the date but nothing crazy. It's not like I'm planning my wedding to Max like everyone else is already. He is nice and funny, but that doesn't mean he's the one.

"Ugh, you are the worst at girl talk Gray," Kylie grunts as she sits back in her seat giving up on me.

"Tell me about it," Bailey laughs.

"Hey," I chide as hit Bailey teasingly in the shoulder.

She laughs at me, but they are both right. I do suck at girl talk, because I don't see a future with most guys I go out with. Seeing a future with someone means a serious relationship, and I'm honestly scared to take a relationship to that level. I'm scared to get my heart broken again. I'm scared to open myself up that much to anyone, especially a man.

I turn to Kylie to see her fake pouting at me. "Sorry Ky, there just isn't much info yet. I know I like him and that's about it," I say honestly. I do like Max, I feel comfortable around him and he's easy to talk to. Plus he isn't half bad to stare at.

She nods at my words with a quick glance to Cale. "Well, that's a start." I ignore her reference to the man who I haven't spoken to in days, and sit back in my seat saying nothing more.

"Whatever," I say as I close my eyes and pretend to sleep for the remainder of the ride.

* * * * *

"Gray," I hear Chase's deep voice whisper at me.

My eyes groggily open to see the car has stopped, and is parked at the beach. I look up to see that I've fallen asleep on Chase's shoulder. I lift my head and wipe at the small drop of dried drool on my lip.

"Sorry," I say as lift my body off of his and sit up straight. Between late night calls with Hayley, and wedding planning all day with Bailey I haven't gotten much sleep lately. I guess I was more tired than I thought with the fact that I dozed off for such a short drive.

Chase waves his hand. "It's no big deal," he shrugs. "Plus you're cute when you sleep."

I laugh at his obvious joke. "Yeah, because drool is cute."

"It can be," he smiles.

We both slide out of the car to meet the others who are waiting on us. Kylie hands me my towel, and we all head down the small wooden bridge to the beach. It's not super crowded yet with it only being early afternoon, but there are more than enough people to make for a fun day. The sun is burning hot, and the sky is as blue as the ocean. I smile inwardly at the how perfect the weather is today. I've needed a day like this, a day to relax and have fun with my sister and friends. The only thing to make this day better would be if Cale wasn't here, but we can't always get what we want.

Kylie's arm hooks with mine as we follow behind Bailey, Cale, and Chase. "He's in a bad mood," she mumbles.

My eyebrows pucker with confusion. "What? Who?" I ask not knowing whom she means.

"Cale," she responds as if I should already know the answer.

I eye the back of Cale quietly trying to gauge some type of reaction from him. From his back I obviously can't tell much, but I do notice the way he trudges forward ahead of everyone. Even ahead of Bailey. But I cast my gaze down from him because I don't care about Cale anymore. We are finished. So who cares if he's upset?

I lift a single shoulder. "Who cares," I say speaking my thoughts.

Kylie purses her lips, but says nothing more though I know she wants to. She knows that there has been weird energy between Cale and me lately, but she doesn't know that it is caused by the biggest mistake I've ever made.

We finally find a spot in the sand that can fit all five of us next to each other. I lay out my towel once again in the middle of Chase and Kylie. Though this time I don't mind being surrounded by my best friends. It's moments like this that make me wish Hayley were here with me. She would love the beach, and Chase and Kylie, and how simple and fun our summer can be. I know she's having the time of her life, but I also know she would love it here with me in Easton.

Cale and Bailey leave to go get some food at the small hut on the beach. So Chase and Kylie and I are left alone relaxing in the sand with the heat of the sun tanning our skin. I dig through the cooler behind me and find a chilled wine cooler.

"Gray, you are lucky we live in a town that never cards," Chase remarks.

I look at him as I swallow the sweet liquid in my mouth with a small grin. "You're right," I agree thinking back to our night at the club. I didn't get carded once the whole night luckily. People usually assume I'm older than I really am, which is fine with me. "But only one hundred and seventy days left and I will be legit," I note.

Kylie laughs at my words. "Not like you're counting or anything," she smirks.

I squish my toes into the sand and shrug. "Don't judge me," I tease. "It's a big birthday," I reason.

"I agree it is a big deal," Chase says as he takes a sip from his beer.

"Thank you Chase," I smile brightly.

"Because it's all down hill after that," he adds.

I look at him with a tilted head. "Seriously," I groan at his comment.

He chuckles. "Hey, it's true."

"Chase is right, what other birthdays do we have to look forward to after this?" Kylie asks.

We all sit there in contemplation at that question. Because after I turn twenty-one the years will roll forward quickly, and next thing I know I will be thirty with a family and kids. Well hopefully. Or I will be alone with ten cats, which is more likely at this point. Wow, they are right after twenty-one it is all down hill.

A shudder rolls through my body, but I immediately push it away.

"Hey," I say to gather Chase and Kylie's attention. They both turn to me. "A toast to twenty-one being the year we can look back at when we are old and tired and say, 'wow that was the year I lived'," I pause. "Okay?" I say as I hold up my drink.

Chase and Kylie nod and hold up their bottles. "To being twenty-one," Kylie says with a wide smile.

"To being twenty-one," Chase repeats.

I giggle. "To being almost twenty-one," I emphasize.

Our bottles clink together loudly and I love it. Right here and right now is perfect, and these are my people.

"What are we toasting to?" I hear Bailey's voice squeak from behind us.

I twist my head to meet Bailey's blue eyes. She's carrying a small white bag, which I know is filled with the best fries in the state. I then turn my gaze to Cale. His eyes hold mine before they flick away. I quickly turn my head back to the ocean before me, and clear my throat. I don't care about Cale, but that doesn't mean I can't hate the tension that now lies between us.

"We were just being dumb," I mumble not wanting to let them on the moment we just shared.

Kylie's gaze hit mine with a questioning look, but I shake my head brushing her off. I don't know why I didn't want to share our toast. But something about it was special to me, and I didn't want to share it with anyone else. Especially Cale.

"Well, I got a ton of extra fries!" Bailey exclaims holding up her bag and shaking it.

She comes and sits besides me on my towel, and opens up the bag. The smell of fresh cut fries hits me, and my stomach growls instantly. "I knew you'd want some," she sings.

I smile as I nudge her with my shoulder. "Thanks sis," I say appreciatively. These fries are my favorite, and the fact that Bailey remembers that makes me beam from within deep inside.

I grab a couple and quietly eat at the deliciously fried food. I notice Cale go to sit by Chase, but I try to not pay too much attention to him.

Bailey plops the bag onto my lap with a sigh, and stands up from my towel. "I gotta run to the bathroom, anyone else need to go?" Bailey asks as she wipes away some sand from her body.

I shake my head continuing to eat the fries Bailey left with me.

"Just go in the ocean," Chase snorts.

Bailey's face scrunches in annoyance. "Eww, I'd rather not," she states as she turns and walks off towards the restroom.

"Didn't seem to like my joke," Chase leans over and mutters at me.

I chuckle dryly. "Yeah, Bailey isn't one for joking about the bathroom," I admit.

He shrugs. "The things you learn about people."

I shove Chase with my hand. "You're stupid," I play.

He narrows his eyes and goes in to grab my wine cooler and takes a gulp. He pulls away from the drink and makes a face of disgust. "No, pretty sure you're the stupid one for drinking that pile of sugar," he states as he hands me back my drink.

I stick my tongue out at him. "Then don't drink it dumbass."

"Believe me, I won't," he laughs.

I shake my head at Chase as I down the rest of my drink. I love how easy it is with Chase. He's like the brother I never had, and I love how I can be myself with him. I honestly can't wait for him to go to Northwestern this fall. I know he is going to fit in great with the school and Hayley. I stand up from my towel to throwaway the bottle in the trashcan a few feet away. I toss the bottle in and turn around and almost run straight into Cale who's standing right behind me.

"What do you want?" I ask confused as to why he is even near me. The way he looked at me when we last spoke is burned into my brain, and I was sure he would never speak to me again.

Cale crosses his arms over his bare chest, and I can't help but let my eyes linger on his bronzed skin for a few seconds longer than needed.

"What's going on with you and Chase?" he asks harshly with a locked jaw.

My mouth opens in shock at his words. I'm taken back by his question. "Nothing..." I trail still baffled at him even talking to me.

"Well it doesn't look like nothing," he sneers. His hazel eyes burn into mine with a mix of emotions I can't read. But the way his eyes hold mine make my skin itch and my pulse race uncomfortably.

"Then what does it look like Cale," I ask my tone turning angry at his accusations.

He huffs in aggravation. "It looks like you were cuddling with him in the car, and it looks like you were flirting with him just now." His body is close to mine, and I can feel the warmth from the sun heating me through him. The heat of his body only spurs the irritation that begins to course through me.

I wet my dry lips, and take a deep breath trying to calm the anger that bubbles within me. "First of all it's none of your business if something is going on between Chase and I, and second of all how dare you think you have the right to ask me even if there is?" I scoff.

He shakes his head in disbelief. "I have a right to know if something is going on between my brother and you." His fists clench, and his tongue swipes against his teeth. His anger only spurs my own.

"And what if there was Cale? What would you do about it?" I ask as I place a hand on my hip.

He opens his mouth, but no words come out.

"Exactly," I push. "You would do nothing because you have no right." I state seeing the realization that washes through his face. He knows he is in the wrong with asking about my relationship with Chase. So why would he even ask in the first place?

"Whatever," he mumbles as he turns and treads back towards our towels.

I squeeze my fists trying to not let the anger take over and ruin my day. But how dare Cale think he can ask me a question like that? He has no input in my love life or whom I date! Cale is nobody to me and deserves no insight into my life or anyone I date.

Kylie comes up to me and places a hand on my shoulder, startling me for a few seconds. "Hey are you okay? Cale just came back looking pissed as all hell," she tells me. I refuse to let myself even look over at Cale. I hope he's pissed, and I don't care if his day is ruined.

I shake my head. "He wanted to know what was going on between Chase and I."

Kylie laughs at my words. "You're just friends," she states like it's obvious. She then pauses, "Wait, you are just friends, right?"

I nod frantically. "Yes, of course! But who does he think he is asking that?"

"Well you two do seem really cozy," she comments.

"We're friends!" I say defensively.

She holds up her hands in justification. "I know, I know but I'm just saying that I can see where he is coming from."

"And where's that?" I ask annoyed.

"He's jealous Gray," she states.

I let out a choked laugh. "Yeah, right Ky," I say sarcastically. She doesn't know what happened between us after the club. She doesn't know the way he looked at me after I yelled at Bailey. And she doesn't know that after all this time that we are finally finished.

"No, seriously," she pushes.

I shake my head. "No, Kylie you don't understand. We are done. Really. He's not jealous."

She shrugs indifferently. "If you say so." And then she turns around and skips back over to her towel.

I stand by the trashcan for a few more minutes trying to take in what just all happened. My anger is slowly fading to pure confusion now because of Kylie's words. I know they aren't true, but in my back of my head I can't help but wonder if maybe she's on to something. But I quickly push the idea of Cale's jealously away, because I don't care if he is or not. I don't care about Cale at all.

"Hey, wanna go for a dip?" Bailey excited voice comes from behind me.

I turn to meet her and wipe on a fake smile. "Aren't we supposed to wait a half hour after we eat?" I ask jokingly.

Bailey rolls her eyes at me. "Come on loser," she mumbles.

Her hand slips in mine and pulls me away from the trashcan. "Hey, that's my line." I play still trying to push the last ten minutes from my head. I lock away the anger Cale instilled in me, and shove away the confusion Kylie laced within me. I push everything away, and let my sister pull me back into a day filled with fun.

She laughs as we race off towards the water. I honestly can't remember the last time we went to the beach, let alone played in the water like kids again. We swam, and splashed, and at one point we were in a dunking war, which Bailey successfully won. I had salt water in my eyes and up my nose, but I couldn't have been happier.

I miss this carefree side of me that used to exist. But now it hides behind a wall of fear. I don't want to hide anymore, I want more fun. Fun with my sister, and even fun with Max.

Bailey and I sit in the sand on the shore with water washing up on us every couple minutes. The ground is firm, and I run my fingers over the sand before my doodles get washed away.

"So," Bailey starts. "Be honest with me."

"About what?" I ask seriously. I hate how my mind races with fear of her asking me about Cale. I hate that every time I'm around her a part of me fears that she knows that I kissed her fiancé.

"Your date with Max!" she squeals. A sigh of relief flies through my body. "I want actual details, please," she begs making puppy dog eyes at me.

I chuckle. "Okay, okay," I surrender.

I sit in the sand and let the waves kiss my legs as I tell my sister about my date with Max. I can't lie it was pretty perfect. The location, the flowers, the lights, and of course Max. Everything about that night was amazing, and it was easily the best date of my life.

But as I tell my sister about my date, all I can think about is my first date with Cale. The beach, the ice cream, our first kiss. It was simple, and nothing compared to my amazing date with Max.

But why can't I stop comparing them?

Chapter Fifteen

6/7/15

"CAN WE RUN by this small boutique before lunch?" Bailey asks as we head off in my car.

I nod. "Yeah, what are you getting?" I question knowing it obviously has something to do with the wedding.

"It's my garter!" she says excitingly.

My eyebrows pucker. "I thought you were wearing mom's garter?" I ask slowly. I have always wanted to wear my mother's garter at my wedding one day since I was young. It's lace and has pearls lining the edges. It's been passed down for years on my mother's side for decades, and it's the most beautiful piece of lace I've laid my eyes on.

"I am! I just had some work done on it," she tells me as she scrolls through her phone. I don't ask any more questions assuming she is having some pearls replaced and such.

I let Bailey direct me to the small boutique that specializes in veils and other wedding accessories. "I'll wait in the car for you," I say to Bailey as I park outside of the store.

She nods and hops out of the car, and starts off toward the entrance.

My phone buzzes and I grab it from my center console. I see I have a text from Max and can't help the smile that slides onto my face.

What are you up 2?

I quickly type a response. Hayley once told me I should wait a few minutes in between texts when responding to a guy so I would seem less eager. But I don't care if I come off eager. I like Max and need to start embracing my feelings for him.

Helping Bailey pick up some wedding stuff and then lunch with her. Wyd?

Texting the most beautiful girl I know that's what I'm doing ;)

Wow.... laying it on thick don't ya think?

It's all I know lol

A small giggle falls from my lips. I look up at the entrance of the store to see if Bailey is out yet, but she's not. I look down at my phone to see Max has texted me again.

So wedding stuff? My offer still stands by the way ;)

I roll my eyes at his text, though a huge grin stays on my lips. I'll keep that in mind :)

Are you busy next week? He texts back.

Nope! I respond way too quickly. I almost wince at how fast I texted back.

Well keep it that way I may have another surprise for you :)

My heart flutters, and my nerves of responding too fast vanish. I can't wait! I text back honestly.

The passenger car door opens and Bailey slides in. "Look, look!" Bailey exclaims as she shoves the small box into my hands.

"Okay!" I laugh at her enthusiasm.

I open the box to reveal a bedazzled garter. My heart and face immediately sinks. The once beautiful piece of antique lace decorated with delicate pearls is gone. In its place is a dyed piece of gaudiness.

"What did you do?" I ask as my heart aches. I always wanted to wear this garter on my wedding day. But now, now that dream is dead.

"I just made some small adjustments," she remarks.

She took everything about the history of this piece of lace, and threw it out to match her awful dress.

I frown, but decide to not push it any further knowing it will just upset Bailey. I don't want to fight with my sister over something so small. But at the same time it isn't small to me. I have been looking forward to this piece of my mother being with me on my wedding day. But now it's gone.

I clear my throat. "Yeah, um it's great," I mumble as I pull out of the store parking lot.

"It will match perfectly with my dress," she sighs.

I nod uneasily. "That's great...yeah."

* * * * *

We finally make our way to the lunch café, and find seats after we grab our trays filled with food. I get potato soup, which they make the best I've ever had in my life here.

"So is everything on track with the wedding so far?" I ask in between bites of my soup. A piece of cheese lands on my cheek and I hastily wipe it away. I always go overboard with the extra cheese.

Bailey smiles at my question. I have been trying a lot lately with my sister, and I think it's starting to show. I do love my sister, and I should be asking more questions about her life.

"I think so! A little over two months left and we have almost everything done," she says.

"That's awesome," I say truthfully. I know planning a wedding can be really hard. And while it can be annoying spending my whole summer planning her wedding, I am impressed at how together she has everything.

She stops eating for a second, and I can see she wants to ask me something. A part of me worries that she might ask about Cale, but I push it away.

In the past I would've ignored her look of questioning and changed the subject to avoid her question. But I'm turning a new leaf and being a better sister to Bailey. "Is there something you want to talk about Bai?" I ask taking the leap.

She takes a sip of her drink before speaking. "Well it's about Cale..." she trails.

"And?" I prompt though my lips purse at the mention of his name.

She shrugs. "Well, I know you two don't really like each other," she says timidly.

I open my mouth to tell her the opposite of just that. But I instantly shut it knowing I can't lie to her about this. "It's not that," I start. I sigh playing with my bread. "I don't want you to get hurt, so I just don't trust him yet."

And what I say is mostly true. I don't want her to get hurt, and I don't trust Cale. But that's also for a whole other reason.

Bailey nods at my words. "I know it's fast, but I do love him," she tells me as her eyes light at the thought of him. My chest clenches at her words, but I also smile at her happiness. It's an odd mix of emotions.

"Then what's going on?" I ask.

She puts down her fork and leans forward onto the table. "He's been weird lately," she says.

I raise an eyebrow. "Weird like how?" I press.

"Umm, weird weird," she murmurs as if that explains everything.

"You're gonna have to be more clear Bai," I say.

"Well, like in bed," she whispers.

My face falls and my skin goes cold. "Oh," is all I can breathe out.

There are certain things I never wanted to know about Bailey and Cale and this is it. Hearing about their romps in the sheets makes me want to throw up my freshly eaten soup. I push my bowl away, and run a free hand through my hair.

Sadly Bailey continues. "Lately when we have sex he's like in this weird daze."

I shudder at the images that enter through my mind. "Dazed how?" I ask unenthusiastically.

"It's like he's a mad man in a rush to no where," she says like it's a bad thing. In my experience a mad man in bed can be quite exciting.

"Well, is it good?" I ask with a shrug.

"Of course, it's always good," she laughs.

I force down the bile that rises through me.

"Awesome," I mutter sarcastically.

"But it's like he can't get off," she says. As soon as the words leave her lips the water I am drinking begins to choke me. I cough a few times as some water flies from my mouth.

"Are you okay Gray?" Bailey asks after my coughs finally quiet. She looks around with an awkward smile at all the onlookers that are staring at me like I'm crazy.

I roll my eyes. "I'm fine," I say loudly to get everyone's eyes off of me.

Bailey looks at me oddly, but says nothing at my reaction.

I take another sip of water to clear my throat. I try to get back on track to our earlier conversation suddenly interested in what she was saying. "What do you mean he can't get off?"

"He does sometimes," she states like it's obvious. "But other times he just rushes off into the bathroom and I hear the shower running, and I don't know it's just odd," she says. "I try to get him to talk to me, but he's been really closed off lately also," she pauses as water fills her eyes.

"Bailey," I say as I place a hand on hers. A part of my mind is still on Cale and the odd distance he is creating between him and Bailey. But I can't focus on that at the moment, because Bailey needs me.

"What if he regrets proposing to me, what if he doesn't want to marry me—"

I cut her off. "Don't even go there Bai! He loves you!" I tell her honestly. It hurts to say but I know Cale does love her, I can see it. I didn't want to at first, but I can't deny it any longer.

"How do you know?" she asks doubtfully.

I wet my lips. "Because I know Bai. It's the way he looks at you," I say.

"How does he look at me?" she asks.

"Like you're the first shooting star he's ever seen," I mumble. I instantly wish I could take my words back because I can see the sudden confusion that coats Bailey's face from my words.

"How do you...where have you heard that?" she asks with the skin between her eyebrows puckering.

I wave my hand feigning dismissiveness. "Oh you know around..." I chuckle awkwardly.

She narrows her eyes at me. "That's what Cale's father says to his mother. It's like their thing...I've never heard anyone else say it before..." she trails.

I swallow the lump in my throat. "I must have heard one of them say it then, like Chase or someone," I lie clumsily.

Bailey nods at my words though I can see she doesn't believe everything I'm saying, but she doesn't question anything either. She shakes her head and clears her throat changing the focus on the conversation.

"So how are you and Chase?" she asks suggestively.

I roll my eyes. "We are just friends," I sing annoyed.

She laughs. "Whatever you say," she shrugs.

"I do say," I push.

"Well Cale thinks—"

I lift a hand cutting her off. "Nope, nope, and nope. Cale needs to stop thinking cause there is nothing going on. Promise." Annoyance flashes through me at the way Cale keeps assuming things are going on with Chase and me. At the same time I'm pissed he thinks he has a right to even ask questions at all. Anything that even remotely lingered between us is over and he needs to realize that, and soon.

"Okay," she drawls.

"Plus I've been texting Max and we are going on another date next week," I tell her.

"Oh! He asked you out again?" Bailey asks happily.

I nod failing at keeping the smile off of my face. Max makes me happy. I don't know if it's his infectious smile, or his silly humor that always raises a giggle from me.

"Is this turning serious?" Bailey asks with a smirk.

At her question a nervous knot forms in my stomach. "I don't know and I don't even want to go there right now," I say. People keep trying to push their agendas onto me and I'm not having it. Why can't I just be having fun? Why does being twenty and dating someone all of the sudden mean wedding bells?

"Well, you could start thinking about the future Gray," Bailey says.

"Why?" I ask as I spin my spoon in my now cold soup.

"No ones getting younger," she comments. She laughs it off like she's making a joke, but I know she's not. Married with two kids by twenty-four is Bailey's goal, and to her I'm slacking because I haven't found a man yet.

A harsh puff of air flies from my nose. "Yup," I mumble as I sit back in my chair.

Bailey continues on with telling me how I need to be looking for a good guy. While at the same time informing me more about the wedding than I care to hear at this point. My mind is on Cale, and why he is acting weird with Bailey. He has been more agitated lately, I have even noticed that. But the question is, why?

My phone buzzes on the table. I see Max has texted me again.

You look beautiful today

I glance around the restaurant strangely, but don't see Max anywhere. A puzzled expression slips onto my face at his words.

How do you know? I text back.

Bailey goes on while I wait for Max's text back.

I don't have to see you to know you look beautiful Grayson

My heart beats a little faster at his words, and a part of me melts a little inside. Maybe picturing a future with Max wouldn't be so bad, but as soon as I think that a wave of nerves crash over the thought.

Nope, too soon.

Chapter Sixteen

6/9/15

"TELL ME SOMETHING," I tell Cale as I slide in closer to his body.

We lay in the back of his truck once again under the dark night sky. I love the way his skin heats mine, and the sound of his heartbeat under my ear.

"Tell you what?" Cale asks humorously.

I bite my lip as I place my leg over his. His hand comes up to my bare hipbone, and his fingers play against my skin making me curl in even closer.

"Please," I beg playfully.

His fingers continue to play against my soft skin. "Okay, I think you're beautiful Gray."

A smile lifts my lips. "Thank you," I flush. "Keep going."

Cale's hand slides further up from my hips until his hand rests below my breast. I feel my heart stop, and my skin rush hot with a sudden need. "I love the way your skin feels against mine," he murmurs into my hair.

"Oh really?" I ask quietly.

"Really. I also love the way you taste," he says next making my throat run dry.

"Taste?" I barely utter out.

"Yes, taste," he repeats. "I could drown in you and enjoy it."

My hand that lies on his chest clutches into the fabric of his shirt at his words. My body clings to him suddenly as a deep need crawls it's way through my body. His thumb continues to caress the under side of my breast making me shudder against him.

"But you know what I love the most?" he asks.

I shake my head unable to form a coherent sentence.

"I love the way you react to my words," he says as he slowly traces over my breast and up my neck till his fingers comb through my hair.

"And how do I react?" I ask breathlessly. I want his hands back on my neck, and on my chest, and everywhere.

"Like you'd let me do anything I'd want to you," he laughs darkly.

I trace my tongue against my lips. "Who says I would stop you?"

I can hear the quiet growl emit from his throat, and his hands now clutch onto my hips. He rolls my body completely on top of his so that our bodies are lined perfectly. I place my arms over his chest and rest my chin on my arms.

Cale's hazel eyes hold mine, and I can't help but fall further into the fire that blazes within them. I love the way he looks at me. I love it so much I could let him stare at me for the rest of my life. It would be quiet, but it would be perfect.

"Tell me more Cale," I say.

He smirks. "Well I love the way you moan when I kiss right—"

I cut him off. "Not what I mean," I blush.

He grins cheekily. "Then what do you mean Gray?"

I sigh. "I don't know, I just want to know more about you I guess," I say with the tilt of a head.

He raises his eyebrows. "More about me?" he questions.

I nod once. "Yes," I state.

"Like what?" he asks unsure.

"Anything," I say softly.

Cale's hands trace over my ass and up until he lands on my waist. I love the way he can't keep his hands of me, it makes me feel wanted and it's a feeling I've never felt before. Cale brings out feelings in me I never knew existed, and it makes me feel excited for what more he could bring out.

"Okay," he agrees as he closes his eyes. I lie atop of Cale and let him think of what he wants to tell me.

I expect something stupid or another way to get me under him since he was almost successful the first time. What I don't expect is what he tells me next.

"When my dad was young he saw a shooting star with his mom. And his mother saw the reaction it drew out of him, and told my dad to wait for the girl that reminds him of that star in that exact moment."

"Why?" I ask.

"Have you ever seen a shooting star Gray?" Cale asks me.

I shake my head in response. Once when I was little Bailey had seen one but I missed it.

He sighs. "It's hard to explain then."

I trace my fingers in a circle on this chest. "Try," I whisper.

He nods. "Okay." I watch his hazel eyes dance as he watches the stars above. "The first time you see a shooting star you almost don't believe you saw it. It goes by so fast and shines so bright that it almost doesn't seem like it exists."

His words wrap around me as I close my eyes and sigh. My body melts in to Cale as my body forms against his. "Tell me more," I breathe.

"Your skin prickles and your pulse races at the bright light that scars the skies for only a few seconds," Cale continues.

"Wow," I exhale. "It sounds magical," I say.

Cale makes a small sound of agreement. "But it only feels that way the first time," he adds.

My lips purse. "Why?"

"Because when you see one after it's not as special. You've seen one before, so who cares. It may be exciting for a second, but you'll never feel the same way you did when you saw it for the first time."

"So that's why your grandma told your dad to find someone who reminds him of that moment," I murmur to myself piecing together his story. It's beautiful and simple and everything I hope to feel one day. Though in the back of my head I know I've felt the exact thing his grandmother spoke about.

I may have not seen a shooting star, but Cale makes me feel exactly the way he described.

"Do you think you will ever feel that way?" I ask Cale. I honestly want to know if he thinks he can feel this way about someone. I know this most likely won't last longer than a summer, but it won't stop me from feeling the way I do about Cale.

I've fallen for him, and I can't turn back now.

His hands lift from my hips to stroke through my blonde hair. I love the way he plays with my hair. The soft caress makes me feel drowsy as I let my body sink into Cale's even further.

"Yeah, I think I could," he whispers after a while.

I don't say anything in response, but that is the moment I know I love Cale Hasting. It is the first time I admit to myself my feelings for Cale, and I don't know if I want to cry or laugh.

I love someone, and even worse that someone is a Hasting.

But instead of letting myself freak-out any further I close my eyes, and let the soft breath sounds of Cale lull me into a deep sleep.

The sound of my phone buzzing wakes me up from my dream filled nap. I sit up breathing heavily hating the way my skin pebbled at the dream I had. Except it wasn't a dream, it was a full on memory. A memory I never wanted to relive because I didn't think my heart could handle it. And I was right. My heart is barely containing itself with the memory of his words against my skin.

My phone buzzes again and I lean over and pull the phone off of the charger. "Hello," I answer groggily.

"Hey G, what's going on?" Hayley's peppy voice sounds from the other line.

"Nothing just waking up from a nap," I mutter as I try and clear the image of Cale underneath my body.

But the images stick around because life hates me. Every time I try and move forward, I get pulled ten steps backward. I cuddle into my bed, and try and let Hayley distract me from the fresh images of Cale that twist through my head.

Chapter Seventeen

6/12/15

"HOLY SHIT!" I shout excitingly in response to what sits in front of Max and myself.

I don't know how Max does it, but somehow every date just gets better and better.

Max laughs at my reaction. "So you're excited?" he asks as uneasiness tinges his words.

I turn to him with a giddy smile lifting my lips. "Yes, yes, a million times yes!" I exclaim as I nod over and over again.

He sighs as the worry that once filled his body is now washed away with relief. "Okay good, I was worried you would think it was dumb..." he trails as he shoves his hands into his pockets. His cheeks flush slightly and I can't help but find him even cuter.

I shake my head. "This is awesome Max," I pause as I meet his green eyes. "Thank you," I tell him honestly.

I told Max on our first date that I haven't been to a carnival in years, and how much I missed them. When I was young my parents would always take Bailey and I to the county carnivals every summer. They held so many good memories for me, but I didn't know telling Max this little piece of information would lead to this.

Max drove for over an hour without letting up on the surprise, even though I begged him to tell me. He took us to another town that is having their annual carnival. The bright colorful lights, the smell of fried food and sticky candy, and the sounds of excited screams fill the air around me making me dizzy with happiness.

I place a small kiss on Max's pink stained cheek, and grab onto his hands pulling him towards the ticket booth eagerly. He trails behind me as I lead him through the small patch of security and into the park.

Max laughs at my eagerness as I pull him into the center of the park where the carnival is being held. "What do you want to do Grayson?" he asks me as we continue to stroll through the crowded carnival space.

My eyes take in the bright flashing lights of the rides, and all the kids running around hyped up on sugar and adrenaline. Max's hand squeezes mine, and the warmth of him reminds me of his presence. I turn to face his jungle eyes and can't help but smile. Max is every girls dream man, and I don't know why he chose me to be with. Cynical and cold me somehow found someone who warms my heart and it makes me tingle with excitement once again.

I turn away from his gaze and look up to see the main attraction of any carnival. The ferris wheel.

I lift a single finger to point at the colorfully bright wheel before us. "I want to ride that first," I say holding back a smile.

He nods once. "Perfect," he smirks slightly and tugs on my hand to pull me towards the ride. We walk over and wait in line with the next group of riders. Couples are scattered around us, and I can't help but smile a bit. I know this is the most cliché thing for a couple to ride, but an overwhelming part of me wants to do this with Max. I want to be cliché for the first time in a long time, and it makes me anxious and excited all in the same moment.

A young teen couple stands next to us and I watch them. The girl can't stop smiling and the boy can't take his eyes off of her. They are young and wildly in love and while a part of me wants to warn them, another part of me wishes I could be them. I wish I wasn't ruined beyond repair and could give my heart away without a second thought. But I can't.

My eyes flicker over to Max who is staring at the busy lights around us, and my heart beats faster. Maybe he can be the one. Maybe he's the one I can finally give myself to.

Immediately my skin goes cold and I drop my eyes at the thought. It's too soon for those thoughts. I barely know him. But what I know is amazing, my mind whispers at me. Suddenly Max is pulling me into the gated area of the ride and my thoughts move away from my greatest fear: Giving my heart to someone who will just crush it again.

The wheel rotates until it's our turn to slip into the cool metal seat. The couple that gets out as we slide in looks at a tad rumpled, and with one glance at Max we both erupt into a fit of hushed giggles. We both notice the guy's miss buttoned shirt and the girl's messy hair.

"Is that why you wanted to ride this?" Max asks as he grips the bar and pulls it down on us. The worker grabs the bar quickly to check it, and we slowly move up so the rest of the ride can fill up.

I chuckle. "Is what why?" I ask innocently while twirling the ends of my long hair around my finger.

Max wraps an arm around my shoulders and pulls me closer. "To seduce me," he whispers against my ear.

A small shiver spins down my spine at his hushed words. Is that why I brought him up here? Did I have an ulterior motive for wanting to ride this ride with Max? I shake my head and turn towards him our faces just mere inches apart. "Do you want me to seduce you?" I ask with the arch of an eyebrow.

His eyes darken slightly. "Maybe just a little," he admits with a small smirk tugging at his pink lips.

My tongue dips out to wet mine in a silent response. I face forward away from Max and straighten my body while still maintaining his arm around me.

We are close to the top before the whole ride is finally full and I let myself sink more in Max's enjoying the comfort he brings my body. The wheel begins to turn slowly as I take in the dark clear night that lies above us. My eyes are trained on the sky looking for something without even knowing what, and then Max's hand lands on my thigh. Innocent or not I'm abruptly tossed into a memory I didn't even know existed because I had tucked it so far away.

"Ohmygod Cale stop!" I giggle quietly as his hand tries once again to trail up the inside of my thigh under the flutter of my sundress.

His warm breath hits my neck. "Just one little touch Gray, please," he begs. "You're just so fucking perfect," he murmurs as my breath shallows and my skin turns hot. My mother taught me a young age to not curse, and to despise when others did it themselves. But when Cale rumbles dirty sayings in my ear I always melt secretly loving the naughty words.

He places a single kiss to my collarbone and I can't help but fall further into his touch. With every kiss I crave more. I love Cale Hasting. I love him so much it hurts. It's just something I haven't told him yet. I'm scared to tell him because what if he doesn't feel the same way. What if he thinks of me just as a fling and I ruin everything? He makes me feel like I can fly and I never want to fall.

Suddenly the ferris wheel jerks and we are moving once again. We are about to reach the top, finally. We are so close to the top that I straighten up and push Cale's wandering hands out from under my dress. I can't be distracted by his devilish touch right now. He grunts in protest but he takes his hands off of me.

"Gray," he groans.

I lean into him and place a chaste kiss onto his soft lips. "Just let me look at the sky," I beg playfully.

Cale leans into steal another kiss from me, and I can't help but linger longer than I wanted. I have to break apart before we get too carried away, which elicits another groan of protest.

"Cale, please," I say quietly.

He tucks a strand of hair behind my ear and lets his fingers linger on the flushed skin of my cheek. "You'll see one when you do Gray," he whispers.

I bite at the inside of my lip as anxiety fills me. I turn to face Cale, his handsome face causing my pulse to race as usual. "What if I don't?"

"You will," he says. "Promise," he shrugs like it's nothing. But he's wrong this means everything to me.

I shake my head. "Don't," I say with my eyes cast to my lap. "You can't promise such a thing Cale."

"Gray, it's not that big of a deal really," he sighs. "It was just a story my grandma use to tell me. If you don't see a shooting star it won't be the end of the world."

I pull away slightly from his touch. His words hurt me a little. I want to see a shooting star. I need to see one, and I have my reasons. I tell myself that I just want to see a shooting star because I'm worried I might fall for someone and then see a shooting star and realize I don't really love that person. I tell myself I want to experience a shooting star for future reference.

But the truth is that I need validation in what I feel for Cale. I'm too scared to say I love him, but if I know what I feel during a shooting star is what I feel for him when he kisses me then I can know for sure. I've never experienced love before, and it's something extremely scary to feel for someone like Cale. He is older, and a Hasting, and has the power to break me if he wants. He owns me so much more than he will ever know, and that realization is the scariest.

Cale wraps his hand around my waist and pulls me into him. And before I can say anything his lips press into mine. They are strong, and assured, and just a little rough, which has me weak immediately.

My hands slide into his hair and grip just a little too hard as I pull him into me. I may be scared to tell him how I feel, but I can show him for damn sure.

His hands slide under my dress and grip at my bare thighs as I throw a leg carelessly over his allowing him more access to under my dress. His hands on my naked skin have always thrown me into a frenzy, and tonight is no different. I bite at his bottom lip playfully when his fingers graze the scrap of lace that lies upon my hips. My fingernails scrape down his neck in response to his fingers tugging at my white undies. I can feel the small raised pink lines I've left in my nails wake on his neck, and for some reason it just turns me on even more.

I lift my hips in response to Cale's hesitant touch as my tongue battles for power with his. We've messed around before and it's gotten heated, but it's never been like this. It's as if every touch of his fingers is hitting a live wire, and my body doesn't know how to respond to such intense need and pleasure.

"Ow ow!"

"Oh yeah, tap that!"

"Ew, no get a room!"

We break apart at the sudden shouts and whistling we hear coming from some guys and a girl above us, and I quickly pull away from Cale in embarrassment. I've never let Cale get so close to touching me in a public place, and that fact that I almost let him makes my body flush. I need to have more control when it comes to Cale, but I know no matter how much I try that with one look I would let him do anything to me anywhere.

My face is hot and I know most likely red as I pull the rest of my body off of Cale. I straighten out of my dress, and press my thighs together lightly to ease the need coursing steadily through my body.

Cale scoots over towards me. "Gray?" he whispers.

I tuck my hair behind my ears in attempt to look unaffected from him and from the embarrassment of those boys. "Yeah?" I ask swallowing down the lump in my throat.

"Did you feel that?" he questions.

My eyebrows knit together in confusion. "Feel what?" I ask.

His hand tangles with mine and I hold on tightly realizing I needed his touch more than I thought. "Feel everything," he smiles. His hazel eyes light up at his words and I can't help but fall into his gaze. "You don't need a shooting star to know what to feel."

I wet my lips and close my eyes, nervous of what I'm about to tell him. "I'm scared of what I feel Cale," I admit. And in that moment I give Cale my heart. I've loved him for a while now, but I still held onto a part of my heart in fear. But not now, now he has everything. Everything to love me, but also everything to ruin me.

Cale lips turn up into a small smile at my words. "Me too Gray, me too," he whispers as his arms wrap around me pulling me closer into his body. Melding out bodies together until his warmth and comfort seeps in mine.

I might've not admitted to loving him. But at the same time I think Cale might've just told me he did. My heart beats steadily as I lean into this perfect mans arms. This perfect man that I love, and maybe just maybe he might love me back.

"Grayson?"

"Grayson are you okay?" I hear finally as Max's hand shakes my shoulder lightly.

I blink my eyes to clear my thoughts of Cale and try and focus on the amazing man in front of me. "Yeah, yeah?" I rasp out trying to shove away the memory of Cale.

"Are you okay?" Max asks as his face scrunches together in worry and laced with confusion.

I shake my head no but mumble, "Yes."

"You sure cause—"

I cut him off. "I'm fine. Just got light headed for a second," I lie. "Would if be okay if we sat down for second after this ride?" I ask unable to look at Max as these old feelings for Cale continue their assault on me.

I hate Cale Hasting so much. Every time I begin to move on and feel something for anyone memories of him come flying back at me. And it's hard to not let them get to me, because who doesn't want to love like they did when they were young? Who doesn't want wild abandon, and sneaking around, and the thrill of being caught? It's addicting that feeling, that thrill, but it's also dangerous. And I need to let it go, I need to let Cale go completely or I will never be able to move on from this hold he still has on me. I thought we were over, but I need to fully let him go for this to be over. For us to be finally out to rest.

I finally glance at Max and all I can see is concern slide over his face. His hand finds mine and covers it with his in a small pass of reassurance. I know he can tell something is wrong, but he says nothing else and nods at my suggestion of sitting down after this ride.

Max again planned the perfect date, and is the perfect guy, and here I am thinking of the worst guy for me. With a sigh I clutch onto Max's hand harder and try and shove my thoughts of Cale away.

I won't let Cale ruin this date. I won't.

But if I were being truthful to myself I would know I already did. I let him ruin everything because I won't let myself forget him. I don't try and think about the man who broke me beyond repair, and in the process the relationships I have with everyone I love including my sister have suffered. I just don't think I realized how deep he was in my veins, how much he still ran through me. The memories burn through me of him and that summer hotter than I ever wanted.

But I'm done sitting in the flames and letting them consume me.

I let my eyes wash over Max and realize he's more than just an attractive guy who makes my heart beat faster. He's the bucket of water I need to douse the flames of Cale that still surround me.

He's just what I needed.

Chapter Eighteen

6/12/15

"THANKS SO MUCH for tonight," I tell Max as he walks me up to the front steps of my house.

The sky surrounding us is so dark tonight, not even one star out twinkling in the distance. The black abyss of the sky paired with the cool ocean air that wraps us is different. Tonight feels different, and I don't know why.

Max's thumb runs over my knuckles making me hold on tighter to his warm hand. "I'm glad you had fun Grayson," he smiles.

After the Ferris wheel incident we sat for a while, and I was finally able to get my head in the right place. Meaning I pulled my thoughts away from Cale and focused on Max where they should've been to begin with. The rest of the night went by perfectly with wild rollercoasters, and obnoxiously large stuffed animals, and tons of fried food. It was perfect, because Max is perfect. I'm the one failing at this so-called relationship.

I clutch the huge stuffed penguin to my side at the memories of tonight. In two dates Max has knocked me off of my feet and it's hard to see him ever topping them, but with Max I'll never know what's up his creative sleeve.

I stop by the front door and turn to face Max, and before I can say anything more he presses his lips against mine. I inhale a sharp breath in shock before melting into the man before me. His lips are soft yet assured, and giving me everything I need because Max is everything I need. I drop the obese penguin that he won for me, and clutch onto his shoulders deepening the kiss before he pulls away. But not before he peppers my jaw and neck with more kisses. I can't help but giggle when his hands poke at my waist and he nips at my collarbone.

Max pulls away from me but keeps his face just inches away from mine. His green eyes dance as they take in my lips and the rest of my face. The silly smile on his face makes me bite my lip in attempts to stop my grin, but it's no help. Max makes me smile, and I like it. I like him, maybe even too much.

I pull away with a sigh, and grab onto my new cuddle buddy as I turn towards the door. "I'll text you," I say as I unlock the front door.

Max smirks at my words. "Not if I text you first," he winks and then hops down the front steps and towards his car.

I pause and watch Max walk away from me. I can't help but stare at the man who is melting my heart slowly from its cage of ice. I nibble at my bottom lip as he casts me one last smirk before I finally tear my gaze away as he speeds down the street. A giddy chuckle escapes my lips, and I head inside while dragging the penguin behind me. I don't even realize the lights are on and someone's in the room with me until I close the door behind myself and turn around to see a narrow eyed Cale.

Suddenly the flames engulf me once again and my insides are crying out to go running after Max. The only person who can save me from the all-consuming fire that is Cale. But I don't show any weakness, and stand tall at the man before me.

"What do you want Cale?" I ask uninterested. Though I clutch onto my penguin as if it's my lifeline in this moment.

He runs his thumb over his bottom lip as he stares at me for a moment longer. His eyes rake over my body as if he's looking for something specific but can't find it.

"Who were you out with?" he asks out of nowhere.

I roll my eyes. "Why do you care?" I counter.

He snorts. "I don't. Just interested since you seem to spreading yourself pretty thin lately," he comments before walking towards the kitchen.

The blood that rushes through my veins flashes cold with shock, and then blazes hot with anger. My jaw falls agape, and my skin crawls with annoyance at his words. "I'm sorry, what did you just say?" I ask harshly as I drop my penguin and stalk after the man in front of me.

Cale turns away from the fridge with a beer gracing his hand. He downs half the bottle in a gulp before his hard eyes meet mine. "You heard me Gray."

My lip curls in pure anger towards this man, and I'm pretty sure steam flies from my ears in a cartoon like manner. Suddenly the flames that surround me are for a different reason. "Please explain to me how I'm spreading myself thin Cale, please," I say sarcastically using my fingers to air quote his outrageous statement.

He sets down his glass bottle on the counter with a loud clank. "Chase... this other dude—"

"Max," I growl cutting him off.

"Yeah whatever, just saying what I see here Gray," he says flippantly.

"Don't call me that!" I shout annoyed at his words.

"Whatever," he mumbles as he finishes off the beer in a large swig.

I stomp over closer to Cale as rage courses through my body steadily. He's under my skin in a way I've never experienced, and I need him out. Now.

"There is nothing going on between Chase and I," I tell him. "How many times do I need to fucking say that?" I curse angrily.

A menacing laugh falls from his lips and snakes around me making my fist clench until my knuckles go white. "Say what you want but I'm not the only one who sees it."

"Who's said something?" I ask confused. Chase is a friend and nothing more. Chase knows that, I know that, yet somehow everyone else can't seem to see that through their thick skulls.

"Bailey and I have talked about it," he shrugs like his words don't hurt me.

I let out a small dark chuckle at his words. "Well Bailey talks to a lot of people about a lot of things Cale," I say with pursed lips and narrowed eyes. I didn't mean to mention my conversation with Bailey ever, and let alone with Cale. But he's invading me in a way he's never done before, and I want to get him back. I want to hurt him, taunt him like he's doing to me. It's wrong, and bad, and I should stop and walk away. But I don't.

Cale doesn't know that during lunch Bailey informed me all about their sex life. It was a moment I never wanted to relive, but just became extremely useful in this warped fight Cale and I are having.

It's Cale's turn to take the defense. His eyebrows scrunch together in confusion at my words, and I can't help the smile that over takes my face. This relationship between us has just turned toxic, and in to an ugly need to hurt each other. It's far from okay, and yet in this moment I'm living off of it.

"What did she tell you?" he questions calmly, but we both know he's anything but.

I lift a single shoulder in indifference. "Something about something," I say with the lift of an eyebrow. "I can't remember honestly."

Suddenly Cale is in front of me, in my face, body too close, and backing me towards a wall. "What did she say Gray?" he rumbles.

"Don't call me that," I counter back. I hate that name. All it does is remind me of a summer I want to forget. I like that Max doesn't know about that summer, and that he doesn't call me Gray. To him I'm Grayson, I'm some new and nice and not afraid of the future.

"What did she say?" he growls again.

"Doesn't feel so great knowing someone's taking about you does it?" I push.

"Gray," he pushes back.

"Son!" I finish for him. "It's Grayson," I emphasize. "Ugh," I groan running both of my hands through my long locks.

"Tell me," Cale urges harder and suddenly I'm back against the kitchen wall, and the smell of beer on Cale's breath wafts over my face.

I place my hands against Cale's chest and shove him away from me as I pull away from the wall and walk away from him. He was too close and I have to get away. My head begins to go fuzzy when he's that close, and I am not making the mistake of letting him get in my head again. I'm over this shit he's putting me through, but suddenly his hand is on my elbow and I'm back against the wall his hand on my elbow so tight it almost hurts. His hazel eyes lock on me dark and probing me for answers. His other hand on the wall beside me locking me into his large body, and again he is too close.

"Why can't you get off with Bailey?" I whisper letting my mind turn fuzzy at the edges. He's making his way in, and if I don't get away soon I'm going to go down the bad road. I'm supposed to be moving on, letting go, and yet here I am falling even more into this toxic battle we have going on.

Cale's eyes go wide at my words and narrow once again until he's glaring at me so hard I feel like I might actually burn from the way his eyes hold onto me. But in this moment I want to burn, because the last time I felt like this was four years ago. And I know I shouldn't, but I love this feeling and never thought I would feel it again.

"I don't—"

My grin turns devilish as I cut him off. "What has you so tangled up that you can't finish? What has you so wound up inside that—"

"Shut up!" Cale yells as his hand bangs against the wall near my head. My heart beats faster at the rage I see growing within this man I used to love. His face is painted red with a vein poking out of his neck violently.

Then I go to a place I never should've gone. I go to a place so far gone I'm even scared of what I've become in this moment. I'm not thinking of Bailey my sister who deserves nothing but the best, of Max the man I truly need to save me from my cold twisted self, I'm only thinking of the past. And the past is a place that once I latch onto sucks me in so fast I begin to drown in its depth. I begin to drown in Cale, and I love it.

"Is it because you're thinking of me?" I say wetting my lips at my words.

Cale's mouth open but no words fall from his perfectly pink lips.

My mouth purses in an attempt to hide my growing smirk. "That's what I thought Cale," I say with a slight tilt of my head and a small bite of my lip. And with that I push off the wall and his hold, and storm off towards my room. I'm playing with flames right now and I know it's going to backfire so badly, but I'm drowning and I don't care. I've gone to the bad place.

I'm just through the threshold of my door when I hear it slam behind me. My body whips around to face a pissed off Cale. His eyes are dark and pointing in on me while his fists clench in at his sides.

"What do you want me to say to that Gray?" His voice breaks slightly.

I'm taken back by his words. "What?" I ask.

He steps closer to me. "What do you want me to say?"

"I don't kno—"

Cale cuts me off. "Do you want me to say that ever since I've seen you I can't stop thinking about you?" His words shock me to no end, and rock my mind like no other. My whole body is twisted and turned around, and I'm lost at how to respond to this man in front of me.

My body burns to reach out and touch him, but I keep my hands to myself. But the tension radiating off of Cale is intense and slowly sucking me in making me want more and more. More of everything I shouldn't have, but have always wanted.

I don't respond to his words. More like I'm incapable of responding.

"Do you want me to say that you invade my every thought? That no matter how much I try I can't get you out of my thoughts. That I'm jealous of any man who even looks at you because every kiss, touch, and moan from you used to me mine and only mine. And—" his words stop suddenly, but his body is right up against mine.

"And what?" I barely breathe aloud.

Cale reaches up with one hand to run his hand though my blonde hair. Something he used to do repeatedly, something I miss more than anything. His hand pulls through my tangled locks until he comes to the end pulling slightly forcing a gasp to fall from my lips.

"You always loved when I was just a little rough with you," his words breathe out surrounding me, hot and heady. His eyes rake over my face as if he is taking me in for the first time, and to be honest I think he is. I don't think he's allowed himself to really look at me, but now he is. And I don't know how to react. "Do you still like that?"

I nod once as loud breaths flutter though my parted lips, and incoherent thoughts run through my fuzz filled head.

Cale leans in until our faces are just mere inches apart. We are so close I can almost taste the beer that still lingers on his tongue. My body burns for more of him when I know I shouldn't. Max flashes in my mind for a second, but is outweighed by the real life Cale in front of me. He's touching me, and so close I can kiss him. It's everything I always wanted again, but everything I shouldn't have.

I love my sister and I shouldn't do this. I really like Max and shouldn't be doing this.

And yet I can't help but still ask, "And what Cale?"

His hand clenches in my hair just as his other hand wraps around my waist and pulls me in closer, and suddenly I'm helpless. I know I should stop him. I know I should say no and push him away, but I just let him control me and lean in even more to his addicting touch. I'm dizzy and he hasn't even kissed me yet.

"And I still want you more than anything. You're still mine Gray." And before I can respond to his words that have me all knotted up inside he kisses me, and I'm once again drowning in Cale Hasting.

But this time I don't want to be saved, and I don't want to stop.

Chapter Nineteen

6/12/15

CALE'S LIPS MEET mine in a mess of toxic need.

We both know we shouldn't be doing this, but nothing can stop us at this point. A meteor could come crashing into my room and I still don't think I could force myself away from Cale. This man in every way is the most delicious poison I've ever had. I know drinking from him will end me, but my god is he tasty though.

His hands bring me in closer and I'm sure at this point that I'm a complete goner. I'm up steam without a paddle, I'm losing myself and fading completely into the man before me, and I don't care. I care about nothing but how I can have more of him, and more of him only.

Before the thought of more was enough to stop me from making this mistake even bigger. But now, now more taunts me. Teases me until all I can think is more, more, more. I need more. I crave more. I will die without more. How can I get more? How deep can I crawl under Cale's skin until I forget where I begin and he ends because all I can think of is more?

More of this perfect man who's imperfectly fit for me.

I lose all concept of where I am or what time it is or even who I am, because all I can focus on is Cale.

Before I know it my body is being pushed towards my desk, and suddenly lifted to sit atop of it. Cale's lips are rough against mine in a way that only he knows I like. I like a little touch of darkness with my kissing, and he knows it. No, he thrives on it. The taste of beer on him makes my head spin in a way I'm afraid I may pass out. He's taking my breath away, literally.

His hands are under my shirt teasing at the soft skin of my waist making me shiver. His fingers pulling at the hem of my tank until it's not enough. He needs more. His strong hands yank it over my head as if he's dying to get one look at what's underneath that flimsy fabric.

Cale's lips land on the skin of where my shoulder meets my neck, and I can't help but sigh. The slight scruff of his unshaven face grazes my skin driving me so crazy that my legs wrap around his body pulling him in closer. I need him closer. I need more. I need everything. I need him.

His teeth graze my skin until he bites down just hard enough to elicit a loud moan from my parted lips. My hands run through his hair and pull at that sensation. I've never been so turned on in my entire life, and if I don't get him right now I may die from the need.

The wet pad of his tongue traces up my neck until my hands land on his face and pull him up to meet my lips once more. But before he kisses me senseless again I trace my thumb over his lips as my eyes hold his. I watch as his eyes flicker down to my lips, and as he gently nips at my thumb causing me to bite my own lip in the process. His eyes are on mine and all over my face at the same time. His hazel eyes are everything as they go as dark as the sky is tonight. I knew something was different about tonight, and I was right. Though I never would've guessed this.

I run my thumb down his bottom lip one last time letting his wet heated breath coat my hand. I lower my hand to kiss him again when Cale utters three words I never expected to hear come from his mouth, ever.

"I love you."

And that's when the glass breaks, the elusion shatters, everything comes to a screeching halt, and the fuzz that once filled my head begins to fade.

My whole body jerks at Cale's words and my hands drop from his face. Tears well up in my eyes before I know it and my chest tightens. "Get out," I whisper.

Cale's eyes look at me with confusion as his hands come up to cup my face. "But Gray—"

I pull away violently from his warm hands, and slide off of the desk and away from the evil man in front of me. "You just had to ruin it didn't you?" I shout.

"Gray, come on don't be this way," Cale begs as he continues to keep getting closer to me. But I hold my hands up in refusal to let him invade my space again.

I shake my head. "Don't be what way Cale?" I ask throwing my hands into the air. "You're engaged to my sister and you tell me you love me!" I exclaim.

"But I do lo—"

"No!" I cut him off stopping him from saying those awful words again. "Fuck you," I say simply.

"Gray—" he starts one last time, but I don't let him finish. I can't.

I point to my bedroom door. "Get out," I tell him as tears threaten to spill over.

Cale takes a step towards me as his mouth opens one last time to speak, but I refuse to let him say anything more tonight.

"Get out now Cale!" I shout angrily as my skin heats with sadness and embarrassment as I realize I'm still just in my skimpy bra. I feel too naked, too bared to this man who isn't mine.

He casts one last look at me that I refuse to decipher so instead I throw my gaze to my feet. I hear his footsteps disappear before I hear the slamming of my bedroom door, and then I break.

My whole body slumps to the floor as the tears I've been keeping at bay finally fall from their holdings. I feel sixteen again, so small and young and inexperienced. I feel lost and without any direction. I feel alone. I feel so alone. I curl up into a ball on the ground and let my sobs wreck though my body quietly. I'm a mess, and I don't know how to fix it this time. I don't know how to fix anything.

The kiss was supposed to be nothing. No, less than nothing. But then Cale had to go and tell me he loved me! Words I dreamed of him telling me for years. Words that meant so much to me all those years ago. Words he never once said to me when I was sixteen and head over heals for him. But now that he's with my sister and beyond the definition of unattainable he says them to me, and I'm spinning uncontrollably down this drain of confusion. And I couldn't take it. I had to get him away from me.

How dare he says he loves me! He wouldn't know what love was if it hit him upside the head with a baseball bat. He is so jaded that I don't even know if he knows how to love. Because love isn't breaking my heart all those years ago, and now saying he loves me when he is with my sister.

God, my sister! I said I wouldn't hurt Bailey anymore and there I go and make out with her fiancé once again. I'm the worst sister in the world, and she doesn't know the half of it. She looks at me with her bright eyes like I'm this amazing woman, and I'm so far from. I'm so lost.

My hands pull through my hair, but now all I can picture are Cale's rough hands running through my locks and I want to scream. I want to run away and never come back here.

I grab the blanket out of the basket that I keep near my desk and drape it over of my body as I lay down against the cool wood floors that surround me. I continue to let tears drip down my face as I wrap my arms around my legs in a way to soothe myself.

I cry and cry and cry until I can't cry anymore, but I still find a way to.

Cale told me he loved me. Words I dreamed of, and prayed for.

He's just four years too late.

* * * * *

6/13/15

"Hey it's Hayley, sorry I'm not here but leave your name and number and I will call you back as soon as I can."

A frustrated sigh leaves my lips as I leave my tenth voicemail for Hayley. "Please call me back," I pause. "As you can tell it's probably urgent!" I say forcefully before hanging up.

I sit on the edge of my bed and try to not focus on last night's events. I chew on my nails as I force images of Cale out of my head. My skin crawls with a dread, and my heart hurts knowing what I've done to my sister once again. Officially making me the worst sister in the entire world.

I shoot Hayley about a million more texts, but of course she doesn't answer. I know she's probably busy, but I need her right now! I need to talk this though with her or I'm about to throw myself in front of a bus because I can't handle the guilt.

I throw on a sweatshirt and some sleep shorts after falling asleep in my clothes from last night. Well my clothes minus my shirt. Again my body flames in disappointment and anger at the events of last night.

I quickly pull a brush through my hair ignoring the small pinches of pain that run through my body at the swift movements, and head out my double doors that lead to the beach. I need some fresh air. I need the salty breeze of the air, and the sounds of waves crashing upon the shore. I need to clear my head because what's in my head may drive me up a wall.

I let the soft sand squish through my bare toes and walk aimlessly down the beach. It's early so not many people are out and about. But I'm just fine with that. I'm not in the mood to run into a million people I know and who will want to ask a ton of questions all about my love life or my sisters. And at this point I don't want to talk about either.

I've gone up the beach, and I'm far from my house now at this point when I spot someone sitting in the distance alone. As I walk closer I realize I know this someone, and they are just a little far from home.

"Chase?" I question as I make my way closer to the Hasting sitting in the sand.

His head turns in shock at seeing me before wiping at his face like he's been crying or something. "Is something wrong?" I ask as I rush over and sit down next to someone who's always been so vibrant and fun loving. And seeing him so down is confusing.

Chase's head is dipped and he refuses to look up at me or meet my gaze.

"Are you okay?" I ask quietly. But his head remains down, and his lips sealed.

I shift and get settled in the sand that now covers my bare legs. I face the ocean letting out a quiet sigh, and sit quietly for a while letting him know that it's okay. Letting him know that I'm here, and I'm not going anywhere.

"You don't have to say anything," I say softly. "But I'm going to talk because I messed up, and I need to talk it through with someone," I tell him as my fingers draw circles in the grains around me.

"What did you do?" Chase asks so quietly I almost didn't here him.

My eyebrows rise in shock at his words. I honestly thought I would be doing all the talking, but maybe just maybe he needs someone to talk it through with him also. So I continue on, because I may not know what's wrong with him. But I know he needs this, he needs someone. Anyone to just sit here with him, and not judge. Because I need the exact same.

I tuck a stray hair behind my ear as my heart aches. "I did something really bad. Something that will hurt someone I love very much," I say my voice cracking slightly at the end as I think of what I've really done to Bailey. What I've permanently done to our relationship.

"When did you do it?" Chase asks.

"Last night," I mumble.

"Why did you do it?" he questions.

His words hit me hard. Why did I let Cale manipulate me again? Why do I always fall for his trap? Why does he mess with my head the way he does? Why is he my weakness? Why, after all he's done to me do I still want him?

"I don't know..." I trail. "I got messed up in the head because I'm confused and because everyone keeps making comments about you and me dating and—"

"We aren't dating!" Chase cuts me off with an angry shout.

I jerk back at his harsh words with eyebrows raised in shock. Silence lingers in the air between us, and I try and find the right words to say. I'm not hurt, just surprised by the outburst. "Chase, I know that we aren't dating," I say slowly. What brought this reaction out of him? I've never acted as if I thought we were dating. He knows about Max for goodness sakes.

"We are just friends," he says as if he's trying to clarify it not only for himself, but for me also.

"I know that also Chase," I say as my face scrunches in confusion. I let out a small chuckle. "If I wasn't so secure in our friendship I would be hurt by that a little," I admit quietly hating how I feel at this moment. I lied. I do feel a tad insecure and small, and I don't like it one bit. "I mean I don't like you that way, but I still find you attractive and I know if I liked you that way I would be lucky to date someone like you," I rumble trying to make sense of my feelings.

"No, I'm sorry Grayson it's just that I know I should find you attractive—"

"But you don't," I finish for him with sagging shoulders. His words shouldn't upset me, but they do for some reason. It's not like I want to date Chase, but him not finding me attractive still stings more than it should. Cale already didn't deem me attractive enough to be with all those years ago, so why would his brother feel any different? But it's a different hurt that lingers around this situation, because I love Chase in a different way than I did Cale. I thought we were friends.

Chase shifts so he's facing me and not the ocean. "No, it's not that—"

"I mean you probably are more into the Kylie or Bailey type, right?" I ask trying to comb through the web of confusion that wraps around this conversation.

He shakes his head. "No, I'm not," he says clearly.

My eyebrows rise in puzzlement at the direction of this conversation now.

He shrugs his shoulders. "I mean I do, and you," he says. "You're all beautiful I know that, but I just can't...I don't," he mumbles unable to find words for the thoughts that are running through his head.

Suddenly everything falls into place. "What about Max?" I ask. I know I can be completely wrong in this moment, but something tells me I'm not.

Chase's eyes grow wide at my words. "What?" he asks breathless.

"Do you find Max attractive?" I ask with the slight tilt of my head.

Chase opens his mouth trying to grasp the right words for this moment. "I mean...what is attractive really?" he stutters awkwardly.

"Chase, do you like boys?" I ask carefully as a gust of wind waves over a small mist from the ocean that lightly hits us. I don't want to make him mad, and I'm not judging. It's just a question.

"No, of course not!" he shouts offended by my words. His face is beat red and his hands lie in fists against the sand. "I like girls," he says through gritted teeth.

"Are you bi?" I ask hesitantly. He's mad at me already so I might as well continue asking. I could be so wrong right now, but for some reason I don't think I am. And I think Chase needs someone here for him, so that's what I'm going to do.

"God, Grayson no!" he barks once again.

I lift my hands in show of surrender. "Okay, okay, okay Chase," I say trying to calm him down. He's all worked up now, and I don't want him to blow up. Especially on me, I'm on his side and just trying to understand where he is coming from. I place a tentative hand on his shoulder. His body jerks away for a second, but then settles against my touch knowing I'm still here for him. "Are you confused?" I whisper.

His sad eyes lift to meet mine glistening with salted tears. "I am," he nods slowly.

My hand that sits on his shoulder gently traces patterns on his back in a soothing manner. "That's okay," I assure him. And it is okay. It takes time to really find out who we are in this world, and sometimes it takes a little longer. Chase has spent so much time in the shadow of his brothers he probably hasn't taken the time to find himself.

"Is it?" he asks as his eyes watch the ocean dance against the sand.

A small smile lifts my lips. "Yes, of course it is," I say with a small pause. "But can I ask you something?"

He doesn't say anything so I take that as my go ahead.

"Have you talked to anyone about this, like your brothers?" I ask softly knowing this may not be my place, but at the same time wanting to show I care about him and what's best for him.

Chase lets out a hard laugh. "Yeah right."

"What?" I ask. "Are you not close to Cale?"

He lifts a single shoulder dismissively to my question. Okay, so not close to Cale.

"What about your other brothers?" I test.

He shakes his head. "Clayton is closer to Cale than I am," he tells me.

"What about your oldest brother?" I question not knowing much about the eldest Hasting.

"Colt is close to no one," he says with a roll of his eyes.

"You're father?" I push one last time.

He turns his head to lock his eyes on me. "I don't want to disappoint him—"

"Chase..." I trail.

His eyes lower to the ground as a tear breaks free and falls into the sand and suddenly becomes lost. "You don't know him Grayson," he whispers.

"But—"

He cuts me off. "You don't," he finishes.

And with that we both face the rolling waves of the ocean, and don't say another word on the subject of Chase and his confusing feelings. It makes me sad that he doesn't feel like he can go to anyone about this. I wonder how long it has been eating him up inside, and how long he has been dying to tell someone. Anyone. I wish he could see what I see, which is a loving family that I know would accept him. Even though he isn't at the point of accepting himself yet, and until then I know how hard it can be to come to terms with certain confusing feelings.

But till then, I will be there for him. I always will be.

"Do you know how you're going to fix the mistake you made?" Chase asks out of nowhere.

My hand that rests on his against the sand grips on tighter. I close my eyes and wet my lips before I open my eyes to the vast sea before me.

I nod my throat dry. "Yes," I rasp. "I do."

And I do. I know exactly what I have to do in this moment.

Chapter Twenty

6/15/15

I SIT ON the beach as the party just up a ways from me hits full swing.

I don't know what it is about tonight, but I'm just not in the mood. But Kylie wanted to come, and I would never let her come to a party by herself. Especially the beach ones. These tended to get more out of control than any other parties Easton's teen population had. Maybe it is the ocean, or maybe the alcohol, but either way these parties are always wild.

I run a finger around my can of beer I am holding. I mess with the tab for a while listening to the swish of the liquid in the can along with the sounds of the waves kissing the beaches shore.

I wish I liked beer. It seems to be the only things these parties supply, but sadly I hate it. The taste is bitter and hard to keep down, but the tingling feeling it causes I can't help but love. I tip the can back to my mouth and take a sip forcing myself to swallow.

"Ugh," I mutter as I make a face of disgust.

"Don't like it?" I hear a boy's voice say in the darkness.

I look up to see a shadow of a person making their way towards me. A wave of nerves flash through me as I realize I'm alone and an easy target for attack. But as he walks further forward the lights on the beach shine against his face, and I realize I recognize him. Kind of.

"It's an acquired taste," he tells me.

I tear my eyes away from the guy, and make sure my phone is on and near me in case he tries anything. I really shouldn't have left Kylie, but she is with Maddy and Ashley and they are way better wing women then I ever will be.

"That's why I'm trying to acquire it," I quip back.

I hear a small chuckle before I see him sit down next to me in the soft sand.

"Why aren't you with everyone else at the party?" He asks as he takes a pull from his can of beer.

"Why aren't you?" I counter instead of answering his question. Because the truth is I'm awkward, and I don't know how to flirt with guys. So Kylie taught me that answering a question with a question is the easiest sure way to flirt, especially for people like me who suck at it. Though I'm not sure why I'm trying to flirt with this guy, I don't even know him.

"Bored," he answers simply.

My eyebrows rise at this mystery guy. "Really?" I ask. "With all those pretty girls over there you're bored?" I say once more not believing his words. I wrap my arms around my knees feeling suddenly feeling insecure about his reasons for sitting next to me.

He lets out a quiet laugh. "What a guy can't get bored at a party?"

I lift a single shoulder. "With pretty girls in skimpy outfits and alcohol in the mix they usually don't," I say truthfully.

"You're not wrong," he concedes. "But tonight I am," he admits.

He shifts and I finally get a good look at this boy in front of me and I realize he isn't a boy. He's definitely older than my sixteen years, but I can't tell by how much. Not too much I realize. His grin is still goofy and young, and he doesn't have any facial hair. Though he could shave. My guess is maybe eighteen years old?

He's really cute. Okay, way more than cute. He's straight up hot, and suddenly I feel flush with him being so close to me. Though he isn't even touching me. My arms tighten even more around my legs as my body fills with anxiety.

His hair is light blonde, and his eyes dark in this light though I can't see exactly what color. The more I look the more he looks familiar. "Do I know you?" I ask with scrunched eyebrows.

The right side of his lips tilts up in a small smirk. My eyes linger for a second on his lips noticing how nice they look before I look away, and my whole body heats with nervousness.

He shakes his head. "I don't think so," he says.

My eyes narrow in on him for a few seconds longer before turning back to the ocean before us. I know I recognize him but I can't place it. But this town is a small place, and everyone knows everyone so I'm sure I've seen him around.

We sit quietly for a while not saying one word as the ocean twinkles in the moonlight cast from above.

I slyly turn my head to see him still sitting next to me. His head is facing the blackened sea and not once glancing at me.

"Did you want something?" I ask awkwardly as my hands fiddle with the small can in my hands. I don't like him just sitting next to me. He makes me nervous for some reason I can't explain.

His head twists to lock his eyes against mine. "Nope," he says quietly as he turns forward once again.

My eyes widen in confusion to this person sitting next to me. Who is this guy?

"Do you have any siblings?" he asks out of nowhere.

I purse my lips in confusion to his sudden question, but answer anyways. "Yeah," I nod. "An older sister. Why?" I ask.

He tilts his head with a small shrug. "Same," he mutters oddly.

"Older, younger, brothers, sisters?" I ask questioning his wording.

He sighs. "Two older brothers and one younger."

My eyebrows lift. "That's a lot of testosterone in the family," I say with a small chuckle.

He smiles. "You're not wrong about that," he admits. He pauses for a few minutes before asking another question. "Do you ever feel like you're living in their shadows?" He asks. His voice is soft almost like he's embarrassed of what he is saying.

I let out a loud breath as I let my body sink into the sand. I let his question roll through my head, and allow myself really think of his question. "Yeah," I mutter. "I do sometimes," I say realizing how true my words are.

Bailey is perfect in every single way to my parents. I know they love me just as much, but it's different with her. She's the oldest, their first born, and it will always be different with them. Just like me being the baby of the family gives me a different position than Bailey.

"I do all the time," he breathes. "I don't ever feel like I'm enough, that my parents are looking for me to be my brothers...but I'm not."

"You're not," I agree with him.

His eyes narrow at my words as if he is shocked. "What?"

I stare straight at him. "You're not your brothers and you never will be," I say. "So stop trying and move on."

"Wow," he says taken back by my words. "I didn't expect those words to come out of your mouth," he comments.

My mouth drops at his words. I'm suddenly aware of how rude that sounded, and this complete stranger probably thinks I'm a bitch now. "Ohmygod, I'm so sorry that sounded awful, but I didn't mean it that way I meant—"

He holds up his hands to stop me. "No, no, no don't worry. I didn't expect that but you're right. I need to get over it."

I shake my head. "I didn't say get over it," I try and correct.

He smiles. "No don't worry about it, I needed a little tough love today."

I place my hands over my face completely embarrassed of my words. "Just go back over to those girls and hit on every single one of them like those dumb Hasting boys do," I mumble to myself more than him. "They seem to love it," I chuckle dryly.

He says nothing. A long silence passes before I finally glance up from my hands. I look up to see the guy grinning from ear to ear at my words. He's still here.

"What?" I ask confused as to his expression.

He laughs as he shakes his head lightly. "Nothing," he says with a smirk. He stands from the ground dusting his pants free of the grainy sand. My body sags slightly in defeat that he's leaving. I don't even know his name but for some reason his presence soothed me. And I liked it. I kind of liked him actually.

"Oh, okay well bye then," I say as I nibble on my bottom lip nervously.

I turn away from him and face the ocean once again assuming he would leave. But he doesn't. He stands next to me for a few lingering seconds before speaking into the quiet night that surrounds us.

"It was really nice to meet you by the way," he says.

I lift a hand in a waving gesture without saying another word knowing I will say something awkward again.

"I'm going to go over and hit on all those girls," he tells me.

I shrug in response without looking at him hating the way his words wash over me.

"Okay," I mutter.

"I'm Cale Hasting by the way." My head whips around to look at the guy who I without knowing just insulted. "See you around." With those last words he leaves me on the beach alone and in shock.

And exactly one week later he asked me out on that very beach. The beach where we first met.

A night I will never forget.

A night I wish I could forget honestly.

I stand in front of Cale's apartment door trying to gather up the courage to knock on his door. The memory of our first meeting wraps around me threatening to strangle me as weak breathes fly from my parted lips. I close my eyes and let the memory hold me hostage for one last second. I let it squeeze my heart and tear my eyes up for one last time before I lock it away. Lock it away for good now.

I can't go back.

I open my eyes, push my shoulders back, and let my knuckles crash against the wooden door before me.

I hear footsteps and as they come closer, and my heart races faster and faster. I've pushed Cale away, I've locked him away, I've told him we're done, but I've never done this. I've never asked him to let me go, to give me up. I've been working on getting away from him all this time, but has he been doing the same? We've been playing this game of push and pull, but neither of us have done anything about our past. So it's time he gives me up, and I do the same. This really needs to end.

The door swings open to reveal a man who isn't Cale, though looks very similar. He has the same dirty blonde hair though his is a little darker and not as short, and hazel eyes, and ridiculously attractive. Must be a Hasting, though the question is which one? I've never met the two eldest Hasting's because they were so much older than me back then. I've seen pictures, but it's been a while. Maybe it's Clayton?

"Hi, I'm sorry is Cale here?" I ask as I shift my weight from foot to foot uneasily.

He lingers for a second watching me as if he's trying to place me. His eyes narrow before twisting his head to shout at who I'm assuming is Cale. "She's here," he says simply.

My eyes widen and my jaw drops in pure shock. "Excuse me..." I trail. "Do I know you?" I ask confused as to why he knows who I am. Surly Cale hasn't been talking about me to his brothers. Or has he?

His eyebrow cocks. "You don't," he states. "But I know you."

Suddenly Cale rushes up to the door behind who I'm still assuming is his brother. "Gray," he breathes with a smile breaking across his perfect face.

My eyes cast down as I force my initial feelings back. I'm on a mission here, and I'm not straying. I know what I need to do. No, what I have to do.

"I'm going to head out," the man says to Cale. His eyes flicker over to me as he leaves the doorframe. "Nice to finally meet you," he sneers before heading down the stairs to the parking lot.

"Same to you," I grumble still confused. "Who was that?" I ask with a harsh edge to my voice as soon as the guy is out of earshot.

"Here come inside and we can talk Gray," he says as he reaches out a hand for me to take. And for a second, no not even a full second less than that, I consider taking it. But I crush that thought immediately and throw it away. Far, far away.

I shake my head. "No, we can talk here and right here only," I say sternly.

Cale's shoulders sag at my words, but he doesn't object. I think he can sense why I'm here, and that I mean business. He tucks his hands into his front pockets. "He's my brother," he says.

"Which one?" I ask.

"Clayton," he breathes.

I nod at his words. "Why does he know who I am?" I question with the tilt of my head.

His eyes flicker away from mine. "Don't worry he won't tell anyone if that's what you're wondering," he says blowing off my question entirely.

I cross my arms. "Of course that's what I'm wondering! You're engaged to my sister Cale!" I whisper yell at him. How can he not understand this?

"Please Gray, just come inside and let's talk some more. I know the other night ended weird but—"

"Let me go," I blurt out cutting him off. The three words so simple yet hold so much power.

His body jerks back at my words as if physically hurt and shocked by them all at the same time. "What?" he breathes.

I take a deep breath, gathering all the courage inside myself to repeat those awful words. "Let me go."

He takes a step towards me, but I step away. And with that single step his face falls and crumbles until I can see the pain clear as day on his face. "I don't understand…" he trails. "What does that mean?" he asks.

"It means let me go," I repeat unable to find the words to elaborate any further. Saying those three words were hard enough, I don't want to say anymore.

"What does that mean Gray?" he shouts at me as his arms fly out in emphasis of his confusion and pain.

Tears wet my eyes and blur my vision. "It means that you ended things with me that summer. You broke me," I say with a cracked voice. "And I worked for years to put myself back together, and I might've not been perfect but I was okay. I was getting on with life because I was moving on from you," I say as tears begin to fall down my cheeks.

"Gray—" Cale starts as he takes another step towards me.

I lift a hand to stop him and his words. "No, I was doing okay with life. But then you got engaged to my sister, and I still thought I would be okay. I thought I could avoid you, but I can't!" I shout. "I can't because you look at me, and you say things to get under my skin like calling me a slut—"

Cale interrupts me. "I did not call you a slut," he specifies.

I shrug and shake my head knowing it doesn't matter, none of his words matter in this moment because I know what I have to do. "You kiss me in kitchens and then say awful things to me..." I say remembering those words he said to me after I yelled at Bailey, and she left us alone in that damn kitchen.

"You said it was over," Cale states.

"I did! And I thought it was because to me it was Cale! I was moving on, I was happy, I was letting you go!" I say at tears continue to fall. "But were you?" I ask.

He opens his mouth as if he doesn't know what to say.

"You aren't," I state. "You ask me about Chase and Max, and get mad when I'm with them, and then you touch me and kiss me and confuse me and say you love me," my voice breaks at the end barely able to say the last three words. I wipe at my face tired of crying, and hating that I'm also crying in front of Cale. I hate showing that side of me, it's weak and he already owns so much of me.

Cale's eyes are wide as he takes in my words. "But I do love—"

"No!" I shout as my heart squeezes. My mind wants so bad to hear those words once more, but my heart can't handle it again. I can't handle finally hearing the words I've dreamed of and him not being mine. He was never mine, not really anyways. Not in a way that truly mattered.

"Gray, listen to me," he starts but I refuse to let him finish.

"Let me go," I cry. "Please," I beg. "I can't do this anymore, I can't live like this, I can't look at my sister every day and remember what we did, how you felt against me, I can't anymore..." I trail. "I fucking can't Cale. Please!"

He walks towards me, and I can't move away because I hit the railing and there's no more space. I'm at his mercy, and he doesn't stop until his body is melded to mine and his hands are holding my face.

"Cale," I cry unable to finish what I was going to say. My whole body physically hurts. He has to let me go, he has to! I can't do this with him anymore. My heart can't be waiting for him for the rest of my life. I can't secretly be hoping he leaves my sister. It's all wrong, and it all needs to end. It has to end. I want to be happy and be able to love someone like Max, but I can't with Cale looming over me and waiting and questioning me. I can't.

"Shh shh shh," he breathes as his fingers wipe at the uncontrollable tears that fall from my eyes. The salty tears wet his hands, but he doesn't stop holding my face and holding me close to him. He dips his face so that he can look at me, and I mean really look at me. His eyes crawl over every inch of my face as if I have the answers to all of life's questions written somewhere on my face. "Let you go," he whispers.

I nod as I choke back another sob. "Let me go," I repeat.

The pad of his thumb caresses my cheekbone tenderly. "I love you Gray—"

I shake my head repeating, "No, no, no," over and over again trying to get him to let go of my face.

Cale won't release my face or my body, and tightens his hold on me refusing to free me of him. "Gray, I love you and that's why I'll let you go," he says finally.

I stop my weak attempts at getting away from him, and still at his words. "What?" I pant.

His bright hazel eyes hold mine, and his lips tremble lightly. "Because you want me to, because I know this can't go on forever, and because I love you so damn much that I just want you to be happy," he pauses as his eyes begin to glisten. "Even if it's not with me." His last words really hit me hard, and more tears begin to fall onto his skin.

"Cale," I breathe his name unable to find any other word for this moment.

He leans forward and places his forehead against mine for a few seconds letting us breathe each other's air one last time before he breaks away, and then he drops his hands from my face.

"I'm letting you go," he says as he squeezes his eyes shut.

"Thank you," I say so quietly I'm unsure if he even heard me.

Cale turns his back on me, and walks back into his apartment. But before he shuts the door behind himself he pauses. "What am I supposed to do now?" He asks unable to look me in the eye. And it hurts, but I accept that this is my life now and that this was what I asked for.

I lift a shoulder. "Go back to before this summer. Before I came and ruined everything," I say trying to come up with some kind of answer for him in this fucked up situation.

"Gray you didn't ruin—"

I cut him off as I head towards the stairs unable to listen to him anymore. "Goodbye Cale," I say.

There's a small pause before he says, "Goodbye Grayson."

And with that tears burst from my eyes because out of everything that just happened that was the worst. Because it made it real.

We are really over. Done. Never again.

He let me go.

So now what do I do?

Chapter Twenty-One

6/20/15

"I'M NERVOUS," Max mutters as I open the door to see his handsome face.

I smile. "Don't be." If anything I should be the nervous one.

"Easy for you to say it's your family," he mutters.

Without saying another word I quickly step outside and close the door behind myself. I place my hands on Max's shoulders, and pull him closer to me so that his warm body is suddenly up against mine. I move a hand to set it on his cheek gently. He tilts his head into my hand, and his jungle eyes light up immediately.

Max moves and his lips land on mine. It's gentle and soft and perfect.

I pull away but not before placing another kiss on his strong jaw. "You still nervous?" I ask, as my body stays pressed up all against his. His heat seeps into my skin making me want just a little more than a kiss.

His hands land on my waist, and they squeeze lightly before pressing even further into me causing a small gasp to fall from my wet lips. The kiss was simple, innocent even. But this exchange is anything but that. Max's eyes and hands light up my body and unexpectedly I want more. Much more, and more is something I've been afraid of with Max. But right now in this moment all I want is him, and his lips on mine once again.

But now isn't that time. Now really isn't the time with my family only a few feet away from our meshed bodies.

"Not so much nervous anymore," he speaks. His voice a little darker, and lower as he alludes to feeling something other than nerves. I can't help the flush that covers my neck because I can feel exactly what he is feeling as he presses his hips into mine further.

I bite my lip and lean into him a little more. "Well then I accomplished my job today," I say with a small smirk playing at my wanting lips.

I quickly give Max another kiss, and pull my body away from his before we can take another step in a direction fueled by lust. He rakes a hand through his hair and takes a deep breath as he tries to calm his body down. Max's eyes narrow at me as if his problem is my fault. "What?" I ask trying to act innocent.

He shakes his head before he grabs my hand and leans down to whisper into my ear, "This is far from over." His words slither around my body, and suddenly my stomach is filled with butterflies and my body with even more anticipation.

I turn so that our noses graze each other's, and I flick my eyes up into his. "Is that a promise?" I ask with a raised eyebrow, and a quick swipe of my tongue against my lips.

Max pulls away so that he is standing upright and facing the front door. He lets out a low chuckle, and with the slight shake of his head a smile touches his lips. And that smile makes my body hum with a feeling I haven't felt in a very long time. A feeling I've never felt for anyone besides one man, and it's scary and nerve-wracking. I want to shove it away, but I don't. I let the feeling settle into my chest and stomach, and I don't do a damn thing about it. I've let go. I've been let go of, and now it's time to seriously move on.

Tonight is really big. Max is meeting the family, and I've never brought a guy home before. Hell, my family didn't even know about Cale. The thought of him immediately makes my heart clench in pain. I haven't seen him since the exchange at his apartment and I'm thankful. I'm also thankful that Bailey was out with friends the night we kissed, and that my parents didn't hear any of our yelling. I can't believe we acted like that when my parents were just feet away sleeping. We were reckless and stupid and I can't believe I let it go that far.

But that doesn't mean it doesn't hurt to still think of Cale. I've been hurt before, so I know I can move on from this. From the pain we both caused each other.

I feel Max's hand hold mine a bit tighter, and my eyes land on the attractive man next to me. I can't help but smile and the thoughts and the pain of Cale Hasting are diminished. Not all the way, but enough. Enough to make the fire lessen.

I pull Max along with me into the house, and then into the kitchen where my parents are waiting. My father almost lost it when I said I was going on another date, third to be exact, with Max and he still hadn't met him. So I agreed we could do some drinks and appetizers together before Max and I left for our date. I know they're interested in who I've been spending my time with when in the past I acted as if I could care less about guys or dating. They don't and will never know the reasoning behind that, but I know they are happy to see me happy.

My parent's faces light up when we walk hand in hand into the kitchen. They immediately stand up and come over to us. "Um...this is Max," I say suddenly not knowing how to introduce him. Do I call him my friend? He's not my boyfriend. Ugh, I already suck at this and we are only a few seconds into the night.

My father comes over first. "It's nice to meet you Mr. Kennings," Max says as they shake hands. My father nods in agreement. I notice him checking Max out as if he will be able to see something wrong with him. I hold in a sigh and the need to roll my eyes at my father.

My mother rushes over next, her floral perfume trailing behind her. "It's so great to meet you Max!" she exclaims shaking his hand also. "You've made our little Gray here so happy lately," she gushes.

"Mom," I murmur in a warning tone trying to get her to ease off.

She gives me a pointed look. "What? It's the truth, and you never bring anyone home so that means he must be really special—"

"Mom!" I say a little too loudly with wide eyes.

She holds up two hands as she takes a few steps backwards. "Okay, okay, okay I'm just saying," she says as he backs off towards the kitchen island.

Max slides an arm around my waist and leans down to whisper, "Gray?" he questions. It's the first time he's ever heard someone address me with the nickname, and a weird feeling hits when the name falls from his tongue. I don't like it, and I don't want him to call me that. Ever.

I shake my head. "Just a family nickname," I whisper back. "You don't need to call me that," I tell him as I pull away from his arm and walk towards my family. When I reach the island I turn to see Max standing in the same spot I left him. His face covered in a mixture of confusion and hurt. I didn't mean to come off rude, but I can't have him call me that name. I love that he calls me by my full name. It doesn't bring up the past, and make me feel sad. It makes me want to look to the future, which I never do. But instead of explaining that to him like a normal person, I shut him down.

I offer Max a small smile before his lips tug in attempts to smile back. He then walks over and stands at the island with me, but his arm doesn't return to its place on my waist. And a small wave of disappointment hits me at the small non-gesture that speaks great volumes.

"Drink?" My father offers Max as he opens the fridge to grab himself a beer. He pauses, "Wait how old are you?" he asks as an after thought.

I chuckle inaudibly. "He's old enough dad," I say knowing this was my father's sly way of getting Max's age.

"I'm twenty-four sir," Max answers right after me. "But I'm driving tonight so I don't need anything," he says. I turn to meet his bright green eyes and smile softly. He definitely just got brownie points for that answer.

"Responsible," my mother says as she smiles a huge hundred-watt smile at Max. She already loves him, and why shouldn't she? Max is amazing. It's me who keeps ruining everything. My mother then waves a hand at the few dips and other appetizers spread in front of us, "Help yourself to anything also."

I grab a small plate and throw some chips and jalapeno dip—my mother's specialty—and some other little appetizers before sitting down at the island next to my date. Max grabbed some chips, but I can tell he is too nervous to eat. Whereas all I do is eat when I'm in any type of mood, especially nervous.

"So do you live in Easton?" My father asks next. He's in interrogation mode and there's no stopping him now.

Max nods. "Yes I do. I have for a few years, but just recently full time," he says. "After I graduated my mom had some surgeries that put her out for a while so I came down to help for a while."

My parents nod at his words listening intently. "That's so sweet," my mother says as she places a hand over her heart. "I only hope if that happened to one of us our kids would be just as willing," she says eyeing me.

I roll my eyes, and immediately regret it as my mother raises an eyebrow at my rude gesture. She hates when I roll my eyes. "That's the oldest's job," I tell her as I shovel some dip into my mouth.

"Oh shush, you better come and help your parents out if we need you," my mother says as she swats at the air in front of her as if she was hitting me.

"So what does your mother do?" My father inquires next because of course the questioning can't end yet. I quickly peak at the clock in the kitchen and see it's somewhat close to the time we need to leave. I silently cheer knowing this is close to being over, though I think I may be freaking out more than Max is at the moment. I know he's nervous, but the anxiousness running through me could rival him. I don't know why I'm so tightly wound. Max is great, and I can tell my mother already likes him, and yet tension still flutters through me.

"She runs a small flower shop downtown, nothing crazy," he answers casually.

My mother claps her hands together in excitement. "Oh, wait is it Flora?" she asks with wide eyes and an even larger smile taking over her face.

Max chuckles at her reaction. "Yes it is," he nods. "You know it?" he asks.

I intercept before my mother can freak out even more. "My mom used to run a shop back home," I tell him. "She loves flowers and knows where to find the best in the area—"

"And your mother's are exquisite, and I'm very picky!" My mother cuts me off as she bubbles over with enthusiasm.

Max smiles at my mother's reaction while I try and hold back another eye roll not wanting to get chastised in front of my date.

"I will have to tell my mom you said so," Max says to my mother.

"Oh, please do," she smiles.

I turn to see my father take a sip of his beer, and open his mouth to ask another question when I decides I've had enough of tonight.

"Ok, well I think it's time for us to head out," I say quickly making sure to intercept my father's nearing question.

"Oh, so soon?" My mother asks sadly. I shake my head lightly. She is already crazy obsessed with Max and this is only our third date. I don't know whether to be overly happy that she loves him, or to feel uneasy that she likes him so much so soon. What if we don't make it? I push the thoughts aside right away and focus on the here and now. I'm trying not to worry so much about the future, but it's hard. Especially when that's all I've done for that past four years.

Max tips his wrist to check his watch before his eyes meet mine. He knows I'm calling this a little early, but I just can't do this anymore so I'm ending it.

"Yeah we have reservations," Max says simply as he slides a hand around my shoulders. He easily goes along with the lie, following me because again he's perfect and I don't deserve him. At all. I know we aren't exclusive or even officially dating, but me making out with Cale didn't just hurt my relationship with Bailey but I know with Max also.

"Well it was great to meet you Max, and I hope we see you again soon," my mother says as she slides off the stool at the island and comes over to hug Max.

My mother then proceeds to place a quick kiss on my cheek before whispering, "Love." And with that she goes back to her stool and her white wine.

My heart races a little faster at her words in happiness and anxiousness at the same time. It's an odd mix of emotions adding to the already weird feelings filling me.

"Nice to meet you again Mr. Kennings, " Max says as he shakes my father's hand goodbye.

"You too Max," my father says with a small smile lighting up his face.

As soon as Max turns to head towards the door my father's eyes meet mine, and he simply nods once in approval of my date. Once again the same mix of confusing emotions run through me, and I don't know whether to cheer or run away. This is the first time my parents are meeting someone I like, and I don't know how to handle it.

Max's hand slips through mine as he leads me out the front door and down into his car, which he opens the passenger door for me. Because even when I'm acting weird he's still a complete gentlemen. Seriously, I don't deserve him.

The driver's side door slams shut as soon as Max is sitting behind the wheel. "What's going on Grayson?" he asks simply.

"I kissed someone," I blurt into the silent air of the warm car. I had debated on whether I was going to tell Max about the kiss or not, but apparently my mouth decided for me in another case of verbal vomit.

"What?" he asks as shock fills his voice.

I don't see his face because I'm keeping my eyes on my lap. I'm too afraid to face him, and his beautiful eyes that always show every passing emotion he's feeling. I can't see the hurt I've caused him.

"I kissed someone last week," I repeat because I don't know what else to say.

Max doesn't say anything. Not one word in response. Silence fills the dead air as the radio drifts around us quietly, yet so loud at the same time.

"I know we aren't anything official, but I still felt like I should tell you," I say whispering the last few words as the nerves weave through me taking my air.

Out of my peripheral I see Max's hands grip the steering wheel tightly. He doesn't say anything for what feels like an eternity, which in reality is probably only a few minutes. "Okay." Is all he says when he finally speaks.

My eyebrows draw together and my body quickly turns to face him in confusion. My eyes meet his jungle green ones for the first time since I blurted those words, and I was right. I can see how hurt he is plain as day in his beautiful eyes and painted across his handsome face.

"Okay?" I question unsure of what his 'okay' really means.

"Okay," he restates. "You ready for dinner?" he asks as he grabs at his seatbelt, but I quickly put out a hand and stop him.

"I don't get it..." I trail.

Max sighs and leans back in his seat letting his head fall back against the headrest. "What do you mean you don't get it Grayson?" he questions, but he doesn't let me answer. "You kissed someone. Does it suck, yes," he states simply. "I really like you, but you're right we aren't anything so I don't have a say in who you kiss in your free time. Now are you ready for dinner?" he asks once again trying to buckle up and drive off and move on. But I once again stop him, because I can't move on.

"No I'm not ready," I tell him.

"Why?" he asks roughly.

"Because you're mad," I answer plain as day.

He shakes his head. "I'm not mad," he tells me.

"Okay, then you're upset with me," I correct.

He rubs a hand over his face. "Yeah, a little bit," he says quietly.

I reach out and place a hand on Max's shoulder. His eyes fall to my hand before lifting to meet mine. "It won't happen again," I tell him.

"How do you know?" he questions.

I close my eyes as the memories of Cale try to come rushing back and ruin me once again. But I don't let them. I keep them locked away where they belong, and that's in the past. And as I open my eyes to meet Max's amazing green eyes I know I'm staring at my future, or at least a part of it.

"I know, because it was a one time thing," I say. "It's over, it's in the past," I tell him reiterating my thoughts.

"The past?" he probes.

I run my tongue over my teeth timidly. "I know I'm not easy Max. I know I can run hot and cold, and come off bitchy at times," I say with a dry chuckle. "But that's because I was hurt a long time ago, and I never really got over it. Well until you," I say truthfully as my hand travels upward from his shoulder to his flush cheek. "It still hurts and I'm still trying and one day I will talk about it. But for now you make me forget, you make me happy, and you make me want more out of life and relationships for the first time in a long time."

Right as the last word leaves my lips Max presses his against mine. It's deep and sensual and everything I need in this moment. As my hand holds his face, his hands weave into my hair pulling me closer to his warmth. His lips slowly play with mine, and it's beautiful. He pulls away just enough so that our eyes can meet. Our hot breathes mix and mingle while I fall deeper into his wild green eyes.

And for the first time I don't compare Max to Cale. I don't compare the kiss, or his eyes, or even the way his hands twisted through my hair.

My mind isn't on Cale. It's on Max, and for the first time since that dreadful summer I let myself fall. Just a little, not a lot. If I need to pull myself back up I can, but I do it. I let myself fall, and it's scary and enthralling at the same time.

"Ready for dinner?" he asks once again.

I smile and press another kiss to his perfectly pink lips. "Yes," I answer. And this time I let him buckle his seatbelt.

Chapter Twenty-Two

------

6 /23/15

"HEY KY!" I call out cheerfully to Kylie as I spot her sitting in the corner booth of the local sandwich shop.

I hold my tray in my hands and make my way over before sliding into the booth seat across from her.

"Hey!" she responds with a large smile. "So glad we are getting lunch. I feel like it's been forever since I've seen you!"

"I know," I agree as my nose scrunches in a tinge of sadness. "It's been too long, and I'm sorry life's been crazy," I tell her as I open up my wrapped sandwich.

"Ugh, same," Kylie responds. "So how has everything been?" she asks before taking a bite of her pita.

I lift a single shoulder nonchalantly. "Fine," I mumble around a bite of my chicken, mozzarella, and tomato sandwich.

"Gray," she nags knowing I'm hiding something.

"What?" I ask innocently. "Everything really is fine," I say trying not to divulge too much into the craziness that has been my life lately.

"What about Cale?" she asks.

"What about him?" I counter.

"Grayson..." she trails knowing something is going on.

I let out a loud frustrated sigh, and place my sandwich back on my tray. I wet my lips before finally speaking. "I um..." I barely get out before dropping my eyes to my lap in shame. I clear my throat, "Something did happen and I don't want you to judge me or—"

Kylie cuts me off with a raised hand to stop my words. "You know I never would Gray," she says. "We all screw up in life," she affirms. "Believe me I know."

I nod knowing she is right, but that I also messed up in a way that I can never take back. "Yeah, well I totally screwed up," I tell her as grief fills my chest at the pain I have of hurting my sister the way I did.

"What happened?" she questions. Her eyes hold mine, and I know I can tell her anything. But that doesn't make it any easier to say the worlds aloud.

"We kissed..." I say awkwardly trying to keep Kylie's gaze, but dropping them to my sandwich as shame fills heart and coats my cheeks red.

"Who kissed?" she pushes not getting what I'm saying.

I give her a pointed look knowing I won't be able to say those awful words again.

"Shut the fuck up!" she exclaims as a hand flies to her mouth in utter shock.

"Kylie!" I scold under my breath at her choice of words. I can feel some eyes on us in the small restaurant as silence rings around us at her outburst, but I try to ignore the stares.

"I'm sorry I just...wow," she breathes her eyes wide in pure disbelief.

"I know I really messed up," I say as my face pulls in disgust at myself.

"So what happened after?" she asks leaning in to me as if I'm about to tell her the secret to the perfect hair day instead of how I screwed over my sister.

"I ended it," I say quietly. "For real," I add more for myself because while Kylie might not know I've tried to end it before, but I do. "I love my sister and what we did wasn't right for anyone," I say. "Not Bailey, or Cale, or myself, or even Max," I add hating the way my I flinch saying Max's name. I really do like him.

"Did you tell him?" Kylie asks as my eyebrows knit in confusion. "Max, I mean," she immediately clarifies. "You aren't exclusive," she points out.

I nod in understanding. "I know we aren't, but I still did because I want to have a relationship with him. I actually like Max," I say honestly.

"He won't ever be Cale," she says. And I know she doesn't say this to hurt me, she says it to be realistic. Max and or any other guy won't ever be Cale, and I've come to realize that maybe that's okay. Maybe that's for the best.

"Exactly," I say frankly.

We sit in silence as my words settle around us. The pain of what I did still weighs heavily on my heart. Cale was my world at one point, but he's Bailey's world now and I have to move on. I thought I was free from the hold he had on me, but this summer has taught me otherwise. I've learned more about myself these past weeks than I have my last two years in college.

It's not easy to get over someone who owns a piece of your heart. But for the first time in a long time I'm actually trying and it hasn't ended in horror yet. And that's all because of Max.

Kylie's eyes meet mine. "So what now?" she asks.

I lift a single shoulder in a shrug. "I help Bailey marry the man she loves," I breathe.

"But if Cale loved her back he wouldn't have—"

I shake my head cutting her off. "No," I start firmly. "He loved her and asked her to marry him. He made that decision to be with her for the rest of his life. He does love her. It's just that—"

"The past is hard to let go of," Kylie finishes for me.

I lean back in the booth, and settle into the cushioned seat. "Yeah, it really can be," I reply. "But I'm doing it. I've let go, I'm moving on with Max."

Kylie plays with her straw wrapper. "So how is that now?"

"It's good," I answer truthfully. "Being with him doesn't make me scared anymore. He blots out the pain of the past and eases my heartache." He is the water that I need in the flames that are Cale Hasting.

"Wow," Kylie exhales.

"He makes me happy for the first time in a long time. I don't know if we have some perfect future ahead of us, but for now—"

"You're happy," she says taking the precise words out of my mouth.

I smile. "I am."

* * * * *

"Hey Gray, is that you?" I hear my father voice shout from the kitchen.

"Yeah, it's me!" I reply as I toss my sandals onto the rug, and shrug off my light cardigan to place it on the hook by the front door.

I make my way to the kitchen to see my father pouring two large glasses of lemonade.

"One of those better be for me," I say playfully. While at the same time not joking at all, because a glass of lemonade sounds perfect right about now.

"Of course," he responds. My father turns and walks towards me to hand me the cold glass. "I was thinking we could sit out on the deck for a while, and talk," he says casually.

I take a sip of the tart drink and nod. "Yeah, sounds good to me," I smile not thinking anything of his request. My father and I used to be very close when I was younger. I was always a daddy's girl, and still am. But with the distance I've put between myself and my family it's been hard to be as close to him as I once was.

We both take a seat on the white wicker chairs on the open deck at the back of our house. We sit in silence as seagulls, waves, and the sound of the ice in our drinks clinking against the glass surround us.

"I'm sorry," my father says out of nowhere.

My face pulls in confusion as I set my glass down. "Dad, what do you have to be sorry for?" I ask completely puzzled by his words.

"I just mean it must be hard and—"

"Dad," I say sitting up in my chair. "I have no idea what you're talking about," I tell him with wide eyes and raised brows. "Is everything okay?" I ask.

"Cale," he says simply.

My lips part in surprise. "What are you saying right now?" I ask taken back.

My father looks right at me, his blue eyes that we share holding mine. "I know Gray," he says gently into the wind.

I drop my gaze into my lap, and try to stop my hands from shaking as a surge of anxiety courses through me. "I don't know what you mean," I tell him as I fist my hands and press them into my lap in attempts to stop the shaking.

"Gray..." he trails.

"Dad, I don't—" I stop myself short. If my father knows then what's stopping me from talking to him about it? He knows, which means I don't need to lie anymore. I raise my eyes to his as tears prick mine. "How?" I ask quietly.

He settles into his chair and takes a sip of his lemonade. "I saw him leave your room one morning through the French doors that lead to the beach one summer years ago," he says calmly.

A low gasp flies through my lips. "Why didn't you say anything?" I question.

He shrugs. "Of course I wanted to say something Gray," he tells me. "You were and always will be my little girl, and some guy leaving your room...." he trails as a grunt flies from his mouth. "I was pissed," he nods. "But," he says unable to finish.

"But what?" I ask.

My father turns so his gaze isn't on the ocean anymore, but me. "You were so happy that summer and I knew," he pauses. "I knew it was because you were falling in love," he finishes.

I run a hand through my tangled hair in disbelief. "Did you know then it was Cale?" I ask.

My father shakes his head. "No, I never saw his face when he left," he admits. "And then you changed," he adds. "You were sad, and I could hear you cry every night, and I knew he broke your heart and I wanted to kill him," he says as his voice goes deadly flat. "Even though I didn't know who he was, he hurt you and that was all that mattered."

"I thought he was the one," I say as a painful ache runs through my chest.

My father fists his hand that lies on the table. "That's young love at its finest," he says gruffly.

"Yeah," I say simply in agreement. "But how did you know? You never saw his face," I say. Are Cale and I just that obvious? But how has no one else figured it out then?

"You're mother mentioned you saying something about shooting stars, and she just couldn't remember where we had heard that before," he says. "But I remembered," he tells me.

I drop my head suddenly remembering telling my parents that phrase. "I said it that summer," I say. My parents and I were talking about the stars, and I told them the story of Cale's father and grandmother. But I told them it was from a friend, but I never said whom.

"You did," he tells me. "But Bailey said it also. She told us the story and said it was from Cale's parents. I had never heard another story like that and the odds were to weird to be a coincidence," he shrugs as the pieces fall into place for me. "And then there's the way he looks at you still," he adds quietly.

"What?" I ask breathlessly almost not even hearing my father over the sounds of the dancing ocean.

He tilts his head. "Gray, I can see it," he says. "He still loves you."

I shake my head fervently hating the way my heart skips a beat at my father's words. My heart wants to believe what's he's saying, but my brain knows better then to fall for those false words. Because I won't, and can't ever go back to the way I felt about Cale. It's too unstable, and wild, and I felt way too much. I also love Bailey too much for that to happen.

"Dad, no," I state. "He doesn't and don't say things like that ever please," I say trying to keep the begging tones out of my cry. "He loves Bailey and she loves him. Nothing more or less."

"Are you sure about that?" he pushes.

"Yes," I say though a voice in the back of my head whispers at me in questioning.

"Okay," he says simply.

"Dad," I start. "I love you and I know I've messed up in the past. But I will never hurt Bailey and she loves Cale, and that's the end of it," I say sternly. "So let's not bring this up ever again," I tell him.

My father takes a sip of the lemonade that's getting warmer by the hot sun, and nods once at my words.

I grab my drink and stand up as I begin to walk back into the house as my father calls out to me, "Gray."

"What?" I ask facing the sliding doors. Refusing to turn around and face him or his next words.

"You're going to be all right," is all he says before I make my way back into the house.

I won't let myself think of that conversation. I can't believe my father never said anything about Cale, and of all times he waits until now. But I won't let it ruin my progress. I'm slowly freeing myself from the hold Cale has on me, and letting myself fall for Max in the mean time. It's not easy, but I'm doing it because I love Bailey and I need to be free.

But as I sit on my bed and stare at the ceiling I can't help but maybe think my father was right about one thing. That I am going to be all right, and that's because of me. Not Cale.

Chapter Twenty-Three

7/4/15

"OHMYGOSH TONIGHT IS going to be so much fun!" Kylie shouts as we make our way down the beach to the bonfire that gets put on every year.

It's the first year my parents actually let me go, and I couldn't be more excited.

Well I could be technically if Cale were here. But he won't show. I asked earlier in the week if he would come to the annual bonfire, and he completely dismissed me and the idea itself. I asked one more time and he got agitated and said no once again. I know he doesn't want anyone to really know about us yet, but one night isn't going to suddenly out us.

I just wanted one night with him. Hidden in plain sight where we could have a wonderful night together. The fourth of July is a magical night. Colors pop and burst across the sky in the flash of an eye and fill the sky like an exploding star. It's mesmerizing and breathtaking, and I can't help but be amazed every single year by them. It's my favorite part of the summer.

I can't stop myself from glancing at my phone to see if Cale had texted me. He hasn't.

I quickly stow my phone back into my purse and try and focus on the night ahead. These beach parties are always fun, but the night of the fourth is when things get crazy. The kind of crazy that gives everyone here enough wild stories to talk about until the next fourth of July wraps around.

"Come on let's get something to drink," I say as I hook an arm through Kylie's and head towards the group of coolers not far from the fire.

Kylie grabs a wine cooler, but I grab a beer because it always makes me think of the night I met Cale. I can't help but smile when the bitter taste hits my tongue. It's still a taste I'm trying to acquire. My best friend gives me a weird look at my choice of drink but I just shrug her off. She wouldn't understand. She knows a little about Cale and I, but I won't ever tell her how deep my feelings run.

Well, at least not yet.

My phone dings and I almost drop my can trying to get my phone out of my purse. Excitement runs though me at the thought the text is from Cale. I finally find my phone in my mess of a bag, and pull it out to only see a new message from my mother. It reads: Be safe and have fun. Love you.

My face drops and so does my heart. I really wanted to spend the day with him. It's the biggest holiday in the summer, and in Easton it's a huge deal.

I shake off the disappointment that creeps in, and take a sip of my beer. Tonight is going to be fun no matter what! It's my first time at the annual fourth bonfire, and even without Cale I'm going to have a night to remember.

An upbeat song blasts over the speakers, and I can't help the way my body sways to the fun beat. It's one of my favorite songs and always a great way to kick off a night.

"Come on let's go dance!" I say cheerfully to Kylie. She downs her drink, and tosses it into the trash bin behind her before following me further down the beach to where everyone else is dancing.

We link hands and begin to jump and dance around playfully. We don't even care what we look like at the moment. We only care about having fun. The song molds into another one and another one until the group around us almost doubles in size. The fireworks won't start for another couple hours, and the night has just begun. Everyone is having fun, throwing their hands in the air, and swaying to the bubbling beats that pour out of the huge speakers.

Suddenly a guy comes up behind Kylie, and places a hand on her hip to stop her movement. She turns her head to get a look at who's stopping her, and she immediately looks back at me with wide eyes. Knowing Kylie as well as I do, I know this means she thinks he's attractive, and he's a cute one even I must admit.

"Hey do you wanna dance?" he asks Kylie and I catch the blush that coats her cheeks.

She looks at me, and I know she's debating with herself on what to do. I know she doesn't want to ditch me, but she thinks he guy is hot, which he is.

I smile. "Go," I tell her.

"Are you sure?" she asks tentatively though her eyes are already on the cute guy and her hand in his.

"Yes, go have fun," I say. "I need another drink anyways," I tell her truthfully. Mine was only half gone before someone bumped into me and I dropped it spilling beer everywhere.

I toss her a quick thumbs up before she turns to the guy, and I turn and head towards the coolers once more.

The sun has finally dipped below the ocean, and darkness surrounds us now. The night is clear and the stars are bright, and I can't help myself from wishing Cale was here.

I reach the cooler and dig through the half-melted ice for another beer. I stand and crack the can when I hear a deep voice behind me speak. "You finally acquire the taste?" the voice says playfully.

I twist on my heel and can't stop the way my face lights up seeing his. He's wearing a pair of khaki shorts, and a navy blue shirt and he's never looked better. Though I think that every time I see him.

"Why are you here?" I ask taking a step closer whilst sipping on my beer.

Cale stuffs his hands into his front pockets. "Let's get out of here," he says with the tilt of his head.

My shoulders sag at his words. "Why?" I ask slowly.

"So we can be together," he says like it's obvious. "I mean that's what you wanted right?" he questions.

I shake my head lightly. "That's not what I wanted Cale," I tell him. "Not at all," I reiterate.

His face scrunches in confusion. "Gray, I don't get it," he says slowly. "You practically begged me to come so we can hang out, but now you're telling me you don't want to hang out..." he trails off.

I toss my half filled beer into the trash and begin to walk away from this conversation and from Cale. "Whatever," I mumble under my breath.

As soon as I take a couple steps away Cale's hand shoots out to grab onto my elbow and stop me. "Gray, I don't get why you're mad at me right now," he says as irritation laces through his tone.

I pull my arm out from under his grasp because I can never think clearly when his hands are on me. "Exactly Cale, you don't get it," I tell him pointedly.

"Can we just talk about this in private?" he asks as his eyes flit around to the party around us.

I look around and not one person is looking at us. They are drinking, and dancing, and having the time of their lives right now. They couldn't care less about us, and yet that's still all Cale cares about.

"No ones even paying attention to us!" I shout aggravated at the whole situation.

"Gray, please just come on," he pleads.

I roll my eyes. "Whatever," I grumble once again.

Cale stomps over to the local burger shack that's shut down for the evening, and we walk to the back of it so we are hidden from the whole party. It's dark behind here besides a single light that illuminates a small about of the area around us.

I lean against the worn wooden siding and cross my arms across my chest. "What Cale?" I ask tersely.

"What is wrong with you Gray?" he questions. "I thought I was doing what you wanted," he says as his palms turn up in confusion.

"No!" I exclaim. "This is never what I wanted Cale! I wanted to spend time with you at a party on the beach with my friends!" I shout at him not getting why he can't understand what I want. I'm not asking him to tell everyone about us, I am asking for just one night. That's all.

He shrugs at me. "I just don't want to go public yet, I already told you that," he says. "What more can I say?" he sighs.

"It's not about being public Cale. You can show up to a party and no one has to know we are together!" I tell him. "There are hundreds of people out there and no one cares what you do, or what I do!" I point out.

"Gray I don't know what to say," he starts. "I'm sorry I just don't know what you want from me right now, I told you—"

I throw my hands in the air in frustration. "I know its just summer and it's fun," I say repeating his words from weeks earlier. "But I can't stop the fact that I like you a lot Cale," I say my voice breaking slightly. "And I want to do fun things with you, and that includes this party."

"I just can't be seen with you yet—"

"Why?" I ask my voice thick and full of tears that want to spill over.

"My family is really strict with everything right now and you're a few years younger—"

"And I'm not good enough am I?" I say finishing his sentence for him.

He stalks forward. "Of course that's not it Gray," he says forcefully.

"Then what Cale? I can't just hide in the shadows and wait for you to—"

His lips cut off my words and I don't stop him. His body pushes into mine until I'm up against the wooden siding and his hands are all over me.

Cale's hands are in my hair pulling me closer as his tongue plays with mine in a mess of wild need. His touch becomes more fervent as his lips press into mine even harder. He is kissing me so hard and with so much desperation that I feel myself melting even further into his touch. I forget about being upset with Cale, I forget about the party, I forget about everything besides his lips and his touch. Because Cale is the drug I never knew I needed or wanted, but I was instantly addicted.

His hands tug at my hair, and hard as if he's having a hard time controlling himself. I love the fact that I'm the one causing him to lose control, and at the same time I need him to lose control. I need him to touch me. I need him to need me, because at times it feels like I'm the only one who feels this way.

Cale's hands roughly pull my blonde locks until my head bends back and I'm at his will. His teeth graze down my neck, and I let out a low moan as heat coils deep within my stomach. When his teeth lightly sink in the curve where my neck meets my shoulder I feel the heat spread between my legs, and Cale is the only one who can ease the fire burning through me.

His lips replace his teeth and soon he's peppering my neck with his perfect mouth. When I feel his hot wet tongue run up my neck I almost lose it. I drop my grip on his messy hair, and run my hands up Cale's chest loving the way his body feels under my touch. I tug on his shirt as I start to shake lightly. "Ohmygod," I gasp as his teeth nip at my earlobe.

Cale's lips caress the shell of my ear as he whispers into my ear. "Let me show you how much you mean to me," he says as his heated breath spills into my ear making me whimper. "Let me show you how good you are Gray," he says almost growling my name out.

Just as the words leave and fall from his mouth one of his hands untangle from my hair. He begins to trail up the soft skin of my thigh while the other hand remains wrapped up in my blonde wisps.

His hand pushes the hem of my dress out of the way as he hooks my leg around his waist and pushes even further into me. Aligning our hips, showing me exactly how much he wants me, how much I mean to him.

The slight fabric of my dress is pushed aside as his hand comes in contact with the thin string on my hip.

A deep grumble sounds deep in his throat as his hand plays with the edge of my underwear. "You are so fucking perfect Grayson." I love the way he curses. I love the way he says my full name against the curve of my neck. I love too much about him to only like him. "Don't ever doubt what I feel for you." I don't want to doubt him, but I do because even what I feel for him scares the hell out of me.

I raise my hands from his chest and settle them on either side of his perfect face. I lift his face from my neck so that his nose grazes mine, and our eyes are locked. I wet my lips with my tongue and let out a deep sigh that mixes with his sweet breath.

"Then show me," I say my voice raspy as I swallow the nerves that want to rise within me. "Show me what you feel for me," I tell him as I let my hips roll lightly into his causing his hand to grip my hip tightly.

"Oh, I will," he tells me. Just before his pink lips press back into mine, and his fingers dive into my underwear and I close my eyes and see a different kind of fireworks.

God, I love the fourth of July.

I blink a few times as the memory fades away into the darkness. My skin is heated in lust and in anger at the memory that moved its way into my thoughts.

My gaze lands across the deck onto Cale and Bailey cuddling under a single blanket as the sky lights up with beautiful fireworks.

I want to love the fireworks, I want to fall into them, and get lost in the sky. But I can't because the reason for the pain of my past and of my heart is sitting right across from me with my sister. I'm over Cale, and yet my heart still aches in moments like this. In moments where I'm alone and he's with her, loving her, touching her.

Damn, I hate the fourth of July.

My phone dings to alert me of a text message. I look down to see the text is from Max. I quickly open it to see: wish I were with you tonight. Miss you

Suddenly my heart doesn't hurt as much anymore, and the sparks in the sky seem just slightly more interesting than they did a moment before.

Chapter Twenty-Four

7/12/15

"AGH, GRAY LOOK at this turnout!" My sister Bailey exclaims as she jumps up and down in excitement.

The house is filled with a ton of our family and Bailey's friends for her bridal shower. The house is decorated with pastel streamers and balloons and table cloths. It's simple and beautiful, and most definitely my mother's choice of decorations rather than Bailey's more extreme taste.

"It's going to be great party Bai," I say truthfully.

Bailey swipes a hand over her white eyelet dress and tucks a strand of dark hair behind her ear. "How do I look?" she asks nervous as if she could ever look anything but perfect even in a simple sundress.

I smile at her. "You look beautiful," I tell her. "Now go mingle before cake and presents!" I chuckle.

She nods at my words. "Okay, okay," she starts. "Thanks," she says with a touch of a smile and walks towards the crowd of guests that continue to fill our house.

I take a deep breath and turn around to see Max leaning a hip against the counter on the other side of the kitchen. He is pouring himself a glass of punch as he snacks on some crackers and cheese. I walk over and slide up right next to him before lifting my gaze to his. The corner of his eyes crinkle just slightly, and I can't deny how much I love the way his green eyes change when they meet mine. They go a shade darker, almost wilder, and I love that I do that to him.

Max immediately hands the drink he was pouring for himself to me. In the most simplest of ways Max always shows me how much he cares. I take a quick sip of the tart punch before setting it down. "Thanks for coming again," I tell him quietly as if we are in our own little bubble. We stand in the corner of the kitchen away from the chatter and the excitement of the party.

He sets down his own drink and wraps an arm around my shoulders pulling me into his body lightly. "Of course Grayson," his deep voice responds. "I'll always come," he comments last and my heart stutters with nerves and anticipation at his words.

I'm still not use to my feelings for him. I know I'm falling for him, slowly but steadily. Yet at the same time it scares the hell out of me. It's hard to remember the exact moment I fell for Cale, because it feels like I fell for him the moment he sat next to me in the sand. It feels like I loved him from the moment he first said my name, or asked me out, or held my hand, or kissed me. That summer was a blur of emotions that ran wild, and it didn't end well. Obviously.

So now trying to be in a relationship, a real honest to god relationship is difficult. I don't know how to navigate myself through these feelings, because I've only felt them once. But as Max swipes his thumb against my neck slowly and absentmindedly my body can't help but sink a little bit more into his, and my mind clears. My worries seem small, and my body hums at peace as my thoughts falls silent. Because this is what falling should feel like, effortless and with no concerns.

"So how was your fourth?" I ask leaning my head against his shoulder. We texted a little back and forth since the summer holiday, but haven't really had a moment to talk. With Bailey's wedding coming up so fast, my mother and I have been running around like chickens with their heads cut off trying to help with the finishing touches.

My head rises slightly as he lifts his shoulders in a shrug. "Fine," he answers simply. "It was fun to see some cousins, but you know how family can get."

I chuckle. "Yeah, I do," I respond understanding exactly where he is coming from. My family can be a bit much at time, or all the time.

Max had gone up to Tallahassee with his mother to see family. He thought he was going to be in town and be able to hang out with my family and me, but his mother had other plans. "Did your mom have fun though?" I ask knowing that she was the reason they went up there. After her surgeries she's been having a hard time getting around hence the reason Max is staying with her and helping her with her shop. But that also means she hasn't been able to go see her family since Easton lies on the opposite side of Florida from them.

"She had the most amazing time, she definitely needed it," he says.

I lift my head and turn to face him. "I'm glad you went then," I say truthfully. "Though I am sad I didn't get to be with you," I admit running my finger over the color of his linen button up. "And you missed the best view in the town," I tease as I playfully bump my shoulder into his.

"What, you?" he asks with a smirk playing at his lips.

I roll my eyes. "I meant the annual firework show," I state but can't help the smile that lifts my cheeks.

Max takes a string of my hair and places it carefully behind my right ear as if he's afraid I might break. His eyes paint over every inch of my face as if he needs to take it all in, as if he can't miss one thing. "No, I definitely missed the best view," he expresses quietly before placing a lingering kiss against the corner of my mouth.

My body runs warm at the action, and my eyes flutter closed at the small gesture. Max pulls back and I place a hand on his flushed cheek. His face and lips still so close to mine, and I love the way his eyes dance between my lips and eyes as if he can't choose where to land his gaze.

"Thank you," I croon.

His eyes narrow as confusion fills his green eyes. "For what?" he questions.

My tongue darts out and wets my lips. "For making me happy," I answer.

Max's eyes soften and a touch of a smile lifts his face, and before he can fully lean back in to kiss me someone stops us. Actually someone's words stop us.

"Oh, well I guess we can all see who will be next up on the engagement train," Bailey says as suddenly a whole house full of eyes land on Max and myself. Sappy smiles and cheers erupt from the crowd that stares at us.

I instantly pull out of his hold. My body may be flushed with embarrassment, but my insides run cold. Max reaches out a hand to stop me, and pull me back to him. Like we can return to that small moment where it felt like we were the only two in the room. But we can't. The moment is so far over, it's gone, and I need space now.

"I um...just need to go grab something," I say as I walk away from the kitchen, the crowd, and Max.

"Grayson..." he trails as he takes a step to follow me. He knows Bailey's words spooked me, though he doesn't know why. He still knows little from my past as I haven't gathered the courage to tell him how beyond repair I was crushed.

"Alone," I tell him pointedly as he takes one more step near me. I turn on my heel towards my room and quickly shut the door behind myself. I slide down against the closed door until I reach the cool wooden floor. I need a minute, and I need moment alone.

I can only heal so fast. I've moved on from Cale, and I'm letting myself fall for Max. I'm opening up my heart, and letting my walls down for the first time in a long time. But the future? That still scares the shit out of me truth be told.

I'm at the age where everyone is finding "the one", and trying to get married as soon as possible. Because soon we will be out in the real world and being alone apparently is frowned upon. But I don't want to be like that. I don't mind me being on my own. Hell, I've been on my own for years, no man needed. I have my family and I have Hayley, what else would I need?

I shut my eyes and take a few calming breaths. I don't want to be afraid of the future, but it's such a scary thing. I can't control the future, I can't control or foresee anything that can happen, and that freaks me out.

Max and I are having fun. I like him a lot. Why does that have to mean wedding bells? Why do people have to automatically assume we will be anything?

I've put all my eggs into one basket before. I fell without fear of the future, and look where that got me.

Suddenly there is a knock at the door. I squeeze my eyes shut and force myself to stand up from the ground just as another loud knock resounds off the door. "Just a minute," I tell whomever is on the other side as I run a hand over my now wrinkled clothing.

I twist the doorknob and open the door to reveal Max. "Max, I—" I start but cut myself off not knowing what to say next. Not knowing how to explain myself.

But he just stalks forward and shuts the door behind himself hastily, and before I can even comprehend what is happening his lips are pressed against mine. I don't know how his hands end up on me, or how he ends up so close that his body is pressed up against mine, but all I know is that I immediately respond. I kiss him back, and I kiss him back with everything.

His lips slowly move against mine and make me forget about the future, and everything else that still worries me. The wall that I have is slowly crumbling, and that's all because of Max. He doesn't give up on me, even though I always give him a reason to. He stays, and while I don't know why I appreciate it more than he can ever know.

Max pulls away, but he lets his lips still lightly brush against mine causing me to shiver in response. "Don't keep running Grayson, I'm here," he whispers to me, against me. "Like I said before, I'll always come."

"Why?" I breathe. "I'm a mess and I know it, and I don't deserve you honestly—"

He cuts me off with his lips once again. Stopping my fears, my doubts, my everything. He silences the worry that wants to rise within me, and fills me with a calm instead. A calm I've craved for so long, but thought I could never have.

"Because," he says once he breaks away. "Because you have this sadness in your eyes that shows when you think no one else is looking, but when you look at me they brighten," he says. "And you don't seem as sad anymore, and I get to be that reason, I want to be that reason," he tells me.

"I'm sorry," I sigh. Because I am sorry, and I don't deserve Max, but I selfish enough to keep him.

"Don't let them scare you Grayson, this relationship is what we want it to be," he declares. "Don't listen to what they're saying. This is ours and it can go no where or everywhere, but just remember that," he pushes.

"It's ours," I repeat his words back to him as he nods his wild eyes holding onto my own.

Then his lips press once again into mine.

Chapter Twenty-Five

7/15/15

I SIT AT the kitchen island with my bowl of cereal as I twirl my spoon in circles in the milk.

I'm not eating any of it. I'm just letting it become a soggy mess as my mind wanders. Because what I do today could change everything, and that scares me like no other. But at the same time I know it's something I need to, something I should've done a long time ago.

I've debated with myself a lot over the past couple of days on whether or not I should do this. But I know if I were in her position, no matter what, I would want to know. And after the talk I had with Max I know I also need this. This secret that I'm keeping isn't helping anyone, especially me.

I hear footsteps coming down the stairs from behind me, and I don't have to turn to see whom it is. "Hey Cale," I mutter before I take a sip of my water.

His steps audibly stop behind me, as if he is stunned that I even said anything to him. But he doesn't realize that I have a lot more to say than just "hi" today.

Cale walks around the island and stops once he is directly across from me. His hazel eyes roam over my face as if he's trying to read my mood, but he won't ever guess what I'm about to say next. His blonde hair is messy, and his t-shirt and boxers just as wrinkled. He obviously just woke up, and he wasn't expecting me.

"I though you would've left with Bailey already for the fitting," he says awkwardly. We haven't spoken much besides pleasantries since the whole admission of love and me forcing him to let me go. It's just easier to keep our distance, especially with the wedding approaching so quickly.

I slide off my stool and walk around to the sink where he stands. "She had an errand to run first, so I said I would meet her there instead," I tell him as I dump my mushy cereal remains into the sink and run water over the bowl.

I switch the water off and turn to face Cale as I cross my arms across my chest. "We need to talk," I announce keeping my face even. I would rather come across cold then show him one ounce of emotion. I'm over Cale. I am.

He takes a step back obviously not liking my words. "About what?" he asks cautiously.

I run my tongue over my teeth all of the sudden nervous to tell him, nervous to actually follow through. But I am, and I do. "I'm telling her the truth," I say not needing to say my sister's name for Cale to understand what I am saying.

His eyes narrow immediately at my words. "What is that supposed to mean?" he questions.

I tilt my head. "I'm telling her everything, I don't want to hide anything anymore," I tell him.

"Why does she need know?" he pushes as he runs a hand over his face. His body is tense, and his hands clench over and over again as if that is the only he can expel the energy running through him right now.

"It's something I need to do Cale, and if I were her I would want to know—"

"Well you aren't her, so you can't really know what she wants can you," he argues cutting me off.

I drop my head. I didn't want to start a fight with him this morning. I just wanted to at least warn him of what I was planning so he wouldn't be caught off guard if Bailey questioned him about that summer. "I'm not going to go into detail with her, or paint you in a bad picture—"

"Oh, really?" he taunts. This time he crosses his hands over his chest as if he doesn't believe me.

I scoff. "No Cale!" I exclaim a tad pissed he would assume I would do such a thing. I may have never been happy about them being together, but I would never ruin my sister's happiness. "She loves you, I wouldn't do that to her," I tell him. I'm not trying to break their relationship up. I'm just trying to free myself from anymore lies. The weight of these secrets has weighed heavily on me for years, and I'm over it. I'm trying to untangle myself completely from Cale and that summer so that I can finally be free.

"Then what are you going to say?" he asks.

I lift a single shoulder. "That we had a summer fling, and it ended," I say simply enough to him. "But it's something I think she deserves to know."

"So why are you telling me this?" he asks as he takes a step towards me.

I take a step backward.

I don't think Cale realized he walked towards me, and when he sees my step back he also takes another away from me. We keep our space from each other because it's safer this way. It's safer than the alternative of falling into a past that may feel good at first, but comes with so much baggage in the end.

I quickly grab my phone and purse off of the counter. "In case she wants to talk to you about it, or if for some reason she doesn't believe me," I say as I start towards the door.

"Why wouldn't she believe you?" he calls after me.

"Who knows, it's Bailey," I say with a shrug as if that explains everything. "So there you go, I told you," I continue as I throw Cale one last look over my shoulder before walking out the door and out to my car.

I turn the music up loudly in my car, and try and block out the way his hazel eyes held onto mine at the very end. I try to block out everything about Cale, because I'm over him. I am.

* * * * *

As Bailey and I walk into I Do, Helen greats us with a full smile and an excited wave. "Well isn't it just my favorite sister duo," she chirps as she claps her hands together.

"How are you today Helen?" I ask as we approach the front desk to check in for Bailey's fitting.

She waves a hand in dismissal. "Oh, you know just another Wednesday afternoon here, nothing too crazy," she says as she types away at her computer.

"And we didn't need to bring anything correct?" Bailey asks Helen as she continues to type away on her phone. She has barely taken her eyes away from her cell since the moment we got here. I know she has emails, and other important wedding stuff to manage, but it's still slightly annoying.

Helen shakes her head in response. "Nope, just your beautiful self," she tells us with another quick smile lighting up her face. She really is the sweetest. "Okay," she tells us as she clicks her mouse one last time. "You are all checked in, and Alicia should be up here soon to grab you both for alterations," she says. "Though it could be a few minutes because I know she has been running slightly behind today, but no worries we will get you in and make sure everything is perfect," she assures us, well more like Bailey. I couldn't care less if this appointment is right on time.

Bailey nods. "It's all good, I have a few more emails to catch up on anyways," she says before making her way to the waiting area sofa.

I raise my eyebrows shocked by my sister's reaction, but follow her to the waiting area nonetheless.

"You were very calm about that," I comment to Bailey as I grab a magazine and begin to flip through the glossy pages.

She sets her phone down for a second and looks at me. "I know right!" she exclaims, as if she is so proud of herself for being an adult about something. I hold in the urge to roll my eyes. "I've been working on my bridezilla-ness lately," she tells me as her eyes cast back down to her buzzing phone. I swear that thing hasn't stopped going off for the past month.

I hold back the laugh that wants to bubble up at her words, knowing that she's being actually serious. "Well that's great Bai," I state simply, honestly not knowing what else to say.

"So you said you needed to talk about something today," she starts. "So talk," she tells me not knowing at all the bomb she is asking me to drop on her right now.

My lips curl inward as I sink back into the plush sofa. "We can wait until after the appointment," I tell her trying to get her to drop the subject. Now really isn't the time or the place to get into this discussion.

She's rapidly responding to some email as her nails continue to tap away on the screen of her phone. How the thing hasn't cracked by her rapid messaging yet is completely shocking.

"No, come on spill," she says still focusing on her phone. "After this I have to run a few other errands, and I'm uber busy the next few days also. So I'd rather you just tell me what you need to tell me now," she expresses.

Nerves crash on me like waves do onto a shore, and I feel my bottom lip begin to quiver at the prospect of saying these words to my sister. My resolve from earlier is quickly dwindling, and I feel myself begin to chicken out. What happened to my determination? But what if Cale is right? What if she doesn't need to know?

No!

Cale is right about nothing. Bailey deserves to know, and beyond that this is something I need to do for my own sanity and future happiness. Something I need to do to continue to move on and focus my attention on Max.

Before I can stop myself I blurt, "I dated Cale."

The incessant tapping that hasn't stopped for a second from Bailey all of the sudden halts. Besides the soft music playing overhead in the boutique there is nothing but a heavy silence that lingers between my sister and myself.

I shift my head lightly to the left to see her big blue eyes that match my own widen as her lips part in a mixture of disbelief and confusion.

"What?" she breathes.

I wet my lips before speaking, not realizing how dry my mouth had become all of a sudden. "Well not dated per say..." I trail uneasy. "More like a fling," I say trying to make it sound better, but I don't miss the way she winces at my choice of the word "fling".

Bailey tucks her dark hair behind her ears and turns to face me as much as she can on the sofa. Her phone still buzzes, but this time she couldn't care less about who's contacting her. "When?" she questions as her face pulls in a look of bitter sadness.

I play with the hem of my tank attempting to avoid my sister's gaze. "Just for a summer," I confess her. "When I was sixteen," I specify.

Bailey was never good at hiding her emotions like I am, and now in this moment is no exception. Deep hurt fills her eyes as her shoulders sag. "Why didn't you tell me?" she demands.

"Because you're engaged and I didn't want to take away from what you have with Cale, but—"

"No," she says stopping my words as well as raising a hand to end my rambling. "Why didn't you tell me about him when you were sixteen?" she asks clarifying her earlier question.

I'm taken back by her words. I shrug not knowing how to answer her question. "I don't know..." I trail. "I didn't tell anybody about it," I tell her almost trying to make her feel better about the situation.

"You told not one person, really?" she says not believing me.

My palms turn up as an exasperated sigh falls from my lips. "Okay, I told one person, but that's it Bai," I tell her adamantly not understanding why she's fixating on this small part of what I admitted. "Seriously, no one knew," I reiterate.

"Who?" she asks simply.

"Who what?" I ask losing track of where this conversation has now headed.

"Who did you tell?" she pushes again.

"Kylie," I finally answer after a long pause. I don't know why it matters whom I told, or that I didn't tell Bailey. Shouldn't she be focusing more on that part that I dated her fiancé?

She bobs her head slowly as her offended eyes finally leave mine and fall back onto her continuously buzzing phone.

"Bailey—"

She cuts me off once more. "I just want to say that I don't even care that you and Cale once had a fling," she starts. "Yes, of course that hurts, but knowing that your own sister felt and obviously still feels like she can't share things with someone who loves them unconditionally hurts even more," she expresses. Her voice is thick as if tears are on the brink, and I can't help the way my heart contracts with a sharp sting.

I want to say something to ease her hurt, and my own aching heart. But no words fall from my parted lips, because there are no words to fix this moment.

"I've missed you so much these past few years," Bailey continues. "And every single time something important happened in my life you were the first person I called Grayson," she says using my full name. Her words breaking as tears begin to fill her emotion filled eyes.

"I don't know what to say," I admit. My throat feels clogged as tears threaten to fall, but I hold the emotion back knowing I don't have a reason to cry right now. Bailey is right. I am in the wrong here. We used to be so damn close, and I broke that bridge the moment Cale walked into my life.

Kylie might've not known the extent of my relationship with Cale, but she at least knew about us. I tore myself not only away from my parents, but also from my sister. The one person who I used to tell everything to, and who is my eternal best friend. I turned my back on the one person who will never not love me, no matter how bad I mess up. Though this time it feels like I might've messed up in a way that's permanent. And not even the pain of Cale breaking my heart can top the way my heart is breaking in this very instant.

"I can still remember the time you ran into my room and told me about your first kiss," Bailey says as a sad smile lifts the corner of her lips. "You were fourteen and you kissed Sawyer Thawten," she sniffles. "You would tell me everything back then. And when all my friends would talk about how much they hated their siblings I was proud to say you were my best friend." Tears openly fall down her face and seeing my sister cry makes me want to break down. And knowing I'm the cause of her pain makes me want to curl into a ball and cry even more.

Guilt, shame, and disappointment drive through my veins, as I feel even worse about myself. I told myself I wouldn't be the cause of my sister's pain, and even after letting Cale go here I still am. I ruined the one great relationship I had, and for what? A fleeting moment of bliss? A broken heart?

"I knew you were seeing someone that summer," she finally discloses to me.

"What?" I ask hoarsely as tears still threaten to spill over.

"You were always gone, and you had this permanent smile on your face that never left and I knew you were in love. And I waited," she says. "I waited for you to come to my room and tell me all about your first love, but you never did," she breaks off her voice filled with a deep sorrow.

I open my mouth to say something, but again no words come out.

"Then you were sad, so sad. And I waited again. I waited for you to come into my room and tell me about the asshole that gave you your first broken heart, but again you never did. You turned away from me, and our parents. And before I knew it you were miles and miles away at a new college with a new best friend," she pauses as a single tear slides down her cheek. "A new sister."

"Bailey—"

But she stands up and tosses her cell into her purse. "I'm sorry I have to go, I need some space," she rushes out.

I quickly stand to stop her, but I know nothing I say can fix what I've done. Nothing can fix how deeply I've hurt her.

"I'm so sorry Helen we need to reschedule," she barely utters out before running out of the boutique.

Helen casts me a look of worry, but I can't even focus on her at the moment. I sit back against the sofa and finally let the tears I have kept at bay openly stroll down my face. The one relationship that was a constant when I was growing up, that literally ran blood deep I ruined. And I finally thought we were making steps towards mending that bond. But then I come in and ram a wrecking ball right into it.

I was so focused on how she would take the fact that I dated Cale, I didn't even stop to think how she would feel about me keeping a whole part of my life from her.

I blame Cale for a lot of things that went wrong in my life, but this right here isn't his fault. This is all mine. I ruined my relationship with my sister, and I have to find a way to fix it. Because my sister may annoy me at times, but she is still my sister and she deserves more than I've been giving her.

So much more.

Chapter Twenty-Six

7/23/15

"WHAT ARE YOU doing here?" I scream as I throw my arms around my best friends neck in pure excitement.

Hayley's arms circle me as she hugs me back just as hard. "Seriously why aren't you in Chicago right now?" I ask confused.

She pulls away as she hoists her duffel bag back onto her shoulder. I had knocked it off in my shock of seeing her face behind my front door.

"When you called the other night I told my supervisor that I needed a few days off," she says. "I told her my best friend needs me," she shrugs simply as if it was that easy.

I toss my arms back around her and give her a big squeeze. "Thank you, thank you, thank you," I repeat quietly as I feel my eyes wet slightly with gratitude.

It has been exactly one week since my big blowout with Bailey at the dress shop. She hasn't been home since, and she's been ignoring my texts and calls. I know I messed up in a way that won't be fixed easily, but I just need her to give me a chance.

"So Bailey hasn't answered you yet, huh?" Hayley asks as she pulls away from my fierce hug.

I shrug trying to play it off, but I know my best friend can see right through me. "I fucked up," I tell her as my whole body sags in defeat.

Hayley tosses her arm around my shoulder and pulls me in to her side lightly. "We usually do with the ones that mean the most," she says quietly. "Now," she continues with a more chipper attitude as she pulls away from me. "Show me to your room so I can set this bag down it's beyond heavy," she says as she heaves the bag back up onto her shoulders.

"What do you have in there?" I ask. "A body?" I joke.

She just smirks at me a throws me a wink. "Wouldn't you like to know," she states. "Now onto your room!" she shouts as she comes up behind me and starts shoving me forward.

I can't help but laugh. It's the first time I've truly felt happy all summer and I needed this. Hayley gets me like no one else does. I understand now that I shouldn't have thrown away my relationship with my sister and forgotten about her while I forged a new one with Hayley. But that doesn't take away from the fact that Hayley was there for me when I was afraid to let anyone in. She stood by my side and never let me feel less, and for that I am forever thankful.

I lead her towards my room and push the door open for her. She quickly drops her bag of bricks onto the floor and flings herself onto my mattress. "Ugh, this feels amazing," she groans into my body pillow.

"Dramatic much?" I tease as I slouch onto the opposite end of my bed from Hayley.

She rolls over so she's on her back and tucks her hands behind her head. "Always," she says as she turns her head to smile at me.

I roll my eyes. "Wow, I can't believe I missed you," I state dryly.

She lets out a small laugh. "I know I'm awesome," she says completely ignoring my sarcastic comment. "Now," she starts as she rolls onto her side to face me. "Tell me about this Max man," she says as she wiggles her eyebrows at me suggestively.

I can't help the grin that blooms onto my lips at the mention of his name.

"Oh, so that good huh?" Hayley drawls with a smirk plastered across her face.

I blush unable to answer.

"So have you two..." she trails as she motions her hands in a lewd fashion.

I playfully shove her hands away. "No, we haven't for your information," I tell her.

"Why not?" she asks as if it's that simple. "He's beyond hot!" she exclaims.

My forehead drags together in confusion. "How would you know?"

"As your best friend it is my duty to know every guy you date so that you are never blindsided," she states.

I let out a single dry laugh. "So you Internet stalked him?" I ask though I already know the answer.

"Oh, I stalked so hard!" she says as she falls into a pit of giggles.

"You're the worst," I play with a smile on my face.

"And you still love me," she sings. And Hayley is beyond right. I do love her and her crazy stalking, and wild boy stories, and her huge heart that makes her a fiercely loyal friend.

I sigh before asking the question I don't really care to ask, but want to seem nice at the same time so ask anyways. "So," I pause. "How's Maxine?" I ask trying to pretend I care even one bit.

"Wow, shocked you even asked about your other bestie," she mocks.

I shake my head slightly. "What can I say," I pause with a small shrug. "I'm trying to become a better person."

"Trying being the operative word," Hayley teases.

I roll my eyes once more. "Whatever," I mumble.

"But for your information she's doing great," she says. "Still quiet, but super sweet."

"As long as you don't like the ginger more than me I couldn't care less how sweet she is," I mumble. I know I should be more mature than this, but something about Maxine's quiet demeanor rubs me the wrong way. I feel like she's always hiding something, when in reality I know she's most likely hiding nothing. Because let's be real, her life is far from interesting.

"Gray—"

I cut her off. "I'm sorry," I start. "I'm trying," I repeat as I play with ends of my dry and sun-damaged hair.

Hayley places her hand on my arm stopping my actions. "While I love the ginger, she will never be you G," she says earnestly.

I try and hide the smile that wants to consume my face at her words, but I can't stop it. This summer has been such a difficult time and it's nice to know that even through these ups and downs our friendship hasn't changed.

"Hey, want to meet some awesome people?" I ask trying to brush off the wave of unwanted emotions that want to rush through me.

Hayley slaps a hand over her chest in feign shock. "More awesome than me?"

I lift a single shoulder. "They are pretty cool..." I trail.

My best friend immediately stands and places her hands on her hips. "Well I must meet these people to double check this, because you know how awesome I am," she says seriously though I can't help but giggle. "These words are hurtful Gray, just hurtful," she speaks as she fakes sadness.

"Hurtful?" I question.

She slaps her hand over her chest once again. "Hurtful," she jokingly reiterates.

I stand up from my bed and link my arm through hers. "Well then we better leave so we can verify my assessment," I tease back.

"Most definitely," she agrees lacing her arm through mine as I lead us out of my house and towards my car.

Hayley's back, and I'm happier then I have been in a long time.

* * * * *

"And who do we have here?" Chase asks as he stands up from the table he's sitting behind.

"Chase," I pause motioning to him. "Kylie, this is Hayley—"

"Ohmygosh Hayley!" Kylie exclaims shooting out of her seat immediately at my words. "We've heard so much about you!"

"Awful things I bet," Hayley winks.

"Oh, the worst obviously," Kylie jokes back instantly as she walks over and envelopes Hayley in a hug.

Hayley laughs at Kylie's words. "I like you already," she declares.

Kylie takes a step back and Chase comes over after. "It's great to finally meet you," he says as he gives Hayley a hug as she returns one just as quickly.

We move to sit down but not before Hayley grabs my arm tightly. "Dibs," she whispers.

My face scrunches in confusion. "On who?"

"Chase, duh," she says as if I'm dumb and blind. "Why didn't you tell me more about this tasty brother," she says as she ogles Chase and rakes her eyes over him.

I want to say something, but I don't. I can't. Because it's not only not my place, but Chase is also confused right now and he might be into Hayley. So I bite my tongue and with a lazy shrug I say, "Just don't see it I guess," I say simply.

She shakes her head in response. "Fine by me," she responds before sitting down right next to Chase at the table.

Besides the unsettling nerves that lace through me about Hayley and Chase, a wave of calmness also hits me. I'm surrounded by people who love me for me, and who will stand by me no matter what. These are the friends everyone waits their whole lives for, and I have mine.

For a fleeting moment I'm happy, and I love it. I want this happiness to last, but for some reason I know it won't. So for now I smile, I sit down, and I enjoy the company of my friends. My people.

Chapter Twenty-Seven

8/1/15

KNOCK. KNOCK. KNOCK.

My knuckles rap against Bailey's bedroom door three times. I tuck a single strand of hair behind my ear as I rock between my heels. Nervousness flutters it's way through my chest as I stand outside of my sister's bedroom door.

"Come in!" I hear my sister's voice call out.

I push the door open to see my sister sitting at her vanity as she curls her dark hair. Bailey's eyes meet mine briefly before focusing on her hair once more. "You look good," I comment as I shut the door behind myself and take a few steps into her room. Tonight is my sister's bachelorette party and we all decided to do little black dresses.

"Thanks," Bailey mumbles in response.

I take a gentle seat on the edge of her bed as she continues to fix her hair and ignore me.

"So," I pause dragging out the single syllable word. "Ask me," I tell her as I play with the hem of my dress anxiously. I don't know if she will go along with what I'm going to do, but I hope she does. Sorry isn't enough for Bailey, I have to show her.

Bailey pauses with her hair as her eyes meet mine in the mirror with a slight puzzled squint.

"Ask you?" she questions slowly.

"Yes," I agree. "Ask me," I state.

"Ask you what?" she asks still confused as to what I'm going on about.

"About Max," I say like it's obvious. "I think I'm falling for him…" I trail as my heart speeds up at my own words. "So ask me about him and our kiss, and he even met mom and dad—"

Bailey's body immediately flips as the curler hits the desk. "Wait, when did he meet them?" she shouts in shock.

"Almost a month ago," I tell her.

"A month?" she exclaims with wide eyes.

I shrug. "You've been busy with the wedding, and I don't know," I say more to myself than her. "It was a step, but I was still scared," I admit.

"And now?" she probes as she stands up from her vanity and comes and sits next to be on her plush bed.

A smile breaks across my lips at the thought of those green eyes and his hands on my hips. "I like him," I whisper. "A lot, and I didn't think it would go anywhere but—"

"It is!" Bailey squeals finishing my sentence.

I nod as her excitement begins to rub off on me.

"And the kissing?" she asks next.

A light blush coats my face and neck in heat.

"Oh, so that good?" she smirks with raised eyebrows.

"He's almost too perfect," I joke with only a slight edge of seriousness.

Bailey sits back against her pillows as she runs her hands down her tight dress. "That's how I feel about Cale," she says quietly almost like she's embarrassed to bring up his name.

"Good," I say as her eyes snap up to meet mine. "Because you are perfect, and you deserve nothing less Bai," I express.

Before I know it her arms are around my neck as she pulls me into her fluffed and curled hair tightly.

"I've missed you so much Gray," she says with tears laced in her voice.

I clutch onto her just as tightly. "I will never not tell you anything again Bai," I state. "And Hayley and I might be close, but she will never be you," I emphasize." And I don't want her to be because you are my sister and you are amazing."

"I love you Gray," she says pulling me in tighter if that's even possible.

"Love you more Bai," I respond.

* * * * *

"DRINK!" Hayley shouts over the loud music at the bar as we all down our tequila shots. My throat burns from the liquor, but the juice of the lime bursts through my taste buds and soothes the fire in my throat.

I giggle with the lime in my mouth as all the ladies cheer with victory for taking their shots like champs.

Bailey stumbles over with her bedazzled sash and flashing penis crown, and falls into me as she gives me a big hug. "Let's do more shots," she mumbles as her words slur slightly.

I shake my head as a smile lifts the edges of my lips. I push her up so that she is facing me and make sure her eyes meet mine. I can always tell how drunk Bailey is by how glazed over her eyes are in that moment. And by the state of her big blue eyes now she's right on the verge of throwing up.

"How about you drink some water and then dance some first," I tell her. "And then we can have more shots, deal?" I ask as a smile coats my lips.

Her head bobs in agreement as I grab one of my glasses of water from earlier off of the bar, and hand it to my sister. I make her down the whole glass before I hand her off to one of her friends from school, and they start dancing like their life depends on it.

Every single set of male eyes is on my sister, her friends, and Hayley. They watch eagerly as my hot friends run their hands down their bodies and shake their asses like it's their job. But as my eyes flick to the side there are just one pair of jungle green eyes that are locked on me and me only.

I walk over to Max and slide right between his bent legs as he sits on a stool at a small table. His eyes watch me carefully as I slowly bite my bottom lip and begin to drag my nails lightly across his jean-clad thighs. I lean in to place a small kiss at the corner of his pink lips, lingering just enough to feel his mouth smile from under mine. He smells incredible and I can't help but want him even more.

"You're drunk," he sings as I pull back so that our noses graze each other.

"I'm the perfect drunk," I counter with a smirk and another graze of my nails. I can see his green eyes turn darker as his hands snake their way around my waist.

"I'm not sure there really is a perfect drunk," he plays as his hands flex and tighten around my waist making me fall between his legs even more. With his body flush against mine I can really feel how much he wants me at this moment, and it makes me feel wild with this sudden need.

"Oh, there is," I confirm as my lips brush his.

A small groan leaves his lips as my body brushes up against his in the most delicious of places. "Do you want me?" I question teasingly.

"More than anything," he answers immediately as one of his hands drop to push behind the fabric of the skirt of my dress. His thumb brushes against my bare skin causing me to let out a small involuntary whimper.

My skin tingles with need as his thumb continues to circle my naked and flushed skin.

"What do you want to do to me?" I ask as I push my teasing to another level. I know I want Max, but in another way I love the teasing and the tension that is between us even more. I'm afraid of what will happen once we take it to the next level. I have been with other guys here and there, but I've only ever slept with one person that I had actual feelings for and it ended in a broken heart. But I know Max, and I'm falling for him. Max wouldn't hurt me...would he?

Once again doubt weaves its way through my body and I hate it, I hate everything about it.

"Grayson," he groans as his eyes fall to my lips tearing me away from the thoughts in my head. "I want to drag you into the bathroom and do so many things to you," he growls as his hand rises even higher under my dress making me shudder against his rough fingertips.

"Then why don't you?" I say as a single finger brushes the zipper on his jeans triggering him to push his hips lightly into my hand on reflex.

Max shakes his head at my words and grabs my hand to stop my teasing movements against him. I lick my lips and smirk as his dark eyes meet mine his hold tightens on my wrist making my breath stutter in excitement. He is so close to breaking and I want him to break, I want him to feel as out of control as he makes me feel. Every emotion I feel for him scares me, and Max always seems so calm and collected and perfect. But I don't want perfect right now. In this moment I need some wild.

"I can't," he states simply.

"Why?" I ask with raised eyebrows.

"Because Grayson," he starts. "You're drunk and this is your sister's bachelorette party and I'm just here to DD," he pauses. "Nothing more tonight."

"Why nothing more," I question again.

His hand is now completely under my dress, but we are so hidden in the corner that no one notices our forbidden touching. His fingers brush against the lace on my hip as my body flushes with white-hot heat.

"Because I want you sober—"

I cut him off, "But I'm not that dru—"

I try and argue but he cuts me off with his words and with his hand sliding around my bare hipbone making me wish he would drop his hand further and release the ache that has been growing steadily all night.

"I want you to feel everything I want to do to you Grayson," he breathes against my lips. "Every touch of my hands on you, and everywhere I want to kiss you" he rasps as his lips moves to graze against my neck making me tremble. "I don't want alcohol to cloud your head when we're together Grayson, I want you there with me completely."

"So you do want me?" I ask quietly as his lips brush my collarbone.

"I want every single part of you under me, on top of me, in the shower..." he lists as he nips at my neck playfully making a small giggle falls from my lips.

"Okay," I agree simply.

"Okay," he replies with a bright smile on his handsome face. "Now go dance with your sister and have the best night, I'll be right here ready for when you want to leave," he says as he takes a sip of the beer he's been nursing all night.

I bring my lips to his and kiss him lightly though my body urges me to push it further, but I don't. I keep the kiss light and playful as my hands circle his neck and taste the slight whisper of beer on his tongue. His hands is out from under my dress and brings them both to my waist as he tugs me closer to his warm body.

He pulls away after a few minutes but not before placing a few more pecks on my tingling lips.

"Go dance," he tells me with a small slap on the ass making me laugh.

"Only if you watch," I play with a wink.

Max smirks. "Wouldn't want to look anywhere else."

My body buzzes as I walk to the middle of the bar and dance until I can't dance anymore with my best friend and my sister.

* * * * * *

"Thanks again for tonight," I tell Max as he helps me put Bailey into bed upstairs.

"No problem at all," he says with a wave like it was nothing. But it was everything. He hung out with a bunch of drunk women all night, and stayed sober to drive us. He then helped me put Bailey and Hayley to bed as they were pretty gone by the end of the night.

I know I definitely don't deserve Max, but I'm too selfish to let him go at this point. We walk downstairs towards the front door as Cale staggers in and my whole body goes cold instantly at the site of him.

It's as if my two worlds are colliding and I don't know how to respond or feel in this moment.

It's been a while since our last conversation about me telling Bailey about our past. And ever since then it's been even more awkward because with Bailey aware of our past he's kept his attention far away from me. I haven't minded the time away though, because it meant time for me to spend with Max and focus on him and only him without fear of the past.

"Hi," I mumble hoping to just bypass him and continue to avoid him until I leave after the wedding.

But Max has another idea instead. "Hey man, Cale right?" he checks as Cale nods in response. "I'm Max, nice to meet you," he says as puts a hand out to shake Cale's hand.

Cale stares at Max's hand for a few long seconds before placing his hand in his and returning his shake.

Ugh, why does Max have to be such a nice guy?

"Nice to meet you too," Cale responds. His voice is even, though his eyes are narrowed in on Max.

"Did you have your bachelor party tonight also?" Max asks.

Cale nods as he stuffs his hands into the front pockets of his worn jeans. Jeans that make me think of that summer, so I quickly avert my gaze and focus on the profile of Max. "Yeah, fun night," Cale simply responds.

Max nods. "Cool, well have a good night," he says as he places his hand in mine and we walk out the front door together.

We reach Max's car and I place my hands on his cheeks and kiss him lightly. I pull back to look into his perfect eyes and can't help the small smile that pulls across my face at the sight of him. "Thank you so much for tonight," I say quietly as if we are in our own bubble.

He places a lingering kiss to my lips in return. "I'll always be here Grayson," he replies easily as he repeats his promise to me.

Max pulls away with one last peck to the lips before he heads to the drivers side of his car and slides in. I toss him a wave and one last look before I skip up the steps and into the front entryway with a huge smile plastered across my lips.

"So that's Max," Cale comments as I close the front door behind me.

And just like that the bubble Max created for me is popped and my smile drops.

My bottom lip folds into my mouth as I itch to run away from Cale and put some much needed distance between us. He's been drinking, and so have I, and last time we mixed those two ingredients we both ended up making a huge mistake.

But that won't happen again. I refuse to let that happen again.

"Yeah, that's Max," I curtly comment back.

I start to head to my room when a hand shoots out to stop me. A hand I know too well.

I rip my arm away and without looking back I say, "Leave me alone."

"Gray," he sighs quietly.

"No," I say harshly while keeping my gaze forward on my bedroom door.

I hear another sigh slip between his lips before I hear his footsteps retreat away from me towards the living room. I can hear the squeak of the hardwood floors, and the sound of his body sinking into the lush sofa, as I stand frozen in relief that he walked away.

Cale walked away, which means so can I.

I didn't fall into his trap or his gaze or his warmth. I get to walk away and continue to focus on my relationship with Max. I get to focus on my happiness.

My hand reaches for the doorknob when Cale says, "I never wanted to leave you."

He says it so quietly. So under his breath, that I almost didn't hear him. I wish I didn't hear him.

My body flips around to face the living room where Cale sits.

"What is that supposed to mean?" I barely breathe out.

His eyes meet mine as his drunken body sinks further into the couch. "It wasn't my idea," he starts. "My dad—"

I raise a hand to cut him off. "I can't hear this Cale," I whisper as my heart clenches between pain and anger and a small piece of hope even slips in. And that hope angers me even more.

Suddenly his body stumbles to a stand and he makes his way over to me, as I stand motionless. As he saunters forward my back hits the door I once believed I would walk through and leave Cale behind, and yet here I am.

His body sways in front of me as the smell of hard liquor and his cologne engulf me in a haze of confusion.

"He found out," he starts referring to his father. "He said you were too young, and the image was bad for the business, and he threatened to take away my inheritance and I was young and stupid—"

"Stop!" I whisper yell at him as I shove my hands against his hard chest.

He pushes forward so that his hands hit the door behind me and encase my head as his eyes flicker up and down my face. "No, Gray you have to know I've always loved you," he urges as his blood shot eyes meet mine. "And that I want you and I made a mistake," he rambles on as his body barely grazes mine.

Tears prick my eyes as my breathing becomes short and filled with anger and uncertainty at his words. My eyes close tightly because I can't stand to look at his face anymore. I can't listen to his lies anymore. I can't listen to him tell me he loves me anymore, I can't listen to anything from him anymore. Because if I do I will fall for what can never happen.

"Gray, it's you and it will always be—"

My eyes fly open finally. "No!" I say once again shoving him in the chest, this time harder.

He tries to grab at my hands, but I pull away.

"No, it isn't me and it never will be," I say forcefully. "You're engaged to my sister and you need to leave me the hell alone," I growl out before I tear into my room and slam the door shut behind me.

I have to stay away from Cale. I have to keep my distance or I will let him break me. I will let him ruin my progress and ruin what I have with Max for one last touch. One last kiss. Cale is my weakness, and I have to stay away to keep my strength.

Tears fill my eyes completely now as I sink to the floor against the door. I pull my legs into my arms and hold them close as I try and comfort myself from the confusion and anger that laces through me.

"Gray, are you okay?" Hayley says sleepily as I hear the rustling of sheets from my bed.

"No," I cry out as sobs wreck through my body and Hayley flies out of bed to wrap her arms around my body.

Why does he always make me feel so much? He makes me feel too much and I hate it.

I hate him.

Except I don't hate him, and that makes me hate myself even more.

Chapter Twenty-Eight

8/4/15

"UGH, I CAN'T believe you're leaving," I groan as I stand in the entryway of my house with Hayley and her bag lying by my feet.

I wrap my arms around her neck and pull her in close. She chuckles as her arms do the same to me.

"I'll see you in less than a week!" she says with a smile as she pulls away.

I nod. "I know, I know," I concede. "But I'll still miss you," I say with a small shrug.

"Same G," she admits to me.

"Thanks for coming again," I say as I pull at her duffel before handing it over to Hayley. I needed my best friend more than I even knew after my awful fall out with Bailey, and even the other night with Cale. She is my rock, and I love her for that.

"Anytime," she says as if it's nothing. "I loved getting to meet everyone," she tells me earnestly.

I roll my eyes jokingly. "You mean Chase," I tease.

Hayley shakes her head. "Chase is a cutie, but for some reason I wasn't feeling it," she says with the scrunch of her nose.

"Maybe you weren't his type," I say with a smirk.

She tosses her long hair over her shoulder and throws me one of her million dollar smiles. "Please Gray," she says with a raised brow. "I'm everyone's type."

I laugh though I know she's speaking the truth. She is what every guy wants, and she usually gets what she wants. I shove her shoulder with mine lightheartedly. "Alright it's time for you to leave now."

Hayley tosses her hand over her chest in feign shock. "What happened to the friend that was already missing me just a few minutes ago?"

"You know I love your crazy ass," I tell her.

She winks. "I know."

She pulls me in for one last hug, but not before whispering, "Four days and the wedding is over and you never have to see him again."

I pull back with a sigh at the thought of Cale. "Four days," I repeat.

"Focus on the future. Focus on Max," she urges. "Gray, you deserve to be happy."

"Do I?" I ask with a scoffing breath hating the doubt that weighs on my conscience daily.

Hayley's hand lands on my shoulder as her eyes meet mine. "More than anyone I know," she says quietly before grabbing her bag and walking out the front door.

* * * * *

"Where are we going?" I question as Cale's hand rests in mine. His fingers lace through my own as we continue to head down the beach.

The water washes up against our feet in a warm greeting as we make our way down the beach. The sky and air around us is pitch black besides the spotlight of the moon cast beside us. The stars shine brightly, and the darkness surrounds us making me feel nervous. Nervous and excited, because the summer is drawing to a close and I want Cale.

I want him to know how I feel, in every single way possible.

"I know a secret little place," Cale simply comments.

"Is this where I find out you're a serial killer?" I joke wryly with a small smirk touching my lips.

Cale let's out a breathy laugh. "Yup, you got me," he responds with the same teasing tone of my own.

I love the way he plays back. I love our banter. God, I love him way too much. But I can't do anything to change that now. I'm too far gone to stop myself from loving him now.

We continue to stroll down the beach as silence wraps around us. But it's not uncomfortable. It's the exact opposite, because it's perfect and calming and everything I feel when Cale has his arms around me.

My eyes are focused on the dark waves rolling up onto the shore when Cale stops walking causing me to pause as well.

I turn to face Cale when I notice the small cave. I drop his hand as I walk forward to the large opening. I run my hand over the smooth rock, and bend down to squat and look into the cave. A plaid blanket lays on top of the soft sand that fills the small rock cavern as well as a few flashlights and pillows.

I stand up and walk the few steps back to Cale.

"What do you expect to happen tonight?" I question with a raised eyebrows.

His face flushes red as embarrassment laces through him. Cale is never embarrassed, far from actually. He is always confident and filled with an ease that even I am jealous of at times. It makes me want to laugh at his sudden shyness.

He rubs a hand down the back of his neck as he continues to turn into a tomato. "No," he sputters out. "I just wanted to do this, I don't know..." he trails as if he's unable to find words. "Nothing has to happen—"

I place my hands on his chest as I rub my thumbs lightly against his heated skin efficiently cutting off his words. "What if I want something to happen," I say as my voice rasps out.

Cale's eyes immediately turn a shade darker as his eyes lock on mine. I want Cale more than anything, more than I've wanted anyone ever, and that should scare me. But it doesn't. It just makes me feel even more needy. We've been messing around all summer, and I'm ready. I'm beyond ready for him, beyond ready for every part of Cale Hasting.

"Gray," he whispers my nickname. It has never sounded more perfect then when he says it. "We don't have to do anything you don't want—"

But I again cut him off as my hands rise to lightly wrap around his neck. "I want everything," I whisper as I take a step closer. My nails graze down his neck loving he way his body trembles against mine. "I'm ready," I breathe as my thumbs reach out to trace over his perfect lips.

God, I want him.

"Do you want me?" I question as my body brushes against his. The air around us fills with a humid heat, and suddenly it's hard to breathe and all I want is the untamed electricity that courses between us. The electric touch that has surrounded us every single day, the fire that I don't want to put out because in the flames I feel at home with Cale. I thrive in his wild flares, because they make me feel alive. Because he makes me feel alive.

He leans in so that his nose grazes mine, and his hands fall to my waist to draw me in even closer. Cale shakes lightly under my touch, and I love the way he's trying to gain his control as it slowly leaves him.

Because that's how I've felt every day since I've met this man. Out of control, on fire, and filled with a thirst only Cale can quench.

"Fuck yes," he growls out and suddenly we are moving backwards towards the cave. "I want you Grayson, more than anything," he continues as he pushes us back even further.

We fall onto the blanket of the stone fort that covers us, and Cale falls next to me.

His chest rises and falls quickly as if he can't catch his breath around me. His eyes flickering from my lips, to my eyes, to my chest, and everywhere in-between like he can't get enough. His hands then grip my wrists and push them up so they lie above my head. "Always you," Cale whispers into my ear making me shiver. "It's only you," he says again as his lips fall against the skin of my neck.

I want to tell Cale that I love him. Tell him that I love him so much, even without seeing a dumb shooting star. But I'm too scared so instead I break away from the hold Cale's hands have on me, and tangle them into his hair and crash my lips against his.

If I can't tell him that I love him, I can at least show him.

And that I do, all night long.

I open my eyes as my breathing begins to slow from the memory that attacked me out of nowhere.

Out of every moment I had with Cale, this is the one I hate to remember the most. The moment I showed him how much I loved him. The moment I gave him every last part of my body and heart. I bared my all to him, and only hours later he decided to crush me in a way that I didn't know was possible. I knew hearts broke, but I didn't know one's soul could as well.

I pull the fleece blanket around my arms even tighter in attempts to sooth myself. I cast my gaze upon the sky and focus on the stars as if the sky can give me answers.

Cale's words the other night wrecked me in a way everything else he ever said or did never had. He tells me he loves me, tells me that it was his father's idea to break up with me, tells me that he only wants me, and yet four years ago if he had told me any of this I would've found a way to work through it with him.

But now I have to push him away and regain my focus as Cale's words once again tear through my heart like a knife.

Max is everything I need to move on, and here I still am letting Cale get to me. I don't understand why I can't get him out from under me, why we are attached, and why my heart just won't let go.

My eyes continue to watch the sky as if I'm looking for something, and then that something comes to me. As if the gods above heard my unknown plea for my secret needs.

My skin breaks out in small bumps, and my heart stops beating as a flash of light burns across the midnight sky.

A small gasp falls from my lips as my heart beats faster and faster just for that single instant. That's the moment tears fill my eyes. I've waited years to see a shooting star, so many long years, and I finally see one. Finally. Years to feel something, anything from a burning flying star, and it's dumb to still want to see it. But I have, I waited and waited to see if this millisecond would affect my life. And it has.

I hate to say it, but Cale was right. My body feels alive, my soul aches for more of this fleeting magical moment. It feels like everything, it feels like life...it feels like love.

I don't know how to take all these emotions that flood my body. But as I close my eyes all I can see is that vivid flash of light that filled the dark night and scarred my memories as well as my heart.

A ringing sound fills the air and my eyes fly open to see my phone buzzing on the table next to me. Max's name flashes across the screen and that's when I know.

My heart sinks and the tears that once filled my eyes begin to run down my cheeks.

I shake my head and I let the phone go to voicemail as angry sobs shake through my body.

"Why, why, why, why, why?" I whisper over and over again as salty drops fall into my shirt dampening my clothes.

"Why can't you be the one?" I ask as my eyes watch the sky hoping to find another answer. But I know that I won't, I know this is it.

I know that it's all over.

Chapter Twenty-Nine

8 /8/15

THE HOUSE IS empty as I sit on the living room couch.

It's the big day. Bailey and Cale are getting married and besides the part of me that dreads attending their big day there is another sense of gloom that lingers within me as well.

I can hear my heart beating in my chest as the deafening silence of the house consumes me.

Suddenly there is a knock on the front door and the loud beating of my heart stops all together. I slowly stand from the couch and try and gain my confidence as I make my way to the front door.

I close my eyes before opening the door to reveal a set of what still is my favorite shade of green.

"Hey," Max breathes as a huge smile breaks ours over his handsome face.

My heart aches even more, but it doesn't break. Because only one man has the power to break me, but also to put me back together.

"Hi," I smile back weakly in response. I stand aside as I open the door even more to let him walk inside.

Max makes his way through the entryway as I close the door gently behind myself.

"So what did you want to talk about?" he questions. "Cause shouldn't you be at the church with your sister by now?" Max's face is filled with a lightheartedness that always shines through him, and I'm about to take that away. God, I hate myself.

I nod. "I told Bai I would meet her there," I say but the words come out rushed and awkward. His face scrunches as worry laces through his expressions. He can tell something is off with me, with us, with everything.

"So what did you want to talk about?" he asks once again. But this time there isn't a smile. Not even the small crack of one. His words are filled with underlying questions and my heart beats even faster.

"Umm..." I trail uncomfortably not knowing how to start. More accurately not knowing how to end something that was so perfect. But just not perfect for me.

"Grayson," he says my name and my whole body wants to grab him and kiss him one last time, but I don't. Because it isn't fair to him, nothing this summer has resulted in has been fair to him. "What's wrong?"

I clear my throat and my hands squeeze into fists as my nails cut into the palms of my hands. "I don't know how to say this Max," I start. "But I can't do this anymore," I finish with a breath I didn't even know I had been holding.

His eyes hold mine as a wave of confusion and sadness roll and tumble through his face. The pain that's evident in his wild eyes makes my eyes tinge with hot tears, but I hold them back. I don't deserve to mourn for breaking a piece of Max. I don't get to mourn when I'm doing almost the exact same thing Cale did to me to Max, who is a better man then I ever deserved.

"Why?" he asks simply.

"Because I leave after the wedding and go back to school in Illinois and you will be down here and—"

"Why?" he asks again cutting off my lame reason. My stupid excuse because I can't say the real reason I can't be with him anymore.

"What I was just saying is why," I tell Max. "Long distance never works and—"

"Stop with the bullshit Grayson and tell me the truth," he demands. "You like to pretend that you have this wall up that blocks out the whole world, and it might. But not me, I see everything," he explains. "Now tell me the truth."

I swallow the lump in my throat and say what I have to say. I didn't want to lie to him like Cale lied to me, but saying the real reason of why I'm ending this isn't any easier. I don't want to hurt him, though I know it's too late for that.

"Because you deserve better then me Max—"

He cuts me off as he takes a few steps towards me making my heart flutter. "No," he states simply but harshly. "You're not ending this cause you're scared of what you feel for me Grayson," he steps closer as he speaks and his hands are on my shoulders before I realize it. "This is ours," he whispers his promise to me once again.

Blurry tears fill my eyes openly now, but I refuse to let them fall. I can't cry, I can't.

He leans in to kiss me and I almost let him. I let his lips graze mine because I'm selfish and I want to feel him one last time. But I don't let it go any further because I know I would let him consume me, and we would go to a point of no return. A point of where he would fall for me completely and I would still be stuck on another man.

I pull away before I let him take this too far, and I take a step away from the comfort of his hands and body.

The comfort I've selfishly taken all summer.

"Max," I begin as my voice cracks from the rising tears that I won't let fall. "You are amazing, and I like you a lot," I pause before saying the next words knowing I'm driving the knife with what I'm about to say. "But I won't ever love you the way I should, the way you deserve."

He takes a step forward, but I take a step backwards. "You don't know what I want let alone what I deserve, that is something only I can choose for myself and you can't just keep running away—"

I throw my hands in the air as I cut him off. "I am running away, I'm always running away because I'm in love with someone who I can never have!" I exclaim.

Max's body sags at my words. "In love?" he asks softly as his eyes slice a piece of my aching heart. "The guy from your past," he comments as if everything is falling into place for him.

All I can do is nod.

Max shakes his head as his jaw locks and his lips flatten into a thin line. I've seen Max upset before, but never pissed. And he is downright pissed at this moment, and he has every right to be.

"He isn't right for me, he broke me, but he is all I want," I say and for the first time I let a tear fall from captivity. "He is all I picture when I close my eyes at night, when I picture my future he is who I see, and I hate it so much," I sigh. "You have no idea how much I hate it Max, because you are amazing and I like you so much, but..." I trail unable to finish.

"But I'm not the one," he finishes for me.

I nod weakly as another tear openly falls down my cheek.

"You keep saying I deserve better, but you do," he urges. "You deserve so much better than this asshole Grayson."

I wipe at the salty tears on my face. "I know," I murmur in response.

"Because he's just going to keep stringing you along," he adds.

"I know."

"If you know then why won't you walk away from this idiot and pick me!" he shouts. My eyes shut in an instinctual flinch. Though not at the force of his voice, but at how right his words hit me in this moment. I know I should walk away and choose Max, but I can't because my heart belongs to someone else. Someone who doesn't deserve my heart like Max says, and yet here I still am.

I open my eyes to meet his beautiful jungle colored ones. Max is amazing, and sweet, and perfect. But I don't want perfect. I've never wanted perfect.

"He makes me feel alive," I tell him.

Max scoffs at my words. "You're just asking to get hurt again."

I don't disagree with him.

He starts towards the front door behind me not able to take anymore from me obviously when he stops cold in his tracks as if something hit him.

Max turns his head deliberately so he is looking straight at me. "Tell me it's not Cale," he breathes.

I drop his gaze as tears fall one after another like a steady rainfall. Like the quiet rain that fell around me four years ago when Cale squashed my heart to pieces.

"When he breaks you're heart again I won't be here to pick up the pieces," he comments. I don't ask how or why he assumed the man from my past was Cale, but he came to that conclusion and I won't lie to him.

I swallow the rest of the tears and force myself to look him square in the face. "I wouldn't want you to," I reply. "Because you deserve better than me," I repeat.

He shakes his head. "No, Grayson you deserve better, but you can't see that," he says. "You can't see what I was able to give you."

"And what was that?" I question.

"A love that was ours," and with those words he leaves and slams the front door behind himself.

My body immediately crumbles to the floor as tears stream down my face and wet my lips.

I don't regret ending things with Max, because I know it was the right thing to do when I couldn't love him the way he loved me.

But that doesn't make it hurt any less.

Max is a great guy, and deserves to be loved with unashamed and wild love. A love that is deep and untamed and needy and amazing. A love that I feel for someone else. Someone I can't have.

A wave of calmness suddenly hits me and I wish I could run out and hug Max. Not because I want him back, but because I want to thank him.

While I don't know if Max truly loved me, I know he fell for me. He treated me as an equal, and comforted me at some of my darkest moments. He made me feel loved for the first time in a long time.

Max and I aren't meant to be, but we were for a small moment. He won't see it yet, but he will one day. Because I needed him to realize that while Cale will always be whom I want, it doesn't mean that I can't find someone else. When I was with Max I would forget the pain Cale caused my heart, I was happy, I was loved.

But I couldn't take that next step. I couldn't fully fall, and maybe that's because Cale is here, around me, surrounding me, suffocating me.

Max showed me I could fall, and though he wasn't the one maybe someone else can.

Maybe I can find love once I leave Easton, maybe I can find another shooting star in my life.

Though I know it will be hard, I have to try because I'm done ruining my life or others for Cale. I love him. I will always love him.

But I can't have him, and I've finally come to terms with that.

A sigh flies through my body as my body relaxes against the wall I'm sitting in front of. Max will find someone better then me, and I hope he realizes I was just a fleeting moment one summer that taught him what true love could be.

Because I've experience true love, and it is in fact like seeing a shooting star for the first time. It's breathless, perfect, and magical, and sadly short-lived.

Chapter Thirty

8/8/15

"TELL ME WHAT needs to be done," I say as I run into my mother at the entryway of the small venue as she hangs up her cell phone. My parents had rented the space for everyone to get ready in before the ceremony on the beach.

"I need help with getting flowers to bridesmaids and boutonnieres for the groomsmen," my mother says as she points to a tray filled with Calla lilies. I smile at her words craving the distraction. The tray sits on the table near her right before her phone starts ringing again.

I pick up the tray as I hear her talk to some guy about shrimp and where he can put it, and she wasn't telling him where to put it for the reception. Seems like everything is right on cue to for the mayhem every wedding ensues.

The men are getting ready in a small room on the opposite end of the building from where Bailey and the rest of her bridesmaids are. I continue to head down the hall when I reach the men's dressing room, and I rap my knuckles lightly against the wooden door.

The door opens to show Cale's older brother Clayton who I've only met once before at his apartment when I told Cale to let me go.

"And we meet again," he comments sourly. He isn't a fan of me, though he doesn't even know me.

"Hi," I say evenly. "I have flowers," I tell him as I lift the small tray filled with their boutonnieres.

He lets out a sigh as he opens the door further for me to walk in. The room is filled with the Hasting men, all of which look too handsome for their own good.

I head over to an empty table as my eyes quickly scan the room. A small sigh of relief slips through my parted lips as I realize that Cale isn't in the room yet.

Ending things with Max wasn't easy, and seeing the one man I love marry my sister isn't any easier. But that doesn't mean I'm going to take away my sisters happiness for my own. So I keep my lips sealed, and set the tray down to unload the boutonnieres for the men.

I turn to face two of Cale's brothers and his father.

They all stand tall in their khaki colored slacks and white button up shirts that make them all look tanner then they actually are. Their skin bronzed, their hair tinted gold, and their eyes warm like honey. The Hasting men are men unlike any other.

They are perfect in a way that completely undoes women, and that's what makes them so dangerous. Even the father being married did nothing to lessen the flirting I know he receives from every single older woman in Easton.

"You all look nice," I comment as I take in the three men in front of me. "But aren't you missing another brother?" I question.

Clayton shrugs before grabbing his glass off of the table behind him. It's filled with amber liquor, and I'm suddenly dying for a shot of whatever he's having.

Mr. Hasting steps forward to grab one of the small flowers for their dress shirts when a voice comes from behind me making my heart stop momentarily.

"Colt always runs late," I hear Cale's voice call out.

I turn my head just barely so I don't see him just yet. Because I can't, I can't get lost in him right now. Not so soon after ending it with Max, everything is too fragile. So I nod simply in acknowledgement of his words, but don't respond verbally.

"Does anyone need help with these?" I ask as I take my eyes quickly over the family motioning my hand to the tray of flowers.

I receive a grunt from Clayton, and Mr. Hasting already has his on, but Chase comes forward with a big smile on his face. "Help a boy out?" he asks with a playful grin.

His easy going smile and bright eyes immediately calm me, and I'm thankful to have him as a friend at this moment.

"Of course," I say returning his smile.

I begin to mess with the pin on the back of the simple white Calla lily so I can pin it easily to his crisp shirt, but my fingers shake lightly making it difficult to open the pin.

"Nervous?" Chase asks with a raised eyebrow.

My eyes meet his before dropping back to the flower. "Just coffee jitters," I lie with a swallow to clear the lump in my throat.

I finally get the pin to corroborate for me, and I keep my eyes fixed on the right side of his chest as I slide the needle through the fabric and clip it into place.

"You look great by the way," Chase tells me getting me to raise my gaze to his kind eyes.

A small smile tilts the ends of my lips in gratitude. "You don't look to bad yourself," I respond back with a wink playfully. I wasn't lying. Chase does look great in his groomsmen outfit.

"So when is your hottie boyfriend making his way over here?" he asks and his unexpected words cause my blood to run cold. This time it isn't for the other guy in the room, it's for the man I hurt today because my heart and mind are stuck on someone who is just out of grasp.

I close my eyes briefly almost afraid to answer, but with Max not showing up today I have to get ready to answer questions about him. So why not start now?

"Um..." I start as a wave of anxiousness washes through me. My eyes instinctively find Cale as he stands right behind his brother Chase, and my eyes meet his as I speak my next words. "We broke up," I answer as if I'm speaking to Cale and only him. As if my words will change anything, even though I know my words don't matter to him.

Cale's eyes widen in response to my words, and not being unable to take anymore of his response I break my gaze from him. I refocus on Chase in front of me as his eyes narrow in on me before tossing a quick glance over his shoulder at his brother who quickly turns the opposite direction. Pretending as if he wasn't watching me, wasn't listening to every word I say, waiting for me to make a move.

Chase's eyes connect back with me with a hint of knowing in his eyes, but I know he doesn't. He may be close, but he knows nothing close to the whole story.

No one does.

Suddenly the door of the dressing room shutting loudly rings through the air and all of our heads snap to the now closed door.

A couple wandering gazes through the air makes it easy for us all to notice Cale is the one who just left. Unease and eyebrows rise as no one says anything, and then their father comes forward.

"He just needed some air," he says as if his son's odd departure means nothing.

"What happened?" Chase asks breaking the silence in the room and refocusing his gaze upon me as he brings the topic back to Max.

I wet my lips and take a step back realizing how close I'm still standing to Chase. The way he's still watching me, and how he watched Cale makes me nervous he might grab onto even an inch of what is going on. Even an inch of what really happened between Cale and myself years ago and even just a few days ago.

It's my sister's wedding day, and nothing will take away from that. Especially me.

"Just didn't work out," I state as I take a few steps towards the door after grabbing the flower tray still filled with long stemmed bouquets for the bridesmaids.

I can tell Chase wants to talk more, and ask more questions. But I'm not ready for that yet, everything is still too fresh. So I have to get away and get some air before I face Bailey. Today is supposed to be the happiest day of my sister's life, the one day she should remember as perfect. And I want to make sure it stays that way.

"Gray—" Chase starts as if he's going to stop me as my hand slips around the doorknob.

"Well if you all don't need anything else," I say faking a smile as my heart suddenly can't find a reason to at the moment. I wait a pause more and when no one stops me I turn the handle. "I'm going to head to Bailey's room then," and with those words I head out the door and down the hall.

* * * * *

I walk back into the building through the French doors that lead out to the beach.

Being in Cale's dressing room for that long was a mistake. After I left I quickly dropped the flowers off in the bridesmaids room right across from Bailey's room and walked straight outside.

I needed air, I needed space, I need to go straight back to Illinois and eat tons of ice cream with Hayley. But I can't, I'm here, and I'm going to make sure today goes smoothly for my sister.

I slowly make my way down the hall and into the suite where Bailey has been getting ready all morning. As soon as the door shuts behind myself I know something is wrong.

I hear hard deep sobs before I enter the small room Bailey is in, and as the pace of my walk increases so does my pulse.

"Bailey what is going on?" I call out urgently. "Is everything okay?" I ask again as I turn the corner and see Bailey in her perfectly white gown sitting on a bench near the window.

She doesn't answer as I rush over to her hunched form. Bailey's body shakes as my arms circle her body trying to sooth her as panic begins to fill my body.

"Bailey," I say quietly. "You have to talk to me," I tell her. "Please," I beg.

She just continues to cry, but her face rises from her hands and her once bright blue eyes are filled with a storm. And she can't stop the rain.

"Did someone hurt you?" I ask as the tears continue to stream down her have mixing with her black mascara making a mess.

"He's gone," she cries through loud sobs as her body finally collapses into me and my arms pull her closer.

"Who's gone?" I ask though I think I know whom she is speaking about. But I need her to specify, I need her to verify my thoughts because who I'm thinking of can break me all he wants. But how dare he break my sister as well.

Her sobs suddenly go silent, but her body still shakes as if they are still flying through her. She lifts her head slowly from my shoulder and closes her eyes momentarily as she tries to take a breath, but is unsuccessful.

"Cale," she stutters out as her eyes slowly open.

My heart squeezes in pain as she says his name. Knots in my stomach ache and they pull tighter as the knots grow. How could he do this to her? How could he hurt in this way? My thoughts spin as the knot pulls making my heart hurt in a way I haven't felt in a while. Because my heart isn't breaking for me this time, it's breaking for my sister.

"Why?" I probe as I hold back hot tears of anger.

Bailey wipes the back of her hand against her damp cheek and smudges of her makeup smear even more.

"Do you know that since you told me that you and Cale were together I never once brought it up to him?" she explains to me as her hands pull out her teardrop diamond earrings. Beautiful, our mothers, and perfect on my sister.

"What..." I trail awkwardly. "Why?"

"I didn't want to know the detail of his past," she explains. "It's his past," she pauses as she twists her engagement ring over her finger in circles. "I thought I was his future."

My heart breaks even more for my sister.

"What happened?" I push lightly needing to know what went down when I wasn't here.

Bailey unclips the silver necklace that hangs delicately around her slim neck, and places it next to her earrings on the nearby table.

"He told me everything about that summer," she says. "How it wasn't just a fling," she says next looking directly at me.

My eyes drop in embarrassment of my lie. When I told Bailey about that summer with Cale I made it seem like less than it was, and that wasn't fair to her.

"Bailey—" I start searching for the words to say to her in this moment.

But she cuts me off. "It's fine Gray," she tells me though her voice is even. "Doesn't matter now, does it?"

"Why did he tell you all of that?" I ask once again needing to know what words occurred between them causing Cale to leave my sister.

"He told me how much he loved you, and how he broke your heart," she tells me as the rain continues to fall from her stormy blue eyes.

"Yeah," I breathe quietly in agreement.

"Cale then told me what happened this summer," she says her voice turning icy towards me. "Everything Grayson," she emphasizes.

Her words cause a few tears to escape and fall down my face in complete shame of everything. Of the lies I've told everyone, of the secrets I've kept, and of everything in between.

"How he cheated on me with you multiple times—" she begins.

"We never slept together!" I exclaim cutting off her words as if they can assuage the guilt that flutters through my veins.

"That doesn't make it better," Bailey says pulling out of my arms and away from me.

"Bailey I..." I trail trying to find the right words but nothing comes because I know she's right. I messed up in a way that is irreversible and betrayed my sister in such a way that I'm disgusted with myself.

She stands abruptly from the bench as she attempts to take a few steps away from me. Though her tight dress stops her actions just slightly from trying to escape me.

"Just go ahead and go!" she yells at me. Her perfectly curled hair falls around her face, as streaks of makeup cut across her face.

"Go where?" I ask confused by her words as I stand from the bench as well. Though I keep a steady distance from her knowing she isn't my biggest fan at the moment.

"After Cale!" she shouts as if it's obvious. "He said he couldn't marry me because he loved you still," she informs me. Her words wash over me making my body run cold, but my heat beat faster. "So there you go, he's free now so go after him," she tells me with a snarl.

I'm frozen by her words, not knowing how to respond when Bailey begins to walk away as fast as she can in her constricting gown.

The sight of my sister walking away from me, angry, and hurt snaps me back to my senses and I leap forward to wrap my hand around her arm to stop her.

"No," I tell Bailey as I stop her from leaving.

Her body pauses as she begins to lightly shake again. I know she's crying and my whole heart hurts for her.

"Just go, please," she begs.

"No," I repeat, but this time stronger.

Bailey turns around to face me as fresh tears trail down her face from her broken eyes. "Why?" she breathes out as her voice cracks.

I drop my hand and step closer to her. "Because you're my sister," I tell her honestly.

She scoffs. "Didn't seem to matter much this summer."

I nod at her words, knowing she's right. So I don't argue. "I messed up this summer, I know I did," I say agreeing with my sister. "But Bailey I'm not going after Cale."

Her eyes meet mine as her eyebrows come together as confusion laced through her expressive eyes.

"But he loves you, and if you love him—"

"Doesn't matter," I say right away, breaking off her words.

"If that doesn't, then what does?" she asks as her shoulders sag in defeat.

I step closer to my sister. "You do," I tell her.

"What?" she questions still baffled by my words.

"You're my sister, and I know I fucked up, but you come first," I explain. "You're hurt, and I'm not leaving your side," I tell her strongly.

Bailey's eyes wet at my words and before I know it she's back in my arms as cries fly from her lips.

I step back to the bench, and bring my sister with me as she cries out all her sorrows on my shoulder.

"I'm still mad," she says through muffled sobs.

"I know," I whisper. "I know."

My sister continues to cry on my shoulder for her heart that is broken, and her love for a man that has been smashed into nothing.

A small part of me wonders what Cale is doing, or if he expected me to follow him after this mess.

But I won't.

I won't pick a man who broke my heart for my sister. I won't ruin what little I have left of my relationship with Bailey for Cale.

Because for the first time in a while I'm going to choose the right person. I'm going to choose my sister, my blood, and my best friend over a heart breaking love.

Chapter Thirty-One

8/31/15

I GRAB MY phone when it rings from the back pocket of my jeans as I walk down the street near my apartment. Fall is beginning to touch the air around the city as the air gets colder and the trees begin to bleed orange and red.

A small smile touches my lips at who is calling me as I swipe my finger against the screen to answer the call.

"Hey sis," I say happily to Bailey. "What's up?"

"Nothing much just wanted to say hi," she says. "I miss you," she whines though I don't find it as annoying as I once did. Maybe that's because my relationship with Bailey is different now. We are different now.

We both went through so much this summer, and when Cale left her she was crushed. I know she truly believed I would chase after her fiancé once he left, but Bailey is my sister. I would choose her over some guy any day of the week.

"I miss you too," I tell her honestly. We spent the last couple weeks of summer break together watching 80's movies and eating enough ice cream to fill a room. I helped soothe her heart, because I know how hard going through this kind of pain alone can be.

"So..." she trails as if she's unsure she should continue.

"Bai..." I drag out copying her same trailing voice. "What did you really call about?" I question.

I hear her take a deep breathe through the phone before she speaks next. "I think I may have met someone," she says awkwardly. Like she's uncertain if she should tell me. Like she's almost embarrassed. "I mean we are just talking, and we're friends, and nothing's happened—"

"Bai," I cut her off and I know she's holding her breath waiting for my next words. "Is he cute?" I finally ask with a smile painted over my lips.

A breathy chuckle leaves her lips as if she's relieved by my question. "Really cute," she responds.

"Well then I'm happy for you," I tell her earnestly. "I do think you should take it slow—"

"And I am!" she says assuredly. "I'm not rushing into anything ever again," she promises. Bailey knows she rushed her relationship with Cale because she got so caught up in him, same thing I did years ago as well.

"Good, but also don't be scared because you deserve an amazing guy by your side," I tell her.

"He's really nice," she says and I can tell by her voice she's smiling. A big goofy all in love smile at that.

I walk up the front steps on my building and make my way inside. "Hey, I'm at home so I'll call you back later," I say to Bailey. "But know I'm happy for you and he better be awesome and not hurt you or I will track his ass down," I tease though not completely knowing full well I would do just that for my sister.

"Okay, tell the roommates I say hi," she responds.

"Love you, oh and Bai," I pause to catch her attention. "You better call me after your first kiss with him."

A dry laugh leaves her lips. "I said we are just friends, and I'm taking this slow," she comments back.

I shake my head though I know she can't see me. "Yeah, yeah, but still," I say.

"I will," she replies. "Love you Gray." With that she ends the call and I tuck my phone back into my pocket.

I pull out my keys and unlock the door to my apartment and am greeted by the smell of pizza.

"Ooh, what's going on in here?" I ask as I walk into the kitchen to set down my purse and open up the box of my favorite pizza from the shop down the street.

I look over to see tequila on the counter and some limes and margarita mix. My eyebrows scrunch together in confusion about what is happening.

"Hello?" I call out. "Are we having a party I don't know about?" I joke.

I hear laughter coming from Hayley's room so I make my way down the hallway and to her door. I slowly open the door to reveal Hayley and Maxine sitting on the edge of the bed and bent over in a fit of giggles.

As soon as the creak of the door rings through the room their heads snap up to meet mine, and their smiles widen.

"You're home!" Hayley shouts as she stands up from her bed and runs over to me. She swings her arms around me and the smell of tequila hits me in full force.

I pull back just slightly. "Oh, wow," I comment with raised eyebrows. "Someone's been drinking," I comment with a smile as my eyes meet Maxine's bright ones. She shrugs as she turns around to grab her margarita, and sips away happily.

Even though I tried to not like Maxine, I couldn't deny that Hayley was right about her. She is beyond sweet, and is probably one of the most caring people I know. She puts others before herself, which is saying something that she wants to hang around Hayley and mine's selfish asses.

When I left for the summer I didn't want anyone moving into my room really so we let Maxine turn the office space into her room. Hayley and her had a great summer together, and while a little on the quieter end Maxine really is a great addition to the group. So we decided to let her keep the office space, to keep up the fun for junior year. Plus it also helped lower the rent for all of us, which is a perk.

"So what's really going on?" I ask as I take in their outfits. They are both dressed in glitzy cocktail dresses, with full makeup and hair perfectly done.

We don't go out a lot, and even when we do we never go this hard unless it's for a special event. And as today is a Monday, and school starts next week, there is definitely nothing special about today.

"What?" Hayley starts as she begins to dig though her closet. "We can't get dressed up and get drunk in our own apartment because we want to?" she asks as if this was completely normal.

A dry laugh escapes my lips as I shake my head. "You both are crazy," I state. I can't believe these are my best friends, but I also wouldn't have it any other way.

Maxine giggles once again at my words as she sips her glass dry. I can't help but smile at her, because a drunk Maxine is pretty funny. Out of all of us she drinks the least, but when she does she does she's a little more open, and cracks more jokes. She's more carefree, and I hope one day she will realize that she can be like that with us all the time. No liquid encouragement from her needed.

Suddenly Hayley turns around and throws a dress into my face. I grab at the fabric and pull it from my head.

"If by crazy you mean crazy awesome, then yes I would agree with you," she says with her hands placed on her hips. "Now put the dress on, and let's drink!" she sings in a cheerful tone.

I shrug my shoulders. "Fine," I agree as if I had a say or if I wanted to say no to begin with. Getting dressed up for no reason, drinking for no reason, and having fun for no reason. Seems like my kind of night.

Maxine slides off the bed to sit at Hayley's vanity to touch up her makeup and Hayley throws herself onto her bed as she begins to scroll through her phone.

I quickly slip out of my jeans and top and toss on the slinky shimmery fabric. As soon as the dress falls around me I immediately feel like I want to take a shot and dance the night away.

Thankfully I had done my hair and makeup before I left the apartment for the day so I am just as done up as they were. "Okay," I say as I give them a little twirl when I catch their attention. "I'm ready to have a three person apartment party," I say with a teasing roll of my eyes.

"Yay!" Hayley cheers and climbs off of the bed as Maxine finishes her touch up of makeup and stands from the bench.

We all head out into the kitchen and Maxine pours us all a shot of tequila. Hayley grabs the salt as I cut up a few more slices of the lime.

Hayley lifts her glass in the air as she shakes her head so her hair falls behind her shoulders. "We drink to those who love us," she proclaims starting off one of her favorite toasts. One we all have heard many times before.

Maxine lifts her glass next. "We drink to those who don't," she continues the toast.

"We drink to those who fuck us," I say as I lift my glass last.

"And fuck those who don't!" We all cheer together as our glasses clink and we take the shots quickly letting the liquor burn our throats.

Hayley turns on the music next, and Maxine begins to mix more margaritas.

I look at my best friend of almost three years now, and realize how lucky I was to meet her and have her in my life.

My eyes then fall on the ginger that I once hated, but now can't help but love. She fits perfectly into our group, and it makes me glad that Hayley had someone like her while I was away this summer.

These are my best friends, my roommates, and my people. The people who when I was lost loved me the most. With their help I found myself, and with that I found a happiness I haven't felt in a long while.

I pour one last shot for myself, and silently toast to more dance parties, more laughs, and a ton of memories to take from this year.

And with that I toss it back easily with a smile.

Epilogue

1 2/5/15

A KNOCK SOUNDS from the front door as Hayley, Maxine, and I sit in front of the space heater we splurged on for the apartment.

It's been an unseasonably cold winter and we have been getting the brunt of it up here lately. Below zero temperatures, and snow several feet tall lining the streets.

"Nose goes," Hayley said as her pointer finger flies to her nose and Maxine quickly follows.

"Shit," I grumble as I shrug off my fleece blanket and stand up from the warmth of the heater.

I make my way over to the door as giggles follow me. "Oh, shut it," I tell my friends who are still well heated.

Our heater is broken, and we are also broke so it's not like we can afford to up the heat in the apartment even if it did work.

Another knock sounds from the door. "I'm coming," I respond as annoyance slices through my voice.

I open the door and my body tense as it waits for the wave of cold to hit me, but as my eyes land on the person in front of me I run cold for a completely other reason.

"Cale," I breathe.

His cheeks and nose are wind blown and flushed as his warm hazel eyes lock on mine. A smile breaks across his still beautiful face. "Hi," he responds simply.

"Uh...um...what?" I rasp out unable to form a coherent question.

It's been four months since I last set eyes on Cale Hasting. Since he ran out on my sister before their wedding because he told her he still loved me.

"Can we talk?" he asks. I think he can see the indecision clear as day on my face as his next words are rushed out. "It will be quick," he says. "Promise," he adds.

I turn my head to look back at my roommates and while Maxine looks confused, Hayley's eyes are wide with shock at the man standing in our doorway.

"Um..." I pause again still trying to put together what is actually happening. I honestly thought I would never see Cale again. A small part of me hoped, but the realistic side of me squashed that hope immediately.

Hayley stands up from the ground quickly coming to my aid helping as my brain stops working from pure shock. "Max and I wanted to check out my room cause...cause—"

"Cause she has this new sweater I wanted to try on?" Maxine finishes for her though her words come out sounding like a question rather then a statement.

"Yes," Hayley agrees swiftly as her eyes widen. "What she said," she adds as they scurry off towards Hayley's room.

As soon as the shut of her door echoes through the hallway my eyes fly back to Cale who might as well be frozen.

"Come in," I say as I step aside. "I guess," I add awkwardly though I say it more to myself then Cale.

He comes in and runs a hand through his hair to shake out the snowflakes that dot his head. Cale's eyes scan the apartment quickly before he turns to face me. It's weird after this summer to see him again. To have him near me, and all his attention on me.

I cross my arms and take a step towards the shut door trying to keep as much space between us as possible. "So," I start as I swallow the nerves within me. "You wanted to talk?"

Cale nods as he slips off his gloves. "Yeah," he says. He clears his throat before speaking, "You look great."

I look down at the hardwood floors of our apartment because his words make my heart squeeze with a feeling I haven't felt in years. It makes me nervous, and it makes me want more of something I shouldn't want. Him.

"Cale..." I start but I can't finish. I don't know what to say or where to go from here.

"I want to apologize," he says after a long pause that hangs in the air between us.

"Apologize?" I question. "What?"

He takes a small step forward, hesitation filling his body as he can sense my discomfort at him in the same space with me. "I was lucky enough to love you that summer," he says as a small smile touches his perfect lips. "You were everything I didn't know I needed Gray. You were beautiful, sweet, and your laugh—"

I cut Cale off because his words make my heart ache with memories of our times together. "Please, I—"

He steps closer. "No, I can't stop," he finishes my unheard words. "I was lucky to have had you and I ruined it because I was young and stupid. I know that. I know I fucked up beyond words, but seeing you again this summer," he pauses as his eyes shut just for a moment. "My whole body felt alive again, and that's because of you. I really did think I loved Bailey, and in small ways she reminded me of you but..." he trails not finishing his words.

"But what?" I ask as my heart beats a mile a minute in surprise at his words.

"But she wasn't you," he finishes. "No matter how much I tried she could never be you Gray, and I know what happened this summer wasn't perfect—"

I scoff cutting him off.

"I know," he agrees. Though my words are unspoken, it's obvious where I am coming from. "I fucked up everything, I went about things wrong, and I'm sorry for everything," he says.

"You should be apologizing to Bailey," I tell him point blank.

He nods in agreement. "You're right," he coincides. "And I have because what I put her through was wrong. I wasn't strong enough to let her go before things went too far."

"Why are you saying all this Cale?" I ask.

He takes one more step towards me. Now he is standing just arms distance in front of me. "Because I love you Gray," he states as if it's simple.

Tears sting my eyes at his words. Words I craved years ago and in a twisted way received this summer. "I...I don't...I..." I stutter unable to form the many thoughts flying through my head and my heart in this moment.

"Tell me you don't love me and I will leave," he tells me.

I open my mouth to state otherwise, but I can't. I know why and so does Cale, I can't speak because my objection would be a lie. I do love him. I will always love him. He is my first love, and I know we shouldn't love like our first love because it's wild and burns too bright. But I want wild, and I want Cale.

Words don't leave my mouth before he rushes the few feet towards me. He doesn't touch me, as he knows it would cross a line too soon for us, but his body comes up close.

"Go on a date with me," he requests.

"What?" I barely breathe out.

"Date," he repeats. "You and me, food, drinks," he says as a smile breaks out over his handsome face.

"I'd have to talk to Bailey—"

"I've already talked to her—"

"What?" I cut him off now.

"Yeah," he says. "I want this Gray, and I want this the right way for once. So I asked her and we talked for a long time and she just wants us both to be happy," he explains.

"I just talked to her yesterday why didn't she mention this?" I ask confused.

"Because I asked her to keep it a secret until I came here to talk to you in person."

"Oh," is all I can breathe out.

"So..." he trails.

"So what?" I ask, my mind racing as I lose track of where this conversation is heading.

"Back to the date I asked you on," he smirks.

Nerves bubble up through my body and a part of me wants to run away from Cale and everything. But the larger part of me is intrigued and wants to go on this date to get some more answers. I was so broken, and honestly a part of me still is from that summer. I won't say I'm all healed up now, but I'm close. I am happy with my friends and no man defines me or my happiness, not even Cale.

If I take this step, even if it turns into nothing I know it will be on my terms. I was lost for years, and it took time to find myself and to find true self-happiness. But I did, and no one can take that away from me.

So I take a gigantic leap. "One date," is all I agree to.

Cale tries to cover up the victorious smile that threatens to break loose on his face. "That is all I'm asking for," he says repeating those exact same words from years earlier that got me in to this mess to begin with.

I want to laugh, I want to cry, and I want to scream and do all three at the same time. But instead I open the door behind myself, and watch Cale walk back into the frozen tundra of Illinois.

"I'll call you tomorrow," he says as he slips on his gloves.

"Okay," I agree quietly. I meet his eyes one last time, with a small smile touching my lips before I close the door placing my back against it. My eyes flutter shut in excitement and nervousness.

I open my eyes when I hear footsteps and see Maxine and Hayley standing in front of me with wide eyes and eager smiles. "What happened?" they almost shout at the same time.

"He asked me out," I answer slowly still in disbelief of what just happened.

"And what did you say?" Maxine asks next.

"I said yes," I respond still breathless.

Sometimes life leads us where we least expect it.

I know it did for me, because it lead me right back to the beginning.

Back to Cale.

•

www.ingramcontent.com/pod-product-compliance
Lightning Source LLC
Chambersburg PA
CBHW072148070526
44585CB00015B/1046